EXERCISE TESTING & PROGRAM DESIGN: A FITNESS PROFESSIONAL'S HANDBOOK

foreword by
Ken Germano

Cedric X. Bryant, Ph.D.
Barry A. Franklin, Ph.D.
Jason M. Conviser, Ph.D.

ISBN: 1-58518-588-4
Library of Congress Control Number: 2001097817

Published by
Exercise Science Publishers
P. O. Box 1828
Monterey, CA 93942
1-888-229-5745
www.healthylearning.com

Throughout this book, the masculine shall be deemed to include the feminine and vice versa. In addition, the publishers have made every effort to trace the copyright holders for borrowed material. If they have inadvertently overlooked any, they will be pleased to make the necessary arrangements at the first opportunity.

The publisher is not responsible (as a matter of product liability, negligence, or otherwise) for any injury resulting from any material contained herein. This publication contains information relating to general principles of medical care which should not be construed as specific instructions for individual patients. Manufacturers' product information and package inserts should be reviewed for current information, including contraindications, dosages, and precautions.

Printed in the United States of America

Special contributor: Donna Manning
Cover design: Karen McGuire
Graphic layout: Roseanne Cowles
Proofreading: Roseanne Cowles, Mary Bischoff, and Misty Patzer

DEDICATION

This book is dedicated to the many fine men and women who dedicate their lives to helping others experience the joys of leading an active, healthy lifestyle.

If you should have any questions pertaining to the information presented in this book, please contact:

American Council on Exercise
5820 Oberlin Drive, Suite 102
San Diego, California 92121-3787
Phone: 858-535-8227 / 800-825-3636
Fax: 858-535-1778
Web Site: www.acefitness.org
Email: acepubs@acefitness.org

FOREWORD

The need for accurate, cutting-edge information was never more important than today. This information, regarding exercise as it pertains to health status, is vitally important for individuals who want to engage in regular exercise. As a leading agency for the promotion of safe and accurate information regarding exercise and physical activity, it is the role of the American Council on Exercise (ACE) to identify the tools and information that fitness professionals need to provide the best service possible for all segments of the population. In *Exercise Testing and Program Design: A Fitness Professional's Handbook*, the authors have compiled a state-of-the-art compendium for fitness professionals, exercise program participants, and sports medicine and allied health professionals. Focusing on such topics as pre-exercise screening, exercise prescription, the components of fitness, and, perhaps most critically, exercise as it relates to individuals with special needs, this *Handbook* is a necessary addition to the library of every fitness professional and exercise enthusiast.

In a society with chronic illness and inactivity on the rise, the health benefits of exercise were never more apparent. In ACE's effort to create industry standards, it is critical to build a synergy of confidence between the fitness and medical communities. Doctors who treat individuals with chronic illnesses must feel confident when they refer patients to fitness professionals. For members of the medical community to have this confidence, however, fitness professionals must demonstrate a high level of competence, skill, and knowledge regarding exercise as a critical element in the treatment of chronic illnesses due, in part, to inactivity. Tools such as the *Fitness Professional's Handbook* will further enhance the continuing education process of fitness professionals and bolster the confidence of both physicians and participants.

ACE recommends this text as a cutting-edge tool for fitness professionals worldwide in their efforts to grow professionally and personally and to effectively deal with a wider and more diverse population. When it comes to advocating exercise and its health and life-sustaining benefits, bravo Drs. Bryant, Franklin, and Conviser.

Ken Germano
Executive Director
American Council on Exercise

CONTENTS

●●●●●●●●●●●●●●●●●●●●●●●●●●●●●●●●

SECTION I

AEROBIC TESTING AND TRAINING

CHAPTER 1

●●●●●●●●●●●●●●●●●●●●●●●●●●

PRE-EXERCISE SCREENING

*P*rior to beginning an exercise program, it is important to evaluate the health status of each client, especially sedentary individuals, to identify any existing medical conditions (contraindications) or risk factors. This chapter focuses on screening and evaluation procedures that, when followed, will allow you to optimize safety during exercise testing and participation and to design an exercise program with minimal risk of medical or physical complications. The primary purpose is not to make medical diagnoses, but to determine if your clients are at high risk for, or experiencing symptoms of, cardiopulmonary or metabolic disease.

Regular exercise is safe and promotes improved health and fitness for most people. Noted Swedish exercise physiologist P.O. Åstrand probably summed it up best with the following quote: "All men and women should submit to a thorough physical exam before deciding *not* to exercise regularly." Many people have one or more known medical conditions that have been diagnosed and/or treated by a physician. If your clients are in this group, then you must rely on your knowledge and/or the clients' physicians for appropriate fitness programs. If, however, the health status of a client has been recently evaluated by a physician and/or a health professional and no existing health problems or major risk factors were found, then he or she is ready to begin (or continue) a fitness program. Most people lie somewhere within this continuum. Many clients do not have any known major health problems or obvious symptoms, but have never had their health status thoroughly evaluated or their health risk properly assessed.

PREPARTICIPATION HEALTH SCREENING

A well-designed health assessment or medical history questionnaire can identify most medical conditions, symptoms, and risk factors that are predictive of future cardiovascular disease or medical conditions. This tool, often referred to as a "health-risk appraisal" (HRA), has a more specific function related to exercise in that it can identify existing medical conditions that have the potential to be significantly exacerbated by physical activity. The American College of Sports Medicine (ACSM) has recommended the following purposes for conducting preparticipation health screening:

- Identification and exclusion of individuals with medical contraindications to exercise.
- Identification of individuals at increased risk for disease because of age, symptoms, and/or risk factors who should undergo a medical evaluation and exercise testing

before starting an exercise program.
- Identification of persons with clinically significant disease who should participate in a medically supervised exercise program.
- Identification of individuals with other special needs.

An HRA must be simple, easily understood, and require minimal time to complete to be practical and effective. It can be self-administered or completed by you and your client. The Physical Activity Readiness Questionnaire (PAR-Q), a relatively straightforward, yet valid query form for screening individuals prior to undergoing exercise testing, has been recommended as a minimal standard for entry into moderate-intensity programs (Figure 1-1). A preparticipation screening questionnaire co-published by the ACSM and the American Heart Association (AHA) is also available for use (Figure 1-2). This questionnaire was specifically designed for health/fitness facilities.

The ACSM also recommends that persons interested in participating in moderate-to-vigorous exercise programs should be evaluated for selected risk factors (Table 1-1) and signs or symptoms that are associated with cardiovascular, pulmonary, or metabolic disease (Table 1-2). The lists are not all-inclusive, but should be used when deciding the level of medical clearance, the need for exercise testing, and the level of supervision necessary for individual clients.

Using age, health status, symptoms, and risk factor information, your clients can now be classified into three primary risk stratifications defined by the ACSM:

- *Low Risk* – Younger individuals (men <45 years of age; women <55 years of age) who are asymptomatic and meet no more than 1 coronary artery disease risk factor (Table 1-1).
- *Moderate Risk* – Older individuals (men ≥45 years of age; women ≥55 years of age) or those who meet the threshold for 2 or more coronary artery disease risk factors (Table 1-1).
- *High Risk* – Individuals with 1 or more signs/symptoms suggestive of cardiovascular and pulmonary disease (Table 1-2), or known cardiovascular (cardiac, peripheral vascular, or cerebrovascular disease), pulmonary (chronic obstructive pulmonary disease, asthma, interstitial lung disease, or cystic fibrosis), or metabolic disease (diabetes mellitus Types I and II, thyroid disorders, renal or liver disease).

EXERCISE INTENSITY

The intensity of your clients' exercise activities is an important factor in assessing their need for additional medical screening prior to beginning an exercise program. The ACSM defines two categories of exercise intensity:

1. *Moderate Exercise* – activities that are approximately 3 to 6 metabolic equivalents (METs; 1 MET = 3.5 ml O_2/kg/min) or the equivalent of brisk walking at 3 to 4 mph for most healthy adults. Moderate exercise can alternatively be defined as an activity performed for a prolonged period of time (approximately 45 minutes), which has a gradual start and progression and is generally noncompetitive. If an individual's exercise capacity is known, moderate exercise corresponds to 40% to 60% of the maximal oxygen uptake.

Physical Activity Readiness
Questionnaire - PAR-Q
(revised 1994)

PAR - Q & You

(A Questionnaire for People Aged 15 to 69)

Regular physical activity is fun and healthy, and increasingly more people are starting to become more active every day. Being more active is very safe for most people. However, some people should check with their doctor before they start becoming much more physically active.

If you are planning to become much more physically active than you are now, start by answering the seven questions in the box below. If you are between the ages of 15 and 69, the PAR-Q will tell you if you should check with your doctor before you start. If you are over 69 years of age, and you are not used to being very active, check with your doctor.

Common sense is your best guide when you answer these questions. Please read the questions carefully and answer each one honestly: check YES or NO.

Yes	No	
☐	☐	1. Has your doctor ever said that you have a heart condition and that you should only do physical activity recommended by a doctor?
☐	☐	2. Do you feel pain in your chest when you do physical activity?
☐	☐	3. In the past month, have you had chest pain when you were not doing physical activity?
☐	☐	4. Do you lose your balance because of dizziness or do you ever lose consciousness?
☐	☐	5. Do you have a bone or joint problem that could be made worse by a change in your physical activity?
☐	☐	6. Is your doctor currently prescribing drugs (for example, water pills) for your blood pressure or heart condition?
☐	☐	7. Do you know of any other reason why you should not do physical activity?

If
you
answered

YES to one or more questions

Talk with your doctor by phone or in person BEFORE you start becoming much more physically active or BEFORE you have a fitness appraisal. Tell your doctor about the PAR-Q and which questions you answered YES.

- You may be able to do any activity you want—as long as you start slowly and build up gradually. Or, you may need to restrict your activities to those which are safe for you. Talk with your doctor about the kinds of activities you wish to participate in and follow his/her advice.
- Find out which community programs are safe and helpful for you.

NO to all questions

If you answered NO honestly to all PAR-Q questions, you can be reasonably sure that you can:

- start becoming much more physically active—begin slowly and build up gradually. This is the safest and easiest way to go.
- take part in a fitness appraisal—this is an excellent way to determine your basic fitness so that you can plan the best way for you to live actively.

DELAY BECOMING MUCH MORE ACTIVE:

- if you are not feeling well because of a temporary illness such as a cold or a fever—wait until you feel better; or
- if you are or may be pregnant—talk to your doctor before you start becoming more active.

Please note: If your health changes so that you then answer YES to any of the above questions, tell your fitness or health professional. Ask whether you should change your physical activity plan.

Informed Use of the PAR-Q: The Canadian Society for Exercise Physiology, Health Canada, and their agents assume no liability for persons who undertake physical activity, and if in doubt after completing this questionnaire, consult your doctor prior to physical activity.

You are encouraged to copy the PAR-Q but only if you use the entire form.

NOTE: If the PAR-Q is being given to a person before he or she participates in a physical activity program or a fitness appraisal, this section may be used for legal or administrative purposes.

I have read, understood and completed this questionnaire. Any questions I had were answered to my full satisfaction.

NAME _____ PHONE _____

ADDRESS _____
STREET   STATE   ZIP

SIGNATURE _____ DATE _____

SIGNATURE OF PARENT_____ WITNESS_____
or GUARDIAN (for participants under the age of majority)

© Canadian Society for Exercise Physiology
Société canadienne de physiologie de l'exercice

Supported by: Health   Santé
Canada   Canada

Figure 1-1. PAR-Q form. Reprinted from the 1994 revised version of the Physical Activity Readiness Questionnaire (PAR-Q and YOU). The PAR-Q and YOU is a copyrighted, pre-exercise screen owned by the Canadian Society for Exercise Physiology. Reprinted with permission.

Assess your health needs by marking all *true* statements.

History
You have had:
___ a heart attack
___ heart surgery
___ cardiac catheterization
___ coronary angioplasty (PTCA)
___ pacemaker/implantable cardiac
    defibrillator/rhythm disturbance
___ heart valve disease
___ heart failure
___ heart transplantation
___ congenital heart disease

If you marked any of the statements in this section, consult your health care provider before engaging in exercise. You may need to exercise at a facility that has a **medically qualified staff**.

Symptoms
___ You experience chest pain or discomfort with exertion.
___ You experience excessive breathlessness.
___ You experience dizziness, fainting, blackouts.
___ You take heart medication(s).

Other health issues
___ You have musculoskeletal problems.
___ You have concerns about the safety of exercise.
___ You take prescription medication(s).
___ You are pregnant.

Cardiovascular risk factors
___ You are a man older than 45 years.
___ You are a woman older than 55 years or you have had a hysterectomy or you are postmenopausal.
___ You smoke.
___ Your blood pressure is ≥140/90.
___ You don't know your blood pressure.
___ You take blood pressure medication.
___ Your blood cholesterol level is >200 mg/dL.
___ You take cholesterol-lowering medication.
___ You have a close blood relative who had a heart attack before age 55 (father or brother) or age 65 (mother or sister).
___ You are diabetic or take medicine to control your blood sugar.
___ You are physically inactive (i.e., you get less than 30 minutes of moderate-intensity physical activity on most days of the week).
___ You are more than 20 lbs overweight.

If you marked two or more of the statements in this section, you should consult your health care provider before engaging in exercise. You might benefit by using a facility that has a **professionally qualified exercise staff** *to guide your exercise program.*

___ None of the above is true.

You should be able to exercise safely in almost any facility that meets your needs without consulting your health care provider.

Figure 1-2. American College of Sports Medicine/American Heart Association Health and Fitness Facilities Preparticipation Screening Questionnaire*

* Adapted from Balady, GJ, Chaitman, B, Driscoll, D, et al. American College of Sports Medicine and American Heart Association Joint Position Statement: Recommendations for cardiovascular screening, staffing, and emergency policies at health/fitness facilities. *Medicine & Science in Sports & Exercise* 30(6):1009-1018, 1998.

2. *Vigorous Exercise* – activities requiring an energy expenditure of >6 METs, which can alternatively be defined as exercise intense enough to represent a substantial cardiorespiratory challenge. If an individual's exercise capacity is known, vigorous exercise may be defined as an intensity corresponding to >60% maximal oxygen uptake.

Table 1-1. Coronary Artery Disease Risk Factor Thresholds for Use With ACSM Risk Stratification*

RISK FACTORS	DEFINING CRITERIA
Positive	
Family history	Myocardial infarction, coronary revascularization, or sudden death before 55 years of age in father or other male first-degree relative (i.e., brother or son), or before 65 years of age in mother or other female first-degree relative (i.e., sister or daughter)
Cigarette smoking	Current cigarette smoker or those who quit within the previous 6 months
Hypertension	Systolic blood pressure of ≥140 mm Hg or diastolic ≥90 mm Hg, confirmed by measurements on at least 2 separate occasions, or on antihypertensive medication
Hypercholesterolemia	Total serum cholesterol of >200 mg/dL (5.2 mmol/L) or high-density lipoprotein cholesterol of <35 mg/dL (0.9 mmol/L), or on lipid-lowering medication. If low-density lipoprotein cholesterol is available, use >130 mg/dL (3.4 mmol/L) rather than total cholesterol of >200 mg/dL
Impaired fasting glucose	Fasting blood glucose of ≥110 mg/dL (6.1 mmol/L) confirmed by measurements on at least 2 separate occasions
Obesity[a]	Body Mass Index of ≥30 kg/m^2, or waist girth of >100 cm
Sedentary lifestyle	Persons not participating in a regular exercise program or meeting the minimal physical activity recommendations[b] from the U.S. Surgeon General's report
Negative	
High serum HDL cholesterol[c]	>60 mg/dL (1.6 mmol/L)

[a] Professional opinions vary regarding the most appropriate markers and thresholds for obesity; therefore, exercise professionals should use clinical judgment when evaluating this risk factor.

[b] Accumulating 30 minutes or more of moderate physical activity on most days of the week.

[c] It is common to sum risk factors in making clinical judgments. If high-density lipoprotein (HDL) cholesterol is >60 mg/dL, subtract 1 risk factor from the sum of positive risk factors because elevated HDL decreases the risk of coronary artery disease (CAD).

* Adapted from Expert Panel on Detection, Evaluation, and Treatment of High Blood Cholesterol in Adults. Summary of the second report of the National Cholesterol Education Program (NCEP) expert panel on detection, evaluation, and treatment of high blood cholesterol in adults (Adult Treatment Panel II). *Journal of the American Medical Association* 269:3015-3023, 1993. (Reprinted with permission from American College of Sports Medicine. *ACSM's Guidelines for Exercise Testing and Prescription*, 6th ed. Philadelphia, PA: Lippincott Williams & Wilkins, 2000.)

Table 1-2. Major Signs or Symptoms Suggestive of Cardiovascular and Pulmonary Disease*

- Exercise-induced ST-segment depression (≥ 1 mm)
- Pain or discomfort in the chest, neck, jaw, arms, or other areas that may be due to myocardial ischemia (poor blood supply)
- Shortness of breath at rest or with mild exertion
- Dizziness or syncope (fainting)
- Orthopnea or paroxysmal nocturnal dyspnea (trouble breathing in certain positions)
- Ankle edema
- Palpitations or tachycardia (rapid heart beat)
- Intermittent claudication
- Known heart murmur
- Unusual fatigue or shortness of breath with daily activities

* Adapted from American College of Sports Medicine. *ACSM's Guidelines for Exercise Testing and Prescription,* 6th ed. Philadelphia, PA: Lippincott Williams & Wilkins, 2000.

Combining a client's risk stratification and exercise intensity, you are now able to refer to ACSM's recommendations to determine if a diagnostic medical examination and an exercise test are appropriate for your client and if a physician's supervision is recommended (Table 1-3). Exercise testing recommendations reflect the risk of adverse cardiovascular events that increase as a function of clinical status (low, moderate, high) and exercise intensity.

It is also important to obtain the lifestyle and behavioral patterns of your clients when first setting up and designing their exercise programs. Note the questions in the Health Status Questionnaire (Figure 1-3) at the end of this chapter.

SAFETY FIRST

For years, many professionals in the medical community have ascribed to three basic rules for rehabilitating their patients. These rules also have direct application for individuals who want to engage in a sound exercise program:

Rule #1. Above all else, DO NO HARM.
Rule #2. Create an environment for optimal healing.
Rule #3. Be as aggressive as you can, without breaking Rule #1.

Obviously, all of the positive benefits of exercise will be inconsequential to your clients if their safety is compromised. To minimize the possibility that such an event might occur, an appropriate HRA should be administered prior to engaging in any type of exercise test or physical activity program for the first time.

An HRA is a tool with the primary purpose to help protect your clients from experiencing any serious adverse events during their participation in exercise. The basic objective of preactivity screening is not diagnostic, but rather to determine risk, whether it is cardiovascular, orthopedic, metabolic, etc. An HRA, if properly used, should be able to:

- Determine if your clients have medical conditions or risk factors that could be exacerbated by exercise.
- Be used to develop appropriate exercise tests and prescriptions.
- Be used to educate and motivate clients to initiate and sustain necessary lifestyle behavioral changes.

Given the many desirable benefits of regular exercise, you may be tempted to "jump" into prescribing an exercise program without spending the necessary time to ensure that the safety of your clients will not be compromised and that you are legally protected. Accordingly, you should view an HRA as a user-friendly form of "safety insurance" ... insurance that you and your clients need and deserve.

Table 1-3. ACSM Recommendations for (A) Current Medical Examination[1] and Exercise Testing Prior to Participation and (B) Physician Supervision of Exercise Tests*

	Low Risk	Moderate Risk	High Risk
A.			
Moderate exercise[2]	Not necessary[3]	Not necessary	Recommended
Vigorous exercise[4]	Not necessary	Recommended	Recommended
B.			
Submaximal test	Not necessary	Not necessary	Recommended
Maximal test	Not necessary	Recommended[5]	Recommended

[1] Within the past year.

[2] Absolute moderate exercise is defined as activities that are approximately 3 to 6 METs or the equivalent of brisk walking at 3 to 4 mph for most healthy adults. Nevertheless, a pace of 3 to 4 mph might be considered to be "hard" to "very hard" by some sedentary, older persons, with or without chronic disease. Moderate exercise may alternatively be described as an intensity well within the individual's capacity, one which can be comfortably sustained for a prolonged period of time (~45 min), which has a gradual initiation and progression, and is generally noncompetitive. If an individual's exercise capacity is known, relative moderate exercise corresponds to approximately 40% to 60% maximal oxygen uptake.

[3] The designation of "Not necessary" reflects the viewpoint that a medical examination, exercise test, and physician supervision of exercise testing would not be essential in the preparticipation screening; however, these should not be considered inappropriate.

[4] Vigorous exercise is defined as activities exceeding an energy requirement of 6 METs. Vigorous exercise may alternatively be defined as exercise intense enough to represent a substantial cardiorespiratory challenge. If an individual's exercise capacity is known, vigorous exercise may be defined as an intensity corresponding to >60% maximal oxygen uptake.

[5] When physician supervision of exercise testing is "Recommended," the physician should be in close proximity and readily available should there be a complication or medical emergency.

---

* Reprinted with permission from American College of Sports Medicine. *ACSM's Guidelines for Exercise Testing and Prescription*, 6th ed. Philadelphia, PA: Lippincott Williams & Wilkins, 2000.

HEALTH STATUS QUESTIONNAIRE

Name:				Phone (H):	
Address:				Emergency Contact:	
				Emergency Phone:	
City:		Zip:		Personal Physician:	
DOB:	Age:	Sex: M F		Physician's Phone:	

SECTION I) MEDICAL HISTORY

1. Mark any of the following for which you have been diagnosed or treated:
    __ Kidney problem   __ Heart problem   __ Phlebitis   __ Concussion
    __ Mononucleosis   __ Cirrhosis, liver   __ Stroke   __ Asthma

2. Mark any medications taken in the last 6 months:
    __ Blood thinner   __ Epilepsy medicine   __ Nitroglycerin
    __ Diabetes medicine   __ Heart rhythm medicine   __ Insulin
    __ Blood pressure medicine   __ Diuretic (water pill)   __ Digitalis
    __ Cholesterol medicine
    __ Other_____

3. List any surgeries you have had in the past (e.g., knee, heart, back, etc.):
    _____
    _____
    _____

4. Have you ever had **back problems**, any problems with **joints** (knee, hip, shoulder, elbow, neck), or been diagnosed with **arthritis**? _____ If yes, describe:
    _____
    _____
    _____

5. Do you have **any other medical conditions** or health problems that may affect your exercise plan or safety in any way? _____ If yes, describe:_____
    _____
    _____

SECTION II) CARDIOPULMONARY AND METABOLIC SYMPTOMS

Y N   Do you ever get unusually **short of breath** with very light exertion?
Y N   Do you ever have **pain, pressure, heaviness**, or **tightness** in the chest area?

Y N   Do you regularly have **unexplained pain** in the abdomen, shoulder, or arm?

Y N   Do you ever have **dizzy spells** or episodes of fainting?

Y N   Do you ever feel "**skips**," **palpitations**, or runs of fast or slow heart beats in your chest?

Y N   Has a physician ever told you that you have a **heart murmur**?

Y N   Do you **regularly** get lower leg pain during walking that is relieved with rest?

Y N   Do you have any joints that **often** become swollen and painful? Where:_____

SECTION III) CARDIOPULMONARY/METABOLIC DISEASE

Y N   Have you ever had a **heart attack**, **bypass surgery**, **angioplasty**, or been diagnosed with **coronary artery disease** or other heart disease? If yes, describe:

_____

Y N   Do you have **emphysema**, **asthma**, or any other chronic lung condition or disease?_____

_____

Y N   Are you an **insulin dependent diabetic**?_____

SECTION IV) CORONARY RISK FACTOR PROFILE

Y N   Have you had **high blood pressure** ($\geq$140 systolic or $\geq$90 diastolic) on more than one occasion?

Please list any **medications** you take for high blood pressure:_____

_____

_____

Y N   Have you ever been told that your blood **cholesterol** was high (200 mg/dL or higher)? Cholesterol level _____

Y N   Do you currently **smoke** 10 or more cigarettes per day?
_____ **cigarettes/day** _____ **years smoked**

Y N   Have you ever been told that you have **high blood sugar** or **diabetes**?_____

Y N   Has anyone in your **immediate family** (parents, siblings) had any heart problems or coronary disease before age 55? Describe:_____

_____

Y N   Do you feel you are more than 20 lbs overweight? _____ What do you feel is your realistic, ideal weight?_____

SECTION V) FITNESS

Circle the average number of times per week you participate in planned moderate-to-strenuous exercise of at least 20 minutes duration (brisk walking, jogging, cycling, swimming, stair climbing, weightlifting, active sports such as tennis, aerobic classes, etc.).

0   1   2   3   4   5   6   7   8   9   10

Y   N   Can you briskly walk 1 mile without fatigue?_____

Y   N   Can you jog 2 miles continuously at a moderate pace without discomfort?_____

Y   N   Can you do 20 push-ups?_____

Please list your body weight:
Now:_____ lbs   1 year ago: _____ lbs   Age 21:_____ lbs

SECTION VI) LIFESTYLE AND BEHAVIORAL

1. Describe any **aerobic exercise** you have done in the past (what, when, how often, for how long)._____
_____
_____

2. Describe any **muscular strength/weight training** you have done in the past (same as above)._____
_____
_____

3. List any major **obstacles** that you feel you will have to overcome to stick with your exercise plan long-term (e.g., what has stopped you in the past)._____
_____

4. Have you ever participated in **aerobic** or **aerobic step** classes?   Yes   No

5. Please list any recreational physical activities (tennis, golf, etc.) in which you regularly participate and how often._____
_____
_____

6. List any **favorite** activities you would like to include in your exercise plan.
_____
_____

7. List any activities that you definitely **do not like** and do not want to include.
_____

8. Which do you prefer?   ___ Group exercise   ___ Exercising on your own

9. List the 2 most important goals or reasons why you want to exercise regularly.

_____

_____

_____

10. Your occupation: _____

11. Do you spend more than 25% of work time at the following (mark all that apply)?
    ___ Sitting at a desk   ___ Lifting/carrying loads   ___ Standing
    ___ Driving   ___ Walking

12. Number of **hours** worked per week: _____ Hours   Any flexible hours?   Yes   No

13. Write in the best exercise times for you during a **typical week**.

	M	Tu	W	Th	F	Sa	Su
AM							
PM							

14. Where do you plan to exercise?   ___ Club   ___ Home   ___ Outside
    Other_____

15. If at home, list all available equipment._____

_____

_____

Figure 1-3. A sample Health Status Questionnaire for preactivity screening to determine health status and readiness for exercise.

Recommended Reading

American Association of Cardiovascular and Pulmonary Rehabilitation. *Guidelines for Cardiac Rehabilitation and Secondary Prevention Programs*, 3rd ed. Champaign, IL: Human Kinetics Publishers, Inc., 1999.

American College of Sports Medicine. *ACSM's Guidelines for Exercise Testing and Prescription*, 6th ed. Philadelphia, PA: Lippincott Williams & Wilkins, 2000.

American College of Sports Medicine. *ACSM's Health/Fitness Facility Standards and Guidelines*, 2nd ed. Champaign, IL: Human Kinetics Publishers, Inc., 1997.

Balady, GJ, Chaitman, B, Driscoll, D, et al. American College of Sports Medicine and American Heart Association Joint Position Statement: Recommendations for cardiovascular screening, staffing, and emergency policies at health/fitness facilities. *Medicine & Science in Sports & Exercise* 30(6):1009-1018, 1998.

Canadian Society for Exercise Physiology. *PAR-Q and You.* Gloucester, Ontario: Canadian Society for Exercise Physiology, 1-2, 1994.

Koeberle, BE. *Legal Aspects of Personal Training*, 2nd ed. Canton, OH: Professional Reports Corporation, 1998.

CHAPTER 2

AEROBIC FIELD TESTS

*A*erobic fitness – sometimes referred to in the scientific literature as cardiorespiratory fitness – can be defined as the coordinated ability of the pulmonary system (lungs), cardiovascular system (heart and blood vessels), and the metabolic pathways within the muscular system to take in, deliver, and utilize oxygen. The more oxygen an individual can take in, deliver, and utilize, the more aerobically fit they are.

The most widely accepted measure of aerobic fitness is an individual's aerobic capacity or maximal oxygen uptake ($\dot{V}O_{2max}$). A reflection of the greatest rate at which one can consume oxygen while exercising, $\dot{V}O_{2max}$ can be assessed in either a laboratory or a non-laboratory setting. When conducted in a laboratory, $\dot{V}O_{2max}$ testing usually involves the direct measurement of the gases expired during progressive exercise to maximal or near-maximal effort. An analysis of the volume of expired air and its oxygen and carbon dioxide levels provides a very accurate measurement of $\dot{V}O_{2max}$. It is also possible to estimate $\dot{V}O_{2max}$ in a laboratory setting without collecting gases by identifying the highest work rate one can achieve while exercising to the point of volitional fatigue (Figures 2-1 and 2-2).

In a non-laboratory setting, assessing $\dot{V}O_{2max}$ involves predicting $\dot{V}O_{2max}$ on the basis of either how well clients perform on a specific performance test (e.g., how fast or how far they walk or run within specific limits) or how they respond (e.g., heart rate) to submaximal exercise. Deciding whether to test in a laboratory or a non-laboratory setting and which assessment procedure to use is largely dependent upon the level of testing accuracy that is required, why the testing is being done, what testing resources (personnel and equipment) are available, and what (if any) unique characteristics your client might have that would preclude or lend themselves to a specific mode of assessment.

Prior to undergoing any exercise test (laboratory or non-laboratory), all individuals should be required to take certain precautionary steps. At a minimum, they should complete a health/medical questionnaire, have their resting blood pressure and resting heart rate measured, and complete an informed consent form. At the present time, one of the most widely used health/medical questionnaires is the PAR-Q (Figure 1-1). The PAR-Q has been used extensively in the exercise science and fitness communities as a screening device to determine whether an individual is an acceptable candidate for an exercise test. A "yes" answer to any of the seven questions on the PAR-Q disqualifies an individual from taking part in an exercise test until he or she obtains appropriate medical clearance.

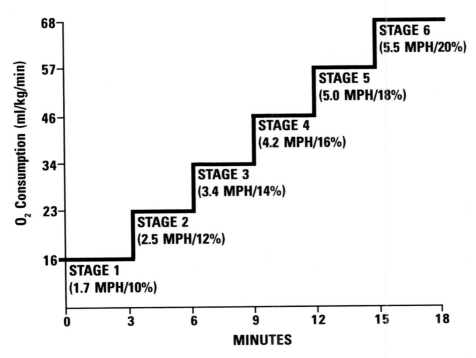

Figure 2-1. The standard Bruce treadmill protocol showing progressive stages (speed, percentage grade) and the corresponding aerobic requirements, expressed as ml/kg/min.

METs	1.6	2	3	4	5	6	7	8	9	10	11	12	13	14	15	16
Balke			2	4	6	8	10	12	14	16	18	20	22	24	26	
Balke		0	2.5	5	7.5	10	12.5	15	17.5	20	22.5					
Naughton	1.0 / 0	0	3.5	7	10.5	14	17.5									
METs	1.6	2	3	4	5	6	7	8	9	10	11	12	13	14	15	16
O₂, ml/kg/min	5.6	7		14		21		28		35		42		49		56
Clinical Status	Symptomatic Patients / Diseased, Recovered / Sedentary Healthy / Sedentary Healthy															
Functional Class	IV	III		II		I and Normal										

In the Balke rows the speed headings are "3.4 Miles/hr" and "3.0 Miles/hr"; the Naughton row speed heading is "2.0 Miles/hr".

Figure 2-2. Metabolic cost of selected treadmill test protocols. A MET is a unit of energy expenditure equivalent to approximately 3.5 milliliters of oxygen consumption per kilogram of body weight per minute (ml/kg/min). Numbers refer to treadmill speed (top) and percentage grade (bottom).

ASSESSING AEROBIC FITNESS IN A LABORATORY

Within a laboratory setting, $\dot{V}O_{2max}$ is usually either directly measured or predicted using indirect means. The direct analysis of expired gases during a maximal exercise (stress) test yields the most accurate determination of $\dot{V}O_{2max}$. Unfortunately, this procedure requires extensive equipment: (1) an exercise testing modality, such as a treadmill, a cycle ergometer, or an independent step-action, stair-climbing machine, on which the work rates are easily quantifiable, can be incrementally increased, and are highly reproducible; (2) a metabolic system for measuring minute ventilation ($\dot{V}_E$) and analyzing expired gases (oxygen and carbon dioxide); and (3) an electrocardiogram for monitoring the electrical activity and heart rate of the subject during the exercise test. Accordingly, the direct measurement of $\dot{V}O_{2max}$ is usually conducted only in research or clinical settings, since it tends to not only be time-consuming and costly (in terms of the equipment), but it also requires specially trained personnel to administer.

ASSESSING AEROBIC FITNESS IN A NON-LABORATORY SETTING

Because laboratory testing is not a particularly feasible method for assessing aerobic fitness for most health/fitness practitioners, several non-laboratory tests to predict $\dot{V}O_{2max}$ have been developed. Among the more commonly employed tests are performance-based measures (e.g., walking and running) and tests that use the heart rate and oxygen uptake responses to progressive submaximal exercise, extrapolated to the age-predicted maximal heart rate.

WALKING TESTS

In recent years, the Rockport One-Mile Fitness Walking Test has gained popularity as a field test for estimating aerobic fitness. This assessment involves having an individual walk one mile as fast as possible, preferably on a track or a level surface. Immediately upon completion of the test, the individual's heart rate is taken using a 15-second pulse count and recorded. The time that it took the individual to cover the one-mile distance is also recorded. Both measurements are then entered in an equation (Table 2-1).

Table 2-1.   Equation for Rockport One-Mile Fitness Walking Test

$$\dot{V}O_{2max}\ (ml/kg/min) = 132.853 - (0.0769 \times BW) - (0.3877 \times A) + (6.315 \times G) - (3.2649 \times T) - (0.1565 \times HR)$$

Where:
- **BW** = body weight in lbs
- **A** = age in years
- **G** = gender: 0 = female, 1 = male
- **T** = time for the 1-mile walk in minutes and hundredths of a minute (e.g., 15 minutes and 45 seconds would be expressed as 15.75)
- **HR** = heart rate taken at the end of the 1 mile expressed in beats per minute

---

RUNNING TESTS

Two of the most widely used running tests for assessing aerobic fitness are the Cooper 12-Minute Walk/Run Test and 1.5-Mile Run Test for time (Tables 2-2 and 2-3). The primary objective in the 12-Minute Walk/Run Test is to cover the greatest amount of distance in the allotted time period. The primary objective for the 1.5-Mile Run Test is for the individual

Table 2-2. Normative Data for the Cooper 12-Minute Walk/Run (M = men; W = women)

Fitness		Age (years)				
		13-19	20-29	30-39	40-49	50-59
		12-Min Run Distance (miles)				
Very Poor	M	<1.30	<1.22	<1.18	<1.14	<1.03
	W	<1.00	<0.96	<0.94	<0.88	<0.84
Poor	M	1.30-1.37	1.22-1.31	1.18-1.30	1.14-1.24	1.03-1.16
	W	1.00-1.18	0.96-1.11	0.95-1.05	0.88-0.98	0.84-0.93
Fair	M	1.38-1.56	1.32-1.49	1.31-1.45	1.25-1.39	1.17-1.30
	W	1.19-1.29	1.12-1.22	1.06-1.18	0.99-1.11	0.94-1.05
Good	M	1.57-1.72	1.50-1.64	1.46-1.56	1.40-1.53	1.31-1.44
	W	1.30-1.43	1.23-1.34	1.19-1.29	1.12-1.24	1.06-1.18
Excellent	M	1.73-1.86	1.65-1.76	1.57-1.69	1.54-1.65	1.45-1.58
	W	1.44-1.51	1.35-1.45	1.30-1.39	1.25-1.34	1.19-1.30
Superior	M	>1.87	>1.77	>1.70>	>1.66	>1.59
	W	>1.52	>1.46	>1.40	>1.35	>1.31

Source: Cooper. *The Aerobic Program for Total Well-Being.* NY: M. Evan & Co., 1982.

Table 2-3. Normative Data for the Cooper 1.5-Mile Run (M = men; W = women)

Fitness		Age (years)				
		13-19	20-29	30-39	40-49	50-59
		1.5-Mile Time (minutes)				
Very Poor	M	>15:31	>16:01	>16:31	>17:31	>19:01
	W	>18:31	>19:01	>19:31	>20:01	>20:31
Poor	M	12:11-15:30	14:01-16:00	14:44-16:30	15:36-17:30	17:01-19:00
	W	16:55-18:30	18:31-19:00	19:01-19:30	19:31-20:00	20:01-20:30
Fair	M	10:49-12:10	12:01-14:00	12:31-14:45	13:01-15:35	14:31-17:00
	W	14:31-16:54	15:55-18:30	16:31-19:00	17:31-19:30	19:01-20:00
Good	M	9:41-10:48	10:46-12:00	11:01-12:30	11:31-13:00	12:31-14:30
	W	12:30-14:30	13:31-15:54	14:31-16:30	15:56-17:30	16:31-19:00
Excellent	M	8:37-9:40	9:45-10:45	10:00-11:00	10:30-11:30	11:00-12:30
	W	11:50-12:29	12:30-13:30	13:00-14:30	13:45-15:55	14:30-16:30
Superior	M	<8:37	<9:45	<10:00	<10:30	<11:00
	W	<11:50	<12:30	<13:00	<13:45	<14:30

Source: Cooper. *The Aerobic Program for Total Well-Being.* NY: M. Evan & Co., 1982.

to run the distance in as short a period of time as possible. For the running tests, normative data are available to provide a reasonably accurate estimate of the aerobic fitness level of the individual who has been tested.

One of the most attractive features of these field tests is that they are very easy to administer. On the other hand, such performance-based tests have some limitations. For example, an individual's level of motivation and pacing ability can have a profound impact on the test results. Of greater potential significance, a certain degree of risk exists during such testing since individuals are encouraged to put forth a maximal effort.

TESTS THAT PREDICT $\dot{V}O_{2MAX}$ BASED ON HEART RATE RESPONSE TO EXERCISE

The primary aim of assessment techniques that predict $\dot{V}O_{2max}$ based on heart rate is to determine the slope of an individual's heart rate response to progressive exercise and use that slope to estimate $\dot{V}O_{2max}$ (Figure 2-3). The YMCA submaximal cycle ergometer protocol is an excellent example of a test that predicts $\dot{V}O_{2max}$ based on heart rate response to increasing exercise work rates. Other protocols involve using a treadmill or a stepping device.

To determine the slope of an individual's heart rate response to exercise, the heart rate needs to be measured at two or more submaximal exercise work levels. Accuracy in

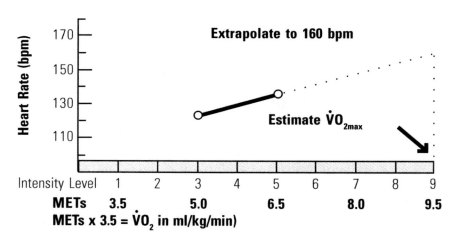

Figure 2-3. Predicting $\dot{V}O_{2max}$ from a series of submaximal heart rate responses.

predicting $\dot{V}O_{2max}$ from submaximal exercise heart rates is dependent upon the following assumptions (which have some limitations):

- *A linear relationship exists between heart rate, oxygen uptake, and work rate.* It is important that the submaximal heart rates are measured between 115 and 150 beats per minute (bpm), because it is within this heart rate range that a linear relationship tends to exist between these variables for most adults. When the heart rate is less than 115, several external factors (e.g., talking, laughing, and apprehension) can greatly influence it. Once the heart rate reaches a level between 115 and 150, external factors influence it much less, and a linear relationship generally exists. On the other hand, once the heart rate rises above 150, the heart-rate/oxygen-uptake relationship becomes curvilinear in many individuals.

- *A steady-state heart rate is obtained for each exercise work rate or exercise intensity level.* Exercising at a given work rate for only a few minutes (usually between 1 to 2 minutes) involves an insufficient amount of time for many individuals to achieve a true steady state. To ensure that a steady state has been achieved, the heart rate should be measured after 3 minutes of exercise at a given work rate and again after 4 minutes of exercise at that work rate. These 2 heart rates should then be compared, and if they differ by >5 bpm, the subject should continue to exercise at 1-minute intervals at the same work rate until 2 successive heart rates differ by less than 5 bpm.

- *The maximal heart rate for a given age is uniform.* Maximal heart rate is the highest heart rate that can be measured when an individual is exercised to the point of volitional fatigue (i.e., exhaustion) during a graded exercise test. An equation has been developed to represent the average maximal heart rate for humans: maximal heart rate = 220 − age (in years). Maximal heart rate can, however, vary greatly among different individuals of the same age. One standard deviation is ±12 bpm, which means that 67% of the population varies an average of ±12 heart beats from the average given by the equation. If an individual's age-predicted maximal heart rate (220 − age) is higher than his or her true maximal heart rate, then the predicted $\dot{V}O_{2max}$ will be an overestimation of the correct or actual value.

- *The mechanical efficiency of exercise (i.e., oxygen uptake at a given work rate for a specific type of exercise) is the same for everyone.* Oxygen uptake at any given work rate can vary by approximately 15% between different individuals. In other words, individuals vary in the amount of oxygen they require to perform a certain exercise work rate. Some individuals are more efficient than others. The average oxygen consumption associated with a given work rate may, therefore, vary significantly from one person to another. Thus, $\dot{V}O_{2max}$ predicted by an individual's submaximal heart rate response tends to be overestimated for those people who are mechanically efficient and underestimated for those individuals who are inefficient at a particular exercise activity.

- *The day-to-day variation in submaximal heart rate is minimal.* Under the best conditions, submaximal heart rate will vary from day to day for a given individual. This normal variation in submaximal heart rate tends to be ±5 bpm.

Much of the exercise equipment available today offers submaximal fitness assessments within their electronic consoles. The previous assumptions would still apply to these tests. However, they can be employed as motivational tools to show clients their improvements in cardiovascular fitness, if used consistently and correctly.

THE REAL TEST

Unless you have the resources for and easy access to a laboratory, you should recognize that no completely valid and reliable method exists for having the aerobic fitness level of your clients evaluated. If, however, individuals are given repeated non-laboratory tests and their heart rate response to a fixed work rate is decreasing over time, it is reasonable to conclude that they are making improvements in aerobic fitness, irrespective of the accuracy of the $\dot{V}O_{2max}$ prediction. Ultimately, the real test of any individual's relative fitness level may be intuitive. As the late T.K. Cureton, a world-renowned exercise scientist, once remarked, "You'll know that you're truly fit when you sense that you are deriving the greatest possible satisfaction from living."

Recommended Reading

American College of Sports Medicine. *ACSM's Guidelines for Exercise Testing and Prescription*, 6th ed. Philadelphia, PA: Lippincott Williams & Wilkins, 2000.

American College of Sports Medicine. *ACSM's Resource Manual for Guidelines for Exercise Testing and Prescription*, 4th ed. Philadelphia, PA: Lippincott Williams & Wilkins, 2001.

Canadian Society for Exercise Physiology (CSEP). Recommendations for the fitness assessment, programming and counseling of persons with a disability. *Canadian Journal of Applied Physiology* 23(2):119-130, 1998.

Howley, E, Franks, DB. *Health Fitness Instructor's Handbook*, 3rd ed. Champaign, IL: Human Kinetics Publishers, Inc., 1997.

Nieman, DC. *Fitness and Sports Medicine: An Introduction*, 3rd ed. Palo Alto, CA: Bull Publishing Company, 1995.

Peterson, JA, Bryant, CX (eds). *StairMaster Fitness Handbook*, 2nd ed. Champaign, IL: Sagamore Publishing Company, Inc., 1995.

CHAPTER 3

THE SCIENTIFIC BASIS
OF AEROBIC FITNESS

*M*uscles involved in exercise produce a significant amount of energy by combining nutrients from food with oxygen. As the oxygen needs of an individual's exercising muscles increase, the lungs supply more oxygen to the blood. The heart, in turn, pumps more oxygenated blood to the working muscles. If a steady supply of oxygen is not produced to meet the energy demands of an activity, an energy imbalance develops, blood lactate (LA) levels rise, blood pH levels decrease, and fatigue occurs. An individual's ability to engage in sustained high levels of physical activity without significant fatigue is determined by the body's ability to deliver oxygenated blood to the muscles, and the ability of the muscles to extract the oxygen from the blood and utilize it for the production of energy in the form of adenosine triphosphate (ATP) (Figure 3-1). A fundamental knowledge of how the body works during different types of exercise is necessary for understanding both the basic concepts of energy production and the physiological adjustments made by the body to meet the increased energy requirements of exercising skeletal muscles.

BASIC CONCEPTS OF ENERGY AND ITS SOURCES

The energy that is required for the normal function (muscle contraction, conduction of nerve impulses, hormone synthesis, etc.) of all living cells in the human body is produced by chemical reactions. These chemical reactions are either aerobic (occurring in the presence of oxygen) or anaerobic (without oxygen). An individual must continually produce energy or the various tissues and organs in the body will cease to function. It would be akin to pulling the plug of an appliance from the electrical outlet.

To clarify the relationship between food consumption and energy production, individuals should think of the human body as a factory. The body must process different raw materials to make its final product — energy. This energy is used by every cell in the body. The three basic raw materials the body uses to produce energy are oxygen, carbohydrates (sugar and starch), and fat. These materials essentially are available in an unlimited supply. Because humans live in a veritable sea of oxygen, an adequate supply is generally not a problem. When individuals eat food, carbohydrates and fat are replenished.

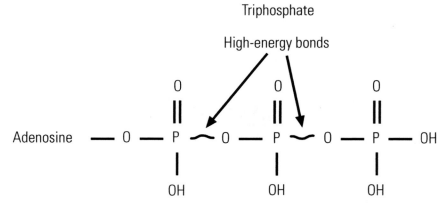

Figure 3-1. Simplified structure of an ATP molecule. The symbol ~ represents the high-energy bonds.

It is important to note that of the three calorie-providing nutrients (carbohydrate, fat, and protein), protein is the only one that the body does not typically use to produce energy under normal circumstances. Protein provides much of the structural basis for cells and is a major component of enzymes (substances responsible for controlling various chemical reactions at the cellular level). If more protein is consumed than the body needs, the excess will be converted into fat, carbohydrate, or both.

Because the amount of energy required at rest is so small, the human body doesn't consume much oxygen. Accordingly, the resting energy needs are easily met by the aerobic system. During the initial stages of exercise, however, the situation changes. When the work demands placed on an individual's body increase, the body needs extra energy immediately. Unfortunately, the rate of aerobic energy production is sluggish (i.e., oxygen must be breathed in, transferred from the lungs to the blood, carried to the heart, and then pumped to the muscles where it actually is needed). Thus, a delay exists in the delivery of oxygen from the environment. If a sudden demand for more energy arises, an emergency backup system exists that permits the body to function until the aerobic "assembly line" speeds up its production. The anaerobic energy system serves this function.

Since a specific amount of work requires a given amount of energy, the body must always have an appropriate level of energy available to meet the demands placed on it. The following descriptive timetable illustrates how energy is produced during the initial stages of exercise and during moderate-intensity exercise.

- When exercise first starts, a very limited supply of energy is present in the muscles for immediate use. During this phase, oxygen is not required.
- Either glycogen stored in the muscles or glucose transported by the blood from the liver can be used without oxygen to provide a limited supply of energy. Lactic acid is the by-product of this anaerobic reaction.
- Most of the lactic acid formed during an anaerobic reaction is released into the blood and transported to the liver, where it is converted back to glycogen and stored.
- As additional oxygen becomes available, the aerobic system is used more and

more. After a few minutes, the aerobic system is able to supply all the energy needed for relatively mild exercise.

- At this time, liver glycogen is converted to glucose and released into the blood to provide fuel for both systems (aerobic and anaerobic).
- Finally, adipocytes (fat cells) release more and more fat, the preferred fuel for the aerobic system.

If the exercise bout is relatively intense, other events take place to ensure that adequate amounts of energy are provided for the working skeletal muscles. The production of energy during exercise at relatively high levels of intensity occurs as follows:

- The speed of the aerobic reactions increases to provide more energy. More carbon dioxide is also produced.
- The faster anaerobic system supplies increasing amounts of energy as the exercise becomes more intense. The intensity of the muscle contractions causes a compression of the small arteries and, in effect, prevents oxygen, glucose, or fat from entering the muscle cell. Thus, the majority of the carbohydrate needed comes from that which is already stored within the muscle itself.
- Eventually, more lactic acid is formed, and increased amounts of lactic acid are released into the bloodstream. As lactic acid levels within the muscles increase, the efficiency of the aerobic chemical reactions are inhibited. When this occurs, inadequate amounts of energy can be produced aerobically. Accordingly, individuals have to either decrease the intensity level of the exercise bout (thereby reducing the amount of energy needed) or rely more heavily on their anaerobic systems.
- Only a small percentage of lactic acid is transformed back into glycogen in the liver; the majority remains in the blood and the muscles. An individual's body can accumulate and tolerate a limited amount of lactic acid. In all likelihood, it is the presence or buffering of lactic acid that causes excessive breathing while exercising, and causes feelings of fatigue and heaviness in the muscles, eventually forcing an individual to stop exercising.

To better comprehend how the body works during different types of exercise, an individual should understand the relative importance of the anaerobic and aerobic systems for energy production. Figure 3-2 provides an approximate idea of the maximal amount of energy a well-trained individual can produce over time, and how that energy is produced.

Although the stored energy can be used to perform a lot of work very rapidly, these stockpiles are essentially exhausted after 10 to 20 seconds. This factor partially explains why individuals cannot run 400 meters as fast as they can run 100 meters, or why weightlifters can lift more in one lift than they can in three lifts without a pause.

The production of energy anaerobically is relatively high (peaking in approximately 40 to 50 seconds), but it doesn't last long because individuals are limited by the body's relative intolerance of lactic acid. After 10 minutes, the amount of energy produced anaerobically is very small.

After 5 to 6 minutes of continuous exercise, the majority of energy the body requires has to be produced aerobically. The longer the duration of exercise, the greater the importance

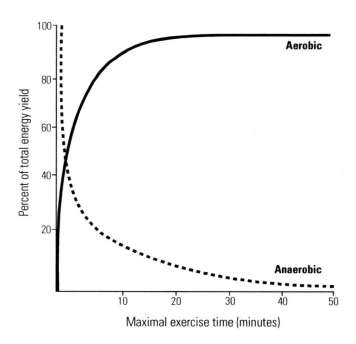

Figure 3-2. Resting contribution of aerobic and anaerobic metabolism during physical activity of increasing duration. During intense activities lasting 1½ to 2 minutes, the ATP-creatine phosphate and lactic acid energy systems generate approximately 50% of the energy, while aerobic metabolism supplies the remainder. A marathoner, on the other hand, derives essentially 98% of his energy from aerobic metabolism during a 50-minute training run. (Adapted from Åstrand, PO, Rodahl, K. *Textbook of Work Physiology*, 3rd ed. New York, NY: McGraw-Hill, 1986.)

of the aerobic system. Any activity over 10 minutes has to be performed aerobically, except for occasional, or brief, increases in work output.

MAXIMAL OXYGEN UPTAKE

If an individual increases the intensity level of exercise, a number of responses will occur. For example, there are increases in heart rate, respiration, and oxygen intake, as well as in the activity levels of other variables. A point occurs, however, beyond which oxygen intake cannot increase even though more work is being performed. At this point, the individual has reached a level that is commonly referred to as the maximal oxygen uptake ($\dot{V}O_{2max}$) or aerobic capacity. This measure is considered to be the best single indicator of aerobic fitness, since it involves the optimal ability of three major systems of the body (pulmonary, cardiovascular, and muscular) to take in, transport, and utilize oxygen. Thus, the higher an individual's level of maximal oxygen uptake, the greater the level of physical work that can be performed.

ENERGY PRODUCTION AND EXERCISE INTENSITY

If the amount of work being performed is progressively increased along the continuum to levels of maximum capacity, the ability to produce energy aerobically will not be able to completely match the energy demands. For most sedentary individuals, this point occurs at a work output requiring approximately half of their $\dot{V}O_{2max}$. In other words, below 50 percent of $\dot{V}O_{2max}$, the "slower" aerobic system can provide all the energy that a person needs. Of course,

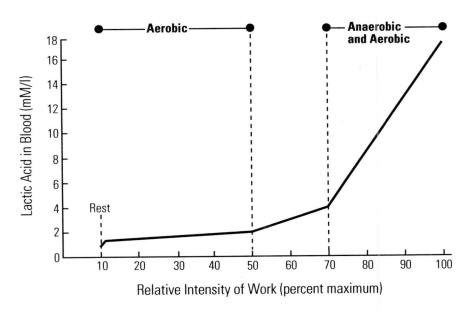

Figure 3-3. Blood lactic acid related to exercise intensity. Skinner, JS. *Body Energy.* Mountain View, CA: Anderson World Inc., 1981. Used with permission.

the human body does not switch over to the anaerobic system all at once, but gradually shifts gears to produce energy at a faster rate. A level between 50 and 70 percent of $\dot{V}O_{2max}$ represents a transition phase for most people. Above 70 percent of $\dot{V}O_{2max}$, the aerobic system does not produce energy fast enough, thereby causing individuals to increasingly rely on anaerobic metabolism.

Another important factor that must be considered when examining the relationship between the production of energy and exercise intensity is lactic acid. Figure 3-3 presents a schematic diagram of the level of lactic acid in the blood relative to the intensity of exercise. The level of lactic acid is a rough indicator of the degree to which anaerobic metabolism is being used. As Figure 3-3 illustrates, lactic acid will begin to rise slowly around 50 percent of $\dot{V}O_{2max}$. Because the increase is not too great, an individual's body can compensate for up to 70 percent of maximum with little trouble. Beyond 70 percent of $\dot{V}O_{2max}$, however, as the buildup of lactic acid becomes progressively more dramatic, an individual will start to get "winded" and fatigued. This factor explains why a person can run at a certain pace (50 to 60 percent of $\dot{V}O_{2max}$) with no problem, but will become exhausted relatively quickly after trying to run faster (80 to 90 percent of $\dot{V}O_{2max}$).

Depending on the intensity and duration levels of the activity, it is important to note that many physical activities require both aerobic and anaerobic production of energy. For example, soccer players who often are required to run for extended periods (i.e., 20 to 30 minutes nonstop) perform aerobic exercise. Obviously, if the activity did not depend on the aerobic system for energy, they would not be able to run for nearly as long. However, when a game situation requires players to sprint after the ball (high-intensity intervals which exceed 70 percent of $\dot{V}O_{2max}$), these athletes are forced to draw upon their emergency (anaerobic) sources. In other words, whether an activity involves the body's aerobic system or its anaerobic system depends on the relative demands placed on the body by that activity at that particular point in time. Anaerobic chemical reactions are primarily used in high-intensity exercise of relatively brief duration (e.g., sprinting short distances or heavy weightlifting), while aerobic chemical reactions are primarily involved in low-intensity, long-duration exercise activities such as walking, cycling, or stair climbing.

Physiological Adjustments to Exercise

The aerobic metabolism of fats and carbohydrates is the preferred and more efficient mode of energy production. This method, however, is limited by the body's ability to transport and deliver oxygen to, and the utilization of oxygen by, the working muscles. Several physiological adjustments are made during exercise. The primary objective of these adjustments is to provide exercising muscle with oxygenated blood for the production of energy. An individual's endurance capabilities will be greatly influenced by the magnitude and direction of these changes.

Cardiac Output

The amount of blood pumped per minute by the heart is referred to as cardiac output ($\dot{Q}$). This measure is indicative of the rate of oxygen delivery to the peripheral tissues (e.g., exercising skeletal muscles). Cardiac output, which is the product of heart rate (HR) and stroke volume (SV), increases linearly as a function of work rate. At rest, $\dot{Q}$ is roughly five liters per minute, but can rise to 20 to 25 liters per minute during exercise in young, healthy adults. This exercise-induced increase of $\dot{Q}$ is due to alterations in both HR and SV.

Heart Rate

Heart rate, one of the two primary determinants of $\dot{Q}$, also rises linearly with work rate. The gradual withdrawal of vagal (parasympathetic nervous system) influences and the progressive increases in sympathetic nerve activity which occur during exercise are largely responsible for the observed increases in HR. At or near $\dot{V}O_{2max}$, HR reaches its peak or maximal value. The equation 220 − age (expressed in whole years) provides a rough estimate of an individual's maximal heart rate (with a standard deviation of ±12 beats per minute). As the equation implies, an individual's maximal heart rate declines with age.

Stroke Volume

Stroke volume is the other primary determinant of $\dot{Q}$, and represents the amount of blood ejected from the heart during each beat. Unlike HR, SV does not increase linearly with work rate. SV increases progressively until a work rate equivalent to approximately 50 to 75 percent of $\dot{V}O_{2max}$ is reached. Thereafter, continued increases in work rate cause little or no increase in SV. Exercise-induced increases in SV are believed to be the result of factors that are both intrinsic and extrinsic to the heart. According to the Frank-Starling law, a greater stretch is placed on the muscle fibers of the heart (due to a greater venous return of blood to the heart during physical activity), resulting in a more forceful contraction of those fibers and, consequently, a greater SV (Figure 3-4). Extrinsic factors such as increased nerve (sympathetic) or endocrine (release of adrenal hormones epinephrine and norepinephrine) stimulation to the myocardium can also contribute to the increased SV that occurs during exercise.

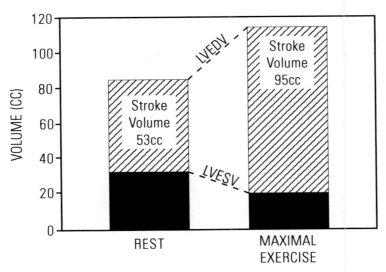

Figure 3-4. Changes in stroke volume from rest to maximal upright exercise is shown in young, healthy men. LVEDV = left ventricular end-diastolic volume; LVESV = left ventricular end-systolic volume. (Adapted from Poliner, LR, et al. Left ventricular performance in normal subjects: A comparison of the responses to exercise in the upright and supine positions. *Circulation* 62:528-534, 1980.)

BLOOD PRESSURE

Systolic blood pressure (SBP) represents the force developed by the heart during ventricular contraction. SBP increases linearly with work rate. In healthy adults, SBP seldom exceeds 220 mm Hg at maximal exercise levels. Diastolic blood pressure (DBP), on the other hand, is indicative of the pressure in the arterial system during ventricular relaxation and reflects peripheral resistance to blood flow. DBP changes little from rest to maximal levels of exercise. Therefore, an individual's pulse pressure (the difference between SBP and DBP) increases in direct proportion to the intensity of exercise. Pulse pressure is important because it reflects the driving force of blood flow in the arteries.

TOTAL PERIPHERAL RESISTANCE

The sum of all the forces that oppose blood flow in systemic circulation is expressed by the term total peripheral resistance (TPR). Numerous factors can affect TPR, including blood viscosity, vessel length, hydrostatic pressure, and vessel diameter. Vessel diameter is by far the most important of these factors, since TPR is inversely proportional to the fourth power of the radius of the vessel. If one vessel has one-half the radius of another and if all other factors are equal, the larger vessel would have 16 times (2^4) less resistance than the smaller vessel. As a result, 16 times more blood would flow through the larger vessel at the same pressure. This factor has important implications for exercise, since certain organs require more blood flow than others during physical activity (e.g., active skeletal muscle).

During exercise, resistance in the vessels supplying the muscles and skin is decreased, resulting in enhanced blood flow to these parts of the body. On the other hand, resistance in the vessels that supply the visceral organs of the body (e.g., the liver, GI tract, kidneys) is increased, which reduces the level of blood flow to those areas of the body. These changes are almost entirely due to intrinsic factors (i.e., the increased metabolic demands of the muscles and the requirement of blood flow to the skin to facilitate heat dissipation). The TPR tends to decrease during progressive dynamic exercise, because vasodilation occurring in the muscles and skin seems to override the vasoconstriction that is occurring in the visceral organs.

ARTERIOVENOUS OXYGEN DIFFERENCE

The arteriovenous oxygen difference is the difference in oxygen content between arterial blood and mixed venous blood. It is a reflection of the amount of oxygen extracted from the blood by the muscles. Obviously, the more oxygen that is extracted from the blood, the more oxygen that is available for aerobic energy production. The oxygen content of venous blood can be reduced to one-half to one-third of an individual's resting level by the exercising muscles. Such a reduction indicates that the muscles are extracting a much higher proportion of the oxygen delivered to them in the arterial blood. Approximately 75 to 85 percent of the oxygen in arterial blood can be extracted during maximal exercise. Aerobic conditioning results in metabolic alterations (e.g., increased capillary density, increased mitochondrial size and density, increased myoglobin content, and enhanced activity of oxidative enzymes) that can enhance the ability of skeletal muscle to extract oxygen.

A MATTER OF CHEMISTRY

By definition, all physical activity involves movement. In turn, sound exercise is often defined as purposeful movement. Because exercise involves the body's muscular system, energy is required. The source of this energy for muscular actions is a series of chemical reactions that involve varying amounts of oxygen and nutrients from food.

Knowing how the body responds to the energy demands necessary for exercise – particularly how the cardiovascular and muscular systems adjust to supply oxygen to exercising muscles – can affect exercisers in a variety of positive ways. For example, such an understanding can enable an individual to be better prepared to select an appropriate exercise mode or to manipulate a particular exercise prescription to achieve a specific personal goal. At the least, such knowledge will provide a clearer insight into why a given exercise bout may vary (i.e., more challenging, less challenging, etc.) from another. Ultimately, a potential by-product of such insight will be to provide a safer and more effective exercise environment for you and your clients.

Recommended Reading

American College of Sports Medicine. *ACSM's Guidelines for Exercise Testing and Prescription*, 6th ed. Philadelphia, PA: Lippincott Williams & Wilkins, 2000.

American College of Sports Medicine. *ACSM's Resource Manual for Guidelines for Exercise Testing and Prescription*, 4th ed. Philadelphia, PA: Lippincott Williams & Wilkins, 2001.

Åstrand, PO, Rodahl, K. *Textbook of Work Physiology*, 3rd ed. New York, NY: McGraw-Hill, 1986.

Rowell, LB. Human cardiovascular adjustments to exercise and thermal stress. *Physiological Reviews* 54:75-159, 1984.

Sharkey, BJ. *Fitness and Health*, 4th ed. Champaign, IL: Human Kinetics Publishers, Inc., 1997.

Wilmore, JH, Costill, DL. *Physiology of Sport and Exercise*, 2nd ed. Champaign, IL: Human Kinetics Publishers, Inc., 1999.

CHAPTER 4

●●●●●●●●●●●●●●●●●●●●●●●●●●

PRESCRIBING EXERCISE

Given the wealth of knowledge regarding the numerous benefits of a physically active lifestyle, it is not surprising that several professional organizations and the majority of health and fitness practitioners strongly recommend that all healthy adults engage in a regular exercise program. The key is to identify a prescription for exercising that is results-oriented, time-efficient, safe, and fosters long-term compliance.

An exercise prescription is a personalized program of recommended physical activity that is designed to enhance, maintain, or restore health and fitness. Specific guidelines for the intensity, duration, frequency, type, and progression of exercise are integral components of an effective exercise prescription.

As a general rule, exercise prescriptions are either self-developed or designed by professionally trained personnel who are employed at health/fitness or medical facilities. Regardless of what course of action is followed, a sound program must be based on the following factors: an individual's health and fitness status, the exercise setting, the program's goals, and the participant's goals. Most facilities administer some type of "health status questionnaire" to gather the information necessary to ascertain which activities will be most appropriate to include in an individual's exercise program. Once an exercise program has been initiated, periodic evaluations of health and fitness status should be conducted to assess a client's response to the exercise regimen and to determine whether adjustments need to be made in the program's design.

The primary focus of this chapter is to provide an overview of the factors that should be considered in developing fitness programs for "apparently healthy adults." The apparently healthy population is generally characterized as being both free of the signs and symptoms of coronary heart disease and able to engage in routine physical activity without evidence of cardiovascular or orthopedic intolerance. Individuals in this category can begin moderate-intensity exercise programs (40 to 60 percent of maximal heart rate reserve) without the need for exercise testing or medical examination, as long as the exercise program progresses gradually and the client is alert to the development of abnormal signs or symptoms (Table 4-1).

As discussed in previous chapters, the PAR-Q has been found to be a valid screening instrument for both submaximal exercise testing and for beginning moderate-intensity and gently progressive (but not heavy or overly challenging) exercise programs. Vigorous exercise (greater than 60 percent of maximal heart rate reserve) is sufficiently intense to represent a substantial challenge to an individual because it will elicit significant increases in specific

Table 4-1. Signs and Symptoms of Exertional Intolerance
Unusual or severe fatigue
Nausea
Difficult or labored breathing (dyspnea)
Dizziness
Lightheadedness
Palpitations (heart rhythm irregularities)
Excessive tachycardia or bradycardia (fast or slow heart rates)
Fainting (syncope)
Tightness or pain in the chest
Unsteadiness
Severe pallor
Mental confusion
Intermittent, severe leg pain (claudication)
Loss of muscle control
Persistent joint or muscle pain

physiologic responses (e.g., heart rate and respiration). At or above age 45 in men or age 55 in women, it is desirable for individuals to have both a medical examination and a maximal graded exercise test before beginning a vigorous exercise program.

DEVELOPING AN APPROPRIATE EXERCISE PRESCRIPTION

Specific goals or desired results can be attained with exercise programs that vary considerably in terms of mode, frequency, duration, and intensity. In addition, some clients will achieve a more rapid rate of improvement than others. For example, clients who have led a sedentary lifestyle should expect to progress more slowly. They should begin exercising at an intensity that can easily be completed, and then gradually increase the amount of work that is performed during a workout. However, if a client has been somewhat active, he or she may progress more rapidly than a sedentary individual whose slower progression is necessary to minimize the risk of injury and to ensure appropriate adaptation in previously inactive muscles. Finally, depending on how his or her body responds (and adapts) to the demands imposed upon it by the exercise program, a client needs to be both willing and able to modify the exercise prescription as appropriate.

WARMUP AND COOL-DOWN PHASES

Warmup and cool-down phases should be an essential part of all exercise programs (Figure 4-1). The purpose of the warmup is to prepare the body, especially the cardiovascular and musculoskeletal systems, for the conditioning or stimulus phase of the exercise session. The warmup phase stretches muscles, helps to increase blood flow, and increases the metabolic rate. Moreover, it may reduce the potential for electrocardiographic signs of strain or serious heart rhythm irregularities (Figure 4-2) that can occur with sudden strenuous exertion. A warmup

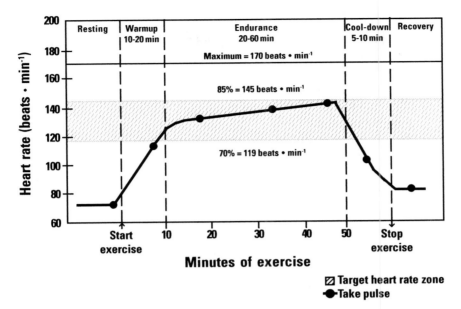

Figure 4-1. Format of a typical aerobic exercise session illustrating the warmup, endurance, and cool-down phases along with a representative heart rate response. At the conclusion of the warmup, heart rate approached the lower limit of the target zone for training, corresponding to 70% to 85% of the peak heart rate achieved during maximal exercise testing. (Reprinted with permission from American College of Sports Medicine. *ACSM's Guidelines for Exercise Testing and Prescription*, 6th ed. Philadelphia, PA: Lippincott Williams & Wilkins, 2000.)

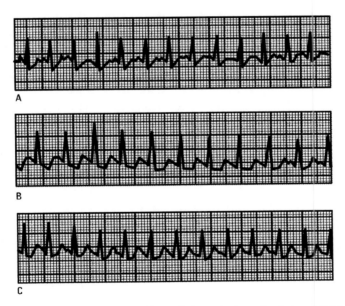

Figure 4-2. ECG recordings obtained from a 35-year-old man. A: At maximal exercise during multistage treadmill testing. B: Immediately after a 10-second run at 9 mph, 30% grade. Significant horizontal to downsloping ST-segment depression is apparent. C: Immediately after a 10-second run at 9 mph, 30% grade, preceded by a 2-minute warmup of jogging in place. ST-segment abnormalities were reduced in severity. (Reproduced from Barnard, RJ, et al. Cardiovascular responses to sudden strenuous exercise: Heart rate, blood pressure, and ECG. *Journal of Applied Physiology* 34:833-837, 1973. Reprinted with permission from the American Physiological Society.)

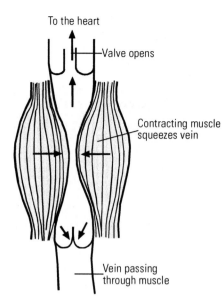

To the heart

Valve opens

Contracting muscle
squeezes vein

Vein passing
through muscle

Figure 4-3. Contraction of skeletal muscle squeezes veins, pumping blood toward the heart. One-way valves prevent retrograde flow.

may also reduce the susceptibility to injury by increasing connective tissue extensibility and improving joint range of motion. Our experience suggests that the best warmup for any activity is to perform that activity, but at a lower intensity (e.g., brisk walking before jogging). Moreover, it is generally recommended that the heart rate response at the conclusion of the warmup be within 10 beats per minute of the lower limit commonly prescribed for the endurance or stimulus phase. The cool-down phase assures that appropriate circulatory adjustments occur, such as the return of the heart rate and blood pressure to near resting levels. Continued movement after moderate or vigorous exercise will enhance venous return (Figure 4-3) by preventing pooling of blood in the lower extremities and eliminate associated side effects (lightheadedness, dizziness, etc.). Dissipation of body heat and the promotion of a more rapid removal of lactic acid are important contributions of the cool-down phase. Light aerobic endurance activities, coupled with stretching activities, provide the fundamental basis for both the warmup and cool-down phases.

The length of the warmup and cool-down periods depends on several factors, including the type of activity engaged in during the conditioning period, the intensity of the activity, and the age and fitness level of the participant. In general, the warmup and cool-down phases last approximately 5 to 10 minutes each. If the client has less time than usual for working out, it is recommended that the time allotted for the conditioning phase of the workout be reduced, while retaining sufficient time for the warmup and cool-down phases.

CARDIORESPIRATORY CONDITIONING

Based on existing scientific evidence and the need for guidelines concerning prescribing exercise for healthy adults, the American College of Sports Medicine (ACSM) developed a position paper on exercise prescription that included the following recommendations regarding the quantity and quality of exercise for developing and maintaining cardiorespiratory fitness and desirable body composition in a healthy adult:

1. *Frequency of training:* 3 to 5 days per week.
2. *Intensity*:* 55/65% to 90% of maximum heart rate (HR_{max}), or between 40/50% to 85% of oxygen uptake reserve ($\dot{V}O_2R$) or HR reserve (HRR). Even a low-to-moderate intensity exercise may provide important health benefits and result in increased fitness in some individuals (those who were previously sedentary and low-fit).
3. *Duration of training:* 20 to 60 minutes of continuous or intermittent aerobic activity. Even short bouts of exercise (i.e., ≥10 minutes) can be highly effective, if repeated. Thus, three 10- or 15-minute exercise bouts can be used to replace one 30- or 45-minute daily exercise session. The actual amount of time spent in exercise generally depends on the relative intensity of the activity. For example, activities involving a lower intensity should be conducted over a longer period of time. The emphasis should be placed on the total amount of work performed, which can be estimated by the caloric expenditure associated with the activity.
4. *Mode of activity:* An appropriate modality for developing cardiorespiratory fitness is any activity that uses the large muscle groups, can be maintained continuously, and is rhythmic and aerobic in nature (e.g., running, jogging, walking, stair stepping, swimming, skating, bicycling, rowing, cross-country skiing, and various endurance games or activities). At the beginning of an exercise program, low-impact activities such as walking, cycling, and stair stepping are generally recommended.
5. *Rate of progression:* In most instances, the ability of the body to adapt to the stresses imposed upon it (sometimes referred to as the training effect) allows individuals to gradually increase the total work done over time. During continuous exercise, increasing the work performed can be achieved by increasing either the intensity of the exercise, the duration of the exercise bout, or both. The most significant conditioning effects are typically observed during the first 6 to 8 weeks of an exercise program. An individual's exercise prescription is normally adjusted as these conditioning effects occur. The degree of adjustment depends on the individual involved, lingering symptoms or fatigue, additional feedback from periodic assessments, and/or the exercise performance of the individual during the exercise sessions.

CARDIORESPIRATORY ENDURANCE ACTIVITIES

The ACSM differentiates between several types of cardiorespiratory endurance activities. Activities like walking, jogging, stair climbing, or cycling (referred to as Group 1 activities) can be easily maintained at a constant intensity. The variability between subjects in terms of energy expenditure is relatively low during these types of activities. In Group 2 activities, such as swimming or cross-country skiing, the rate of energy expenditure is much more related to the individual's skill or proficiency at the activity. Although the level of intensity involved in Group 2 activities tends to vary between individuals, a person can maintain a relatively constant intensity while engaging in this type of activity. On the other hand, Group 3

* Note: The designation 55/65% or 40/50% suggests that the minimum or threshold intensity probably lies somewhere between these two numbers (i.e., between 55% and 65% or between 40% and 50% of the maximal heart rate and oxygen uptake or heart rate reserve, respectively).

activities (e.g., tennis, basketball, racquetball), by their very nature, are highly variable in intensity, both between individuals and within a specific individual.

The type of activities (Group 1, 2, or 3) prescribed for an individual will directly depend on the results of that individual's health-risk assessment and current fitness level. For example, Group 3 activities are generally not prescribed for previously sedentary or at-risk individuals or those with cardiovascular, pulmonary, or metabolic disease, because such activities can vary considerably in intensity.

Intensity of Exercise

Perhaps the most important component of an exercise prescription is the exercise intensity. The prescribed intensity must be sufficient to overload the cardiovascular system, but not so severe that it exceeds the cardiovascular system's adaptive capabilities. For the apparently healthy individual who wants to develop and maintain cardiorespiratory fitness, the ACSM recommends that the intensity of exercise needs to be between 55/65 to 90 percent of maximal heart rate, or between 40/50 to 85 percent of oxygen uptake reserve or heart rate reserve. It is generally accepted, however, that the intensity threshold for a training effect is at the low end of this continuum for those who have been sedentary, and at the high end of the scale for those who are physically active. Exercise intensity can be monitored by simply measuring the rate at which the heart beats during exercise, by subjectively rating the level of physical exertion using the Borg Rating of Perceived Exertion (RPE) scale, or ideally using both as complementary methods.

Determining Exercise Intensity by Target Heart Rate

How fast the heart should beat during exercise depends on the age and fitness level of the client (Table 4-2). Generally, the measured maximal heart rate of 70 to 85 percent is considered optimal for endurance exercise training. If your clients are just starting a training program, they should exercise at the lower end of the intensity rate (60 to 70 percent maximal heart rate). When this level becomes less challenging (usually after three to six months), they should gradually increase the exercise intensity until they reach the middle of the range of their maximal heart rate (70 to 80 percent). As their level of aerobic fitness continues to improve, they may adjust the exercise intensity toward the higher end of the range (80 to 90 percent), if appropriate. Another method for prescribing exercise intensity is presented in Table 4-3. This method, which is referred to as the heart rate reserve or Karvonen method, provides a heart rate that approximates the same percentage of the $\dot{V}O_{2max}$. Individuals should avoid exercising above their target heart rate range, because it could place them at a greater risk for injury. As a general rule, if individuals are unable to comfortably carry on a conversation while exercising (a.k.a., the "talk test"), they should reduce their exercise intensity regardless of the heart rate response. The "talk test" tends to err on the side of conservatism and can be very helpful in ensuring that the intensity of an exercise bout is not unduly excessive.

To measure heart rate during exercise, clients should stop approximately every 5 to 10 minutes during the workout to count their pulse (heart rate). You could also count their pulse for them, but it is important for them to become familiar with their level of intensity and how it corresponds to their heart rate. Pulse rate may be counted by palpating the carotid

Table 4-2. Target Heart Rates Using the Percent of Maximal Heart Rate Method*

Age (years)	HR$_{max}$[1] (beats/min)	HR$_{max}$ Method	
		70%	85%
80	140	98	119
70	150	105	128
60	160	112	136
50	170	119	145
40	180	126	153
30	190	133	162
20	200	140	170

Note: Calculated for age-adjusted estimates of maximal heart rates for 20- to 80-year-olds (220 – age).
[1] When possible, maximal heart rate should be measured directly to avoid potential error when prescribing exercise intensity.

* Adapted from American College of Sports Medicine. *ACSM's Guidelines for Exercise Testing and Prescription*, 6th ed. Philadelphia, PA: Lippincott Williams & Wilkins, 2000.

Table 4-3. Target Heart Rates Using the Heart Rate Reserve Method*

Age (years)	HR$_{max}$[1] (beats/min)	Resting Heart Rate					
		60 (beats/min)		70 (beats/min)		80 (beats/min)	
		Heart Rate Reserve Method					
		60%	80%	60%	80%	60%	80%
80	140	108	124	112	126	116	128
70	150	114	132	118	134	122	136
60	160	120	140	124	142	128	144
50	170	126	148	130	150	134	152
40	180	132	156	136	158	140	160
30	190	138	164	142	166	146	168
20	200	144	172	148	174	152	176

Note: Calculated for age-adjusted estimates of maximal heart rates for 20- to 80-year-olds (220 – age) using the heart rate reserve methods, at 3 different resting heart rates (60, 70, 80 beats/min).
[1] When possible, maximal heart rate should be measured directly to avoid potential error when prescribing exercise intensity.

* Adapted from American College of Sports Medicine. *ACSM's Guidelines for Exercise Testing and Prescription*, 6th ed. Philadelphia, PA: Lippincott Williams & Wilkins, 2000.

Table 4-4. Category and Category/Ratio Borg Scales for Ratings of Perceived Exertion (RPE)*

Category Scale		Category/Ratio Scale	
6		0 Nothing at all	No Intensity
7 Very, very light		0.3	
8		0.5 Extremely weak	Just noticeable
9 Very light		0.7	
10		1 Very weak	
11 Fairly light		1.5	
12		2 Weak	Light
13 Somewhat hard		2.5	
14		3 Moderate	
15 Hard		4	
16		5 Strong	Heavy
17 Very hard		6	
18		7 Very strong	
19 Very, very hard		8	
20		9	
		10 Extremely strong	Strongest Intensity
		11	
		* Absolute maximum	Highest possible

* Copyright Gunnar A. Borg. Reproduced with permission. For correct usage of the Borg scales, it is necessary to follow the administration and instructions given in Borg, G, *Borg's Perceived Exertion and Pain Scales*. Champaign, IL: Human Kinetics Publishers, Inc., 1998. Copies of the scale(s) with instructions can be obtained directly from Dr. Borg: www.borgperception.com.

artery. To do so, individuals should place the middle and index fingers below the jaw line in the groove adjacent to the Adam's apple. Gentle pressure should be applied, because when excessive pressure is applied to the carotid artery, the heart rate will decrease rapidly and, as a result, not accurately reflect exercise intensity. In fact, some individuals could become lightheaded or pass out. To avoid this risk, heart rate can also be measured by palpating the radial artery on the thumb side of the wrist. When taking the pulse during (or immediately after) exercise, individuals should count for 10 seconds, and then multiply by six. If the pulse rate is below an appropriate target range, the exercise intensity should be gradually increased. However, if the pulse rate exceeds the upper end of an appropriate target heart rate range, the intensity of the exercise bout should be decreased.

DETERMINING EXERCISE INTENSITY BY RPE

Exercise intensity can also be monitored by using the Borg Rating of Perceived Exertion (RPE) scale (Table 4-4). Available evidence suggests that RPE, like heart rate, can be effectively used to prescribe and monitor exercise intensity. For example, regularly exercising at an RPE of "moderate" or "strong/heavy" has been shown to significantly improve aerobic capacity. When exercising at a "moderate" level, clients can typically pass the "talk test" and engage in the activity for a sustained period of time. When exercising at a "very strong" level, however, individuals' heart rates tend to be relatively high. As a result, it is difficult for them to talk or exercise for an extended period of time.

DURATION OF THE EXERCISE SESSION

The duration of exercise refers to the amount of time (in minutes) at which the proper intensity level should be maintained. Typically, a conditioning phase lasts for at least 20 to 30 minutes, which corresponds to the amount of time required for the improvement or maintenance of functional capacity. Individuals just beginning an exercise program should start with approximately 10 to 20 minutes of aerobic activity. On the other hand, clients who are more fit can exercise for a longer period of time (20 to 30 minutes). The optimum duration of an exercise session usually depends on the intensity of the workout. Moderate-intensity activity should be conducted over a longer period of time (30 minutes or more) and training at vigorous intensities should last for at least 20 minutes. ACSM recommends a target range of 150 to 400 kcal of additional energy expenditure per day in physical activity and/or exercise.

FREQUENCY OF EXERCISE SESSIONS

Frequency of exercise refers to the number of exercise sessions per week. While some studies have been able to demonstrate improvements in cardiorespiratory fitness with an exercise frequency of less than three days per week, such improvements tend to be minimal. It appears that the body responds best to three to five days per week of moderate-to-vigorous intensity aerobic exercise with sessions lasting at least 20 to 30 minutes. The traditional recommendation of a "work-one-day-and-rest-one-day" routine remains a valid approach for clients who desire improved cardiorespiratory fitness. However, for previously sedentary individuals, the frequency of exercise should initially be prescribed at three days per week. Fewer than three sessions per week would not provide the training stimulus for significant improvement to occur. On the other hand, more frequent sessions would place them at undue risk for orthopedic injuries and expose them to a cumulative exercise workload that might have a negative effect on their exercise adherence. Clients who desire to increase their frequency of training should do so gradually, depending on age, fitness, personal needs, interests, and exercise objectives.

MODE OF CARDIORESPIRATORY EXERCISE

Activities should be selected on the basis of a client's functional capacity, interest, time, personal goals, and objectives. A fitness program usually starts with easily regulated activities, such as walking, exercise cycling, or stair stepping, so that the proper exercise intensity can be achieved and maintained. When exercising three to four days a week for 30 to 40 minutes a day at the appropriate intensity, any activity utilizing large muscle groups can be incorporated into an exercise program designed to enhance an individual's level of cardiorespiratory fitness. The greatest improvements in VO_{2max} occur when the exercise involves using large muscle groups over prolonged periods in activities that are rhythmic and aerobic in nature, especially in individuals who are initially unfit.

RATE OF PROGRESSION

The recommended rate of progression in an exercise program depends on several interrelated factors, including fitness, health status, age, needs or goals, tolerance to the current level of training, and support provided by friends and family. The ACSM defines three distinct stages of an exercise prescription:

1. *Initial conditioning stage:* This stage typically lasts 1 to 4 weeks, but may be longer depending on the client's adaptation to the exercise program. To avoid undue muscle soreness, injury, discomfort, and discouragement, the ACSM suggests that novice exercisers train at an intensity corresponding to 40% to 60% of HRR. The duration of the session may begin with approximately 15 to 20 minutes and progress to 30 minutes. Exercise frequency is suggested to be 3 to 4 sessions per week. Individual, realistic goals should be defined early in the exercise program, with a system of both intrinsic and extrinsic rewards.

2. *Improvement conditioning stage:* This stage normally lasts 4 to 5 months, and is the period during which exercise progression is most rapid. For example, the intensity level is progressively increased to the target range of 50% to 85% HRR while the duration of the exercise session is increased as frequently as every 2 to 3 weeks until the client can exercise at a moderate-to-vigorous intensity for 20 to 30 minutes continuously. The frequency and magnitude of increments are dictated by the rate at which adaptation to the conditioning program occurs. Exercise frequency is suggested to be 3 to 5 sessions per week. The goal of the improvement conditioning stage is to provide a gradual increase in the overall exercise stimulus to allow for significant improvements in cardiorespiratory fitness.

3. *Maintenance conditioning stage:* When the desired level of conditioning is attained, the maintenance stage begins – usually after the first 6 months of training. At this time, the emphasis is often refocused from an exercise program primarily involving fitness activities to one that includes a more diverse array of enjoyable physical activities.

A PRESCRIPTION FOR LIFE

Exercise can be a valuable tool in improving relative health and functional status. For your clients to receive the health and fitness benefits of engaging in a regular exercise program, you need to first identify any risk factors that may influence the design of their exercise programs. Based upon a comprehensive analysis of their personal exercise needs and interests, you should then develop an individualized program of exercise that will meet their unique requirements. This program should closely adhere to the primary prescription variables (e.g., frequency, intensity, duration, and type) for a scientifically formulated exercise regimen. Periodically, the manner in which your client's body has adapted to these variables should be reevaluated. Whenever necessary, adjustments should be made in exercise prescriptions. In so doing, clients will be given an individually tailored prescription for life – a prescription for optimal health and well-being.

Recommended Reading

American College of Sports Medicine. *ACSM's Guidelines for Exercise Testing and Prescription*, 6th ed. Philadelphia, PA: Lippincott Williams & Wilkins, 2000.

American College of Sports Medicine. Position Stand. The recommended quantity and quality of exercise for developing and maintaining cardiorespiratory and muscular fitness, and flexibility in healthy adults. *Medicine & Science in Sports & Exercise* 30(6):975-991, 1998.

Howley, ET, Franks, BD. *Health/Fitness Instructor's Handbook*, 3rd ed. Champaign, IL: Human Kinetics Publishers, Inc., 1997.

Nieman, DC. *Fitness and Sports Medicine: An Introduction*, 3rd ed. Palo Alto, CA: Bull Publishing Company, 1995.

Noble, BJ, Borg, GA, Jacobs, I, et al. A category-ratio perceived exertion scale: Relationship to blood and muscle lactate and heart rate. *Medicine & Science in Sports & Exercise* 15:523-528, 1983.

Peterson, JA, Bryant, CX (eds). *StairMaster Fitness Handbook*, 2nd ed. Champaign, IL: Sagamore Publishing Company, Inc., 1995.

Sharkey, BJ. *Fitness and Health*, 4th ed. Champaign, IL: Human Kinetics Publishers, Inc., 1997.

Thomas, S, Reading, J, Shephard, RJ. Revision of the Physical Activity Readiness Questionnaire (PAR-Q). *Canadian Journal of Sports Science* 17:338-345, 1992 (based on the British Columbia Department of Health, PAR-Q Validation Report), 1975.

CHAPTER 5

CONDITIONING THE UPPER BODY

*T*he beneficial effects of exercising on a regular basis are well-documented. Not only has exercise been shown to enhance our ability to perform daily activities without undue fatigue or injury, it has also been found to help decrease the risk of developing several chronic medical conditions, including coronary heart disease, Type II diabetes, hypertension, and obesity. Common sense dictates, however, that to achieve maximum benefits from exercise, a person must engage in a physical conditioning regimen that adequately addresses all of the body's fundamental functional needs. Such a regimen involves at least two considerations.

First, your client's exercise program should include activities designed to develop the four basic components of physical fitness: aerobic fitness, muscular fitness, flexibility, and body composition. A person's exercise regimen should be inclusive because the ability to perform daily activities involves a combination of these components, rather than a single component.

Second, an exercise program should condition both lower and upper extremities. Because the dynamic nature of most activities of daily living usually involves intermittent, interchangeable involvement of both the legs and arms, your clients may compromise the ability of their conditioning program to meet their needs if the exercise regimen does not address both the lower and upper extremities.

THE REAL CHALLENGE

Conditioning the upper body, however, is a far more challenging task than exercising the lower body. Several physiologic factors contribute to the differences in prescription. The muscles of the arms, for example, are substantially smaller than those of the legs. Accordingly, people have disproportionately less muscle mass in their upper extremities and a lower overall level of aerobic and muscular fitness in their upper bodies than in their lower bodies. The issue is further compounded by the fact that, unlike the musculature of the lower extremities, a person generally isn't required to use his/her upper-body muscles as much. For many individuals, this exacerbates the comparatively deconditioned state of their upper extremities even more. Human nature being what it is, many exercisers respond to this imbalance by simply concentrating their conditioning efforts on the lower extremities – an area of the body where they are assured of more noticeable progress.

Such an approach appears to be rather shortsighted. Research has shown, for example, that many individuals (particularly older adults and cardiac patients) lack the physical strength and self-assurance to perform their daily activities effectively. Without the training effects of an upper-extremity conditioning program, these individuals may never gain the functional capability and confidence to engage in those activities attendant to a normal lifestyle.

An even more relevant issue, from a health-risk perspective, involves the performance of relatively intense activities in which the arms are the prime movers. For example, certain arm exercises, such as carrying heavy groceries or shoveling snow, can be particularly risky for some individuals, especially those with cardiac problems. The combination of dynamic and static arm exercise, especially in a cold weather environment, may produce an imbalance between myocardial oxygen supply and demand. Furthermore, there is a tendency for such exercise to induce a Valsalva maneuver (i.e., expiring against a closed glottis), which places even greater strain on the heart.

The physiological impact of a sustained Valsalva maneuver can be detrimental for some individuals. For example, breath-holding initially causes a decrease in arterial blood flow due to an increase in intrathoracic pressure. As venous return of blood is inhibited, heart rate increases rapidly along with a rise in peripheral vascular resistance. When the strain created by the activity subsides, an overshoot in blood pressure occurs because of the sudden increase in stroke volume and elevated peripheral resistance. An additional problem arises from the fact that the sustained muscle contraction involved in moderate-to-vigorous arm activities may elicit a pressor response that also elevates blood pressure. Activities involving the upper extremities may also contribute to the pressor response because of their effect on blood flow (i.e., vasoconstriction) through these relatively small muscle groups. For anyone with an already compromised cardiovascular system, these physiological changes could provoke ischemic ECG changes, angina pectoris (chest pain), potentially dangerous heart rhythm irregularities, or combinations thereof. However, these risks may be lessened by an enhanced level of upper-extremity fitness.

SPECIFICITY OF AEROBIC-TYPE TRAINING

Cardiorespiratory and metabolic adaptations to exercise training are largely specific to the muscle groups that have been trained. In a classic study, J.P. Clausen and colleagues demonstrated that leg training caused a significant decrease in the heart rate response to leg exercise, but not to arm exercise. Conversely, arm training resulted in a decreased heart rate response to arm exercise, but not to leg exercise (Figure 5-1). Similar "muscle specific" adaptations have been shown for blood lactate and pulmonary ventilation. These findings suggest that a significant portion of the aerobic conditioning response is the result of peripheral rather than central (heart and circulatory) changes, including cellular and enzymatic adaptations that increase the oxidative (aerobic) capacity of chronically exercised skeletal muscle.

The lack of transfer of training benefits from one set of limbs to another challenges the common practice of limiting aerobic exercise training to the legs alone. This practice also fails to consider the fact that many activities of daily living require arm work to a greater extent than leg work. Accordingly, a strong case could be made for individuals to condition their arms as well as their legs (particularly those individuals who rely on their upper extremities for occupational or recreational tasks) to elicit improvements in cardiorespiratory and hemodynamic responses to both types of work.

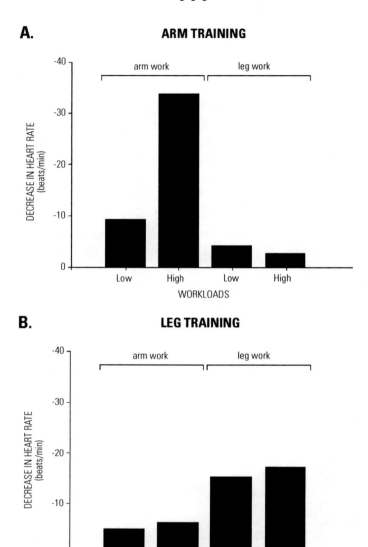

Figure 5-1. A: Arm training on the cycle ergometer reduced the heart rate during arm work but not leg work. B: Similarly, leg training was associated with a lower heart rate response during leg exercise but not during arm exercise. Adapted from Clausen, JP, et al. The effects of training on the heart rate during arm and leg exercise. *Scandinavian Journal of Clinical and Laboratory Investigation* 26:295-301, 1970. (Reprinted with permission from American College of Sports Medicine. *ACSM's Guidelines for Exercise Testing and Prescription*, 6th ed. Philadelphia, PA: Lippincott Williams & Wilkins, 2000.)

Fortunately, conditioning the arms has been found to be just as safe as leg training. Recent studies involving cardiac patients suggest that the upper extremities respond to aerobic exercise conditioning in the same qualitative and quantitative manner as the lower extremities, showing comparable relative decreases in submaximal heart rate and blood pressure and increases in peak oxygen uptake for both sets of limbs when the same exercise training intensity, frequency, and duration are used for the arms and legs (Figure 5-2).

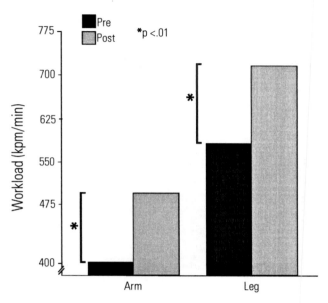

Figure 5-2. Average work loads (kpm/min) during maximum arm and leg exercise testing before and after upper/lower extremity training in men with previous myocardial infarction. Peak power output during arm and leg ergometry increased 24% and 23%, respectively. (Adapted from Franklin, BA, et al. Trainability of arms versus legs in men with previous myocardial infarction. *Chest* 105:262-264, 1994.)

PRESCRIBING UPPER-EXTREMITY AEROBIC EXERCISE

Several guidelines exist for prescribing aerobic-type exercise for the arms, including those that apply to the following variables:

- The appropriate training heart rate
- The work rate that will elicit a sufficient metabolic load for training
- The proper training equipment/modalities

ARM EXERCISE TRAINING HEART RATE

Although the prescribed heart rate for arm training should ideally be based on the results of a progressive exercise test of the upper extremities, this may not always be feasible. Research indicates that a slightly lower maximal heart rate is typically obtained during arm exercise than during leg exercise testing. As a result, an arm exercise prescription based on a maximal heart rate obtained during leg ergometry may result in an inappropriately high target heart rate for upper-extremity training. As a general rule, the prescribed exercise heart rate for arm training, based on a maximal heart rate obtained during leg exercise training, should be reduced by approximately 10 beats per minute, and perceived exertion should be used as an adjunct intensity guide.

APPROPRIATE WORK RATES FOR ARM TRAINING

In estimating the appropriate work rates for arm training, it is important to emphasize that although maximal physiologic responses are generally greater during leg exercise than arm exercise, the heart rate, blood pressure, oxygen uptake, and perceived exertion for arm exercise are higher for any given submaximal work rate. As a result, an exercise work rate considered appropriate for leg training will be too high for arm training. A work rate approximating 50 percent of that used for leg training is generally appropriate for arm training. For example, an individual exercising at 100 watts (one watt approximates six kilogram meters per minute) for leg training would train at 50 watts for arm training. Even though the work rate for the arms is considerably lower than the power output for the legs, heart rate and the rating of perceived exertion would generally be comparable or slightly lower.

ARM EXERCISE TRAINING EQUIPMENT/MODALITIES

Specially designed arm (Figure 5-3) or combined arm/leg ergometers are commonly used for upper-extremity training. Other equipment used for upper-body training includes rowing machines, weight-training devices, wall pulleys, light dumbbells, ladder-climbing simulators, and cross-country skiing simulators. Walking or jogging while pumping hand-held 1- to 3-pound weights can also be used to facilitate training of the upper extremities in an aerobic manner. The pumping action and the hand-held resistance have been shown to elicit significantly greater increases in heart rate, oxygen uptake, and caloric expenditure over conventional walking or jogging at comparable speeds without the hand-held weights.

SPECIFICITY OF RESISTANCE TRAINING

Increases in muscular fitness that are the result of resistance training are specific to the type of contraction used while training, the range of motion (ROM) through which training occurs, the velocity of muscular contraction during training, and whether the exercises performed are done unilaterally or bilaterally. The aforementioned examples of specificity of training are

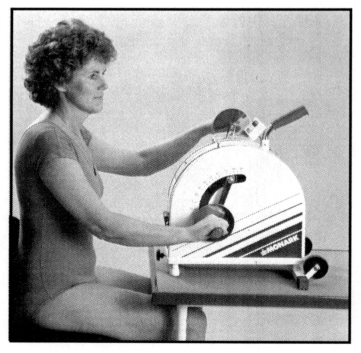

Figure 5-3. The Monark® Rehab Trainer 881E is one of the arm/leg ergometers commonly used for upper-extremity training.

all at least partially attributed to neural adaptations. However, for specificity of the type of contraction and the velocity of contraction, evidence suggests that resistance training also has specific effects on the contractile properties of the muscle.

Basically, muscle activity can be grouped into two fundamental categories: static and dynamic. In a static (commonly referred to as isometric) contraction, the muscle attempts to shorten against a fixed or immovable resistance. Thus, no movement of the skeleton occurs and the muscle neither shortens nor is forcibly lengthened. A dynamic contraction, on the other hand, involves movement and can be either concentric (where the force produced by the muscle is sufficient to overcome the resistance and shortening of the muscle occurs) or eccentric (where the muscle exerts force, lengthens, and is overcome by the resistance).

Exercising a muscle group with dynamic actions (e.g., lifting weights) produces relatively large increases in dynamic muscle strength, but only small increases in isometric contraction strength. And, isometric training improves isometric strength more than dynamic strength. A limited number of studies have shown similar improvements in isometric strength through a full ROM following both isometric and dynamic training when the dynamic training involved slow, controlled repetitions through a full ROM.

Specificity of resistance-type exercise training also involves selecting an exercise that will develop the specific muscle(s) or a specific body area. Correct technique must also be emphasized when performing resistance-type exercises. If a person compromises the proper mechanics for doing an exercise, he or she is likely to achieve suboptimal results from a physical conditioning program.

PRESCRIBING UPPER-EXTREMITY RESISTANCE EXERCISE

Designing a program of resistance-type exercises to develop the upper body should identify the following factors:

- What muscles to condition
- Which exercises will safely and effectively train each of those muscle groups
- An exercise prescription that will elicit the desired training response
- Which training equipment/modalities will best suit needs and interests

THE MUSCLES OF THE UPPER EXTREMITIES

Balance is an important factor when designing an exercise program. When formulating a strength-training program, balance refers to developing both a specific muscle and its antagonist, the muscle that opposes the action of that specific muscle (e.g., the pectoral muscles are "opposed" by the latissimus dorsi muscles). By ensuring that your client's training efforts address muscular balance, you not only decrease the chances of injury, you also increase the likelihood of enhancing functional performance.

A comprehensive strength-training program includes all of the primary muscles that assist in performing various bodily movements. The best way to prevent upper-body muscular imbalances from occurring is to train all of the major muscles of the upper extremities, with particular emphasis on areas that are weak. At a minimum, a training regimen for the upper body should involve the following muscles: latissimus dorsi, rhomboids, erector spinae, pectorals, deltoids, internal and external obliques, rectus abdominis, biceps, triceps, and forearm flexors.

CONDITIONING THE MUSCLES OF THE UPPER EXTREMITIES

Your client's upper-body strength workout should be limited to one exercise per major muscle group. Performing multiple exercises for the same muscle may be counterproductive both physiologically and psychologically, and can expose novice exercisers to an undue risk of injury. An overview of the common exercises for the various muscles of the torso, including the lower back, is listed in Table 5-1.

Table 5-1. Common Strength-Training Exercises for Selected Muscles of the Upper Body*

Parts of the Body	Exercises			
	Free Weights	Multi-station Machines	Variable Resistance Machines	Buddy/Stick Exercises

Shoulder	Dumbbell Upright Row
	Bench (Chest) Press
	Lateral Raise
	Front Raise
	Dumbbell Shoulder Press
		Upright Row
		Bench (Chest) Press
		Military Press
			Arm Cross
			Seated Row
			Seated Press
			Lateral Raise
				Bent-Arm Fly (buddy)
				Front Raise (buddy)
				Bent-Over Side
				    Lateral Raise (buddy)
				Lat Pulldown/Shoulder
				    Press (stick)

Upper Back	Dumbbell Upright Row
	Dumbbell Shoulder
	    Shrug
		Upright Row
		Shoulder Shrug
		Seated Row
			Seated Press
			Seated Row
				Shoulder Shrug
				Back Pulldown/Bench
				    (Chest) Press (stick)
				Bent-Over Side Lateral
				    Raise (buddy)

Lower Back	Barbell Squat Barbell Dead Lift Stiff-Legged Dead Lift	Back Extension	Back Extension	Leg Press (buddy)
Side (back)	Dumbbell Bent-Over Row Dumbbell Pullover	Lat Pulldown	Pullover Pulldown	Lat Pulldown/Shoulder Press (stick)
Chest	Bench (Chest) Press Dumbbell Press Dumbbell Fly	Bench (Chest) Press	Arm Cross Chest Press	Bent-Arm Fly (buddy) Front Raise (buddy)

Biceps	Dumbbell Bent-Over Row
	Dumbbell Biceps Curl
		Upright Row
		Biceps Curl
		Lat Pulldown
			Biceps Curl	Biceps Curl (stick)
				Lat Pulldown/Shoulder
				    Press (stick)
				Back Pulldown/Bench
				    (Chest) Press (stick)

Triceps	Bench (Chest) Press
	Dumbbell Kickbacks
	Dumbbell Overhead
	    Triceps Extension
		Triceps Extension
		Bench (Chest) Press
			Seated Dip
			Triceps Extension
				Triceps Extension (stick)
				Lat Pulldown/Shoulder
				    Press (stick)

Forearm flexors and extensors	Wrist Curl Reverse Wrist Curl	Wrist Curl Reverse Wrist Curl		
Abdominals			Abdominal Curl	

* For a detailed explanation of how to perform these exercises, refer to Peterson, JA, Bryant, CX, Peterson, SL. *Strength Training for Women*. Champaign, IL: Human Kinetics Publishers, Inc., 1995. Reprinted with permission.

AN APPROPRIATE EXERCISE PRESCRIPTION

Because strength training is essentially an art, as opposed to a science (i.e., a number of ways exist to manipulate the various strength-training variables to induce a desired conditioning response), you have many choices about how to structure your clients' strength-training protocols to address such critical quantitative measures as how many repetitions and sets should be performed per workout, how much resistance should be used, and how often they should work out. If you don't have a preferable workout "recipe" that they like to follow, an excellent starting point is the recommendation of the ACSM, which states that, at a minimum, a healthy person (under age 50) should perform one set of 8 to 12 repetitions using 8 to 10 different exercises twice a week.

UPPER-BODY STRENGTH-TRAINING EQUIPMENT/MODALITIES

A variety of equipment is available to help your clients achieve the objectives of their strength-training regimen. When used properly, almost all of the traditional forms of resistance-type equipment can enable a person to meet reasonable training goals.

CONDITIONING FOR A PURPOSE

As in all human endeavors, proper planning can have a substantial impact on the ultimate outcome of one's exercise efforts. Properly designed programs enable people to be better prepared to adequately address specific individual needs. Perhaps the late Dr. Herman K. Hellerstein, renowned cardiologist, summed it up best when he stated, "There are few occupations that require sustained walking or jogging." Some examples he gave were "protective service personnel, mail carriers, police officers, and their fugitives!" By helping your clients to meet the challenge of upper-body conditioning, you'll maximize the crossover of training benefits to real-life situations.

Recommended Reading

Brzycki, M. *Maximize Your Training*. Chicago, IL: Masters Press, 2000.

Clausen, JP, Trap-Jensen, J, Lassen, NA. The effects of training on the heart rate during arm and leg exercise. *Scandinavian Journal of Clinical and Laboratory Investigation* 26:295-301, 1970.

Fardy, PS, Webb, D, Hellerstein, HK. Benefits of arm exercise in cardiac rehabilitation. *The Physician and Sportsmedicine* 5:30-41, 1977.

Franklin, BA. Aerobic exercise training programs for the upper body. *Medicine & Science in Sports & Exercise* 21(S):141-148, 1989.

Franklin, BA, Hellerstein, HK, Gordon, S, Timmis, GC. Cardiac patients. In: Franklin, BA, Gordon, S, Timmis, GC (eds), *Exercise in Modern Medicine*. Baltimore, MD: Williams & Wilkins, 1989.

Franklin, BA, Vander, L, Wrisley, D, Rubenfire, M. Trainability of arms versus legs in men with previous myocardial infarction. *Chest* 105:262-264, 1994.

Peterson, JA, Bryant, CX (eds). *StairMaster Fitness Handbook*, 2nd ed. Champaign, IL: Sagamore Publishing Company, Inc., 1995.

Peterson, JA, Bryant, CX, Peterson, SL. *Strength Training for Women*. Champaign, IL: Human Kinetics Publishers, Inc., 1995.

CHAPTER 6

CROSS-TRAINING PRINCIPLES AND GUIDELINES

*A*s the public's knowledge about the benefits of exercise continues to grow, so does the demand for diversified programming. Not only must fitness programs appeal to a wider group of people than ever, but they must also be varied enough to hold the interest of exercisers and to promote overall fitness without injury.

The best way for personal trainers to meet this need is through the development of cross-training programs. From a clinical standpoint, cross-training enables individuals to place significant demands on the heart and circulatory system, since it typically involves aerobic-type activities. Cross-training produces a variety of chronic adaptations, including increased cardiac output and blood volume plus a greater number of red blood cells which ultimately enhances the body's ability to transport oxygenated blood to the exercising muscles.

However, oxygen delivery is only part of the process, since the muscles used in performing a particular physical activity must be able to extract oxygen from the blood, and then use it to produce the energy needed to power human movement.

In response to engaging in aerobic-type cross-training on a regular basis, several significant changes take place within the muscle cells:

- The number and size of mitochondria (organelles in the muscle cells that produce ATP for energy) increase.
- Concentration of important oxidative enzymes (within the mitochondria that are involved in the production of ATP) increases.
- The amount of glycogen (carbohydrate) stored in the muscle increases.
- The amount of triglycerides (fat) stored in the muscle increases.
- The ability to oxidize fat from primarily muscle-fat stores, but also from adipose tissue stores, increases. This enhanced ability to use stored fat results in less glycogen depletion, less lactic acid accumulation, and, concomitantly, less muscular fatigue and better endurance.

These changes, called peripheral adaptations, help the muscles to contract repeatedly and more efficiently during exercise. Peripheral adaptations are activity-specific (i.e., they differ from activity to activity). For example, trained distance runners cannot transfer their high level of endurance for running to swimming because the peripheral muscular adaptations required for optimal performance are different for swimming.

The combined effect of peripheral and central adaptations determines the quality of performance. Improving one without the other, however, produces limited improvements in sport-specific performance. Accordingly, while cross-training may offer certain advantages for the typical fitness enthusiast, it may also have a few limitations for competitive athletes. As a result, individuals who know exactly what they want from their exercise efforts are better able to decide whether to engage in cross-training.

The Benefits of Cross-training

Incorporating several different forms of exercise in a training program can be an excellent way to develop the various components of fitness. The following are among the numerous benefits of cross-training that have been documented:

- *Reduced risk of injury.* By spreading the cumulative level of orthopedic stress over additional muscles and joints, individuals are able to exercise more frequently and for longer durations without excessively overloading particularly vulnerable areas of the body (e.g., knees, hips, back, shoulders, elbows, and feet). Persons who are particularly prone to lower-leg problems from running long distances should consider incorporating low-impact activities such as stair climbing, cycling, and swimming into their regimens. It should be noted, however, that competitive cross-trainers can experience certain overuse injuries due to inadequate muscle rest, an unbalanced workout schedule, or both.
- *Enhanced weight loss.* Individuals who want to lose weight and body fat should engage in an exercise program that enables them to safely burn a significant number of calories. Research has shown that such a goal, in most instances, is best accomplished when individuals exercise for relatively long durations (i.e., more than 30 minutes) at a moderate level of intensity (i.e., 60% to 85% of maximal heart rate). Overweight individuals can effectively achieve a reduction in body weight and fat stores by combining 2 or more physical activities in a cross-training regimen. For example, such a person can exercise on a stair climber for 20 to 30 minutes and then cycle for an additional 20 to 30 minutes.
- *Improved total fitness.* Cross-training can include activities that develop muscular fitness, as well as aerobic conditioning. While an individual's muscular fitness gains will typically be less than if he/she participated only in strength training, the added benefits of improving muscular strength and endurance can pay substantial dividends. For example, research has shown that resistance training can help individuals prevent injury, control body weight, and improve functional capacity.
- *Enhanced exercise adherence.* Research on exercise adherence indicates that many individuals drop out of exercise programs because they become bored or injured. Cross-training is a safe and relatively easy way to add variety to an exercise program. In the process, it can play a positive role in promoting long-term exercise adherence by reducing the incidence of injury and eliminating or diminishing the potential for boredom.

CROSS-TRAINING GUIDELINES

Whether individuals exercise for fitness or because they are competitive athletes, the essential fundamentals of cross-training are the same. Individuals can choose to vary their exercise programs from workout to workout by engaging in different types of activities, or they can simply add a new form of exercise (e.g., resistance training) to their existing workout routines.

One of the easiest ways to incorporate cross-training is to alternate between activities (e.g., run one day, stair climb the next, cycle the next). Exercisers can also alternate activities within a single workout (e.g., walking on a treadmill for 10 minutes, exercising on an elliptical trainer for 10 minutes, and cycling for 10 minutes — for a total of 30 minutes of exercise). Table 6-1 provides examples of typical cross-training workout schedules. As can be seen in the examples, at no time do consecutive workouts involve high-impact activities (e.g., running).

Making a cross-training program effective is basically a function of adhering to established exercise guidelines. If individuals engage in 20 to 60 minutes of aerobic exercise at least three days a week at an intensity level of approximately 60 to 90 percent of maximum heart rate, they will become more aerobically fit. According to guidelines published by the

---

Table 6-1.   Examples of Aerobic Cross-training Workout Schedules for a Week

A 3-day workout schedule with a single activity per day

Monday:	Exercise on a stair-climbing machine for 20 to 30 minutes
Wednesday:	Jog for 30 minutes
Friday:	Exercise on a stair-climbing machine for 20 to 30 minutes

A 3-day workout schedule with multiple activities per day

Monday:	Exercise on a stair-climbing machine for 10 minutes
	Ride a stationary exercise cycle for 10 minutes
	Run on a treadmill for 10 minutes
Wednesday:	Walk on an inclined (or graded) treadmill for 20 minutes
	Exercise on an elliptical trainer 10 minutes
Friday:	Jog for 15 minutes
	Swim for 15 minutes

A 5-day workout schedule with multiple activities per day

Monday:	Exercise on a stair-climbing machine for 20 to 30 minutes
Tuesday:	Perform a total-body strength-training circuit
Wednesday:	Jog for 30 minutes
Thursday:	Perform a total-body strength-training circuit
Friday:	Exercise on a stair-climbing machine for 20 to 30 minutes

American College of Sports Medicine, individuals should perform at least 8 to 10 exercises that condition the major muscle groups of the body twice a week to enhance muscular fitness.

MIXING IT UP

From the inception of physical conditioning programs, mankind has been searching for a "better" way to train. Apparently, nothing has been held sacred in the pursuit of the best way to achieve maximal training results – contemporary conditioning tools, updated exercise prescriptions, newer training environments, and heightened levels of hands-on assistance.

In the past 10 years, a substantial number of exercise enthusiasts have discovered cross-training to be an alternative and improved method of exercise (Figure 6-1). Unlike many previous attempts to discern how to improve training, cross-training has been found to be a highly safe, relatively enjoyable method. In fact, most cross-training enthusiasts proudly proclaim that "they'll never go back" to single-activity training. To these individuals, many of the inherent problems that occur in a standard exercise regimen can be easily remedied by adhering to the advice: "If your workout needs fixing, fix it up by mixing it up."

Figure 6-1. One of the easiest ways to begin cross-training is to alternate between various types of exercise activities.

Recommended Reading

American College of Sports Medicine. *ACSM's Guidelines for Exercise Testing and Prescription*, 6th ed. Philadelphia, PA: Lippincott Williams & Wilkins, 2000.

Bray, B. Cross training. *American Fitness Quarterly* 9(2):8, 60, 1990.

Brzycki, M. *Cross Training for Fitness*. Indianapolis, IN: Masters Press, 1997.

Burke, ER. The wisdom of cross training. *National Strength and Conditioning Association Journal* 16(4):58-60, 1994.

O'Shea, P. The science of cross training: Theory and application for peak performance. *National Strength and Conditioning Association Journal* 16(4):58-60, 1994.

Stamford, B. Task-specific training vs. cross training. *The Physician and Sportsmedicine* 19(7): 113-114, 1991.

SECTION II

MUSCULOSKELETAL TESTING AND TRAINING

CHAPTER 7

• •

MEASURING
MUSCULOSKELETAL FITNESS

*G*iven the critical role that the muscular system plays in helping individuals to perform activities of daily living (at home, work, and play), the importance of being able to recruit muscles to do what one wants, when one wants, cannot be overemphasized. Collectively, this capacity is referred to as muscular fitness.

Most exercise scientists contend that muscular fitness should be viewed as two distinct components of physical fitness: muscular strength and muscular endurance. Muscular strength is generally defined as the ability of a muscle or a muscle group to exert maximum force. Muscular endurance, on the other hand, is the ability of a muscle or a muscle group to exert submaximal force for an extended period of time. The first step in assessing muscular fitness involves identifying which muscle-related component of physical fitness you want to measure — muscular strength or muscular endurance.

Muscular fitness is usually assessed by tests that employ specific devices for measuring muscular strength and endurance or by calisthenic-type exercises. Most testing that employs devices is conducted in a laboratory, rather than a field setting, because using devices often requires trained personnel and is relatively expensive.

Calisthenic-type tests, on the other hand, can be performed in a non-laboratory setting. This type of testing usually requires little or no equipment, can be performed almost anywhere, enables several individuals to be tested simultaneously, and involves body movements that are more functional in nature.

USING DEVICES TO MEASURE MUSCULAR FITNESS

A number of devices for measuring muscular fitness have been developed, including dynamometers, cable tension meters, electromechanical and hydraulic devices, and resistance machines. Deciding which device to use can involve several factors, including the cost and availability of the apparatus, the level of expertise required to use it, the muscle or muscle group to be tested, the type of information desired, and for what purpose the findings will be used.

MEASURING MUSCULAR FITNESS WITH CALISTHENICS

In certain situations, calisthenic-type tests may offer a more appropriate means for assessing muscular fitness. These tests involve measuring how well (quantitatively) an individual can perform calisthenic-type exercises (e.g., push-ups, chin-ups, pull-ups, dips, and sit-ups) in terms specific to the muscle-related component being assessed. When dynamic muscular strength is measured using a calisthenic-type test, for example, the maximum amount of weight that can be lifted in excess of body weight for one repetition must be determined. On the other hand, assessing dynamic muscular endurance through the use of a calisthenic-type test involves determining the maximum number of repetitions of each exercise that can be performed. Because using calisthenic-type testing for muscular endurance has been popular over the years with several organizations (e.g., the U.S. military, the President's Council on Physical Fitness and Sports), normative data are available that allow you to compare the results of your clients' performance to other groups.

FIELD TESTS FOR MEASURING MUSCULAR STRENGTH

Unquestionably, the most widely used field test for evaluating muscular strength is the one-repetition maximum (1-RM) test. This test has traditionally been used to assess dynamic strength by determining how much weight an individual can lift during a single repetition. This approach to measuring muscular strength usually involves performing three or four exercises that are representative of the body's major muscle groups. For example, performing a bench press or an incline press is frequently used to assess the strength of the torso (upper-body) muscles, while a squat or a leg press is typically performed to ascertain hip-leg (lower-body) strength.

However, conducting the test is often easier than interpreting test results. Once you've obtained your clients' 1-RM results, you face the dilemma of deciding what, if anything, the data mean. For example, are they an accurate reflection of how much work was actually performed in the weight room? Do they provide a reliable means for evaluating the effectiveness of strength-training efforts or current strength level? Do they give you a logical means for comparing one client's strength level to another's? The answer is, at best, questionable.

How much work is performed in the weight room and how strong a client actually becomes are affected by a number of genetic factors that are beyond his or her control. In other words, what goals you help your clients to achieve in the weight room will be relative to their current musculoskeletal fitness and genetic capabilities. Demonstrating a specific strength achievement is relative to such factors as the length of the arms, the proportion of fast-to-slow twitch fibers, the ratio of muscle length to tendon length, the insertion point of the muscle on the skeletal lever involved, and the level of neuromuscular efficiency.

In addition to the restraints that genetic factors impose on 1-RM testing, a more serious limitation is that it can be dangerous. Safety can become a major concern if your clients attempt to exceed the physiological capacity of their bodies or if the lifting techniques expose them to undue risk of injury.

Unfortunately, the trial-and-error method of increasing the weight in the 1-RM approach, particularly if it's combined with a herculean effort to validate an unrealistic exhibition of strength, often leads to attempting to use too much weight in assessment efforts, risking injury. Performing a 1-RM lift with a relatively heavy weight can place an inordinate level of stress on the muscles, bones, and connective tissues. The 1-RM approach to strength testing can also increase blood pressure to dangerous levels. Lifters, particularly at the upper end of the trial and error 1-RM method, tend to hold their breath while performing the exercise (i.e., Valsalva maneuver), an action that increases blood pressure beyond what is normally encountered when lifting less (submaximal) resistance.

Another safety issue involved in 1-RM testing is that if your clients attempt to lift too much, they may compromise the proper techniques for performing the exercise, and injure themselves. For example, one of the most common problems attendant to 1-RM testing is back injuries, which can occur as a result of the 1-RM bench press test. When using excessively high loads, individuals arch their backs during the lift, thereby placing undue stress on the lumbar spine. Finally, in a few isolated instances, individuals have been injured when they lost control of the weight at some point in the 1-RM lift. Accordingly, if you decide to perform 1-RM testing on your clients, you must be a competent spotter to help them maintain control of the weight during the exercise and to provide feedback regarding adherence to proper breathing and lifting techniques.

Given that individuals have their own unique genetic potential for achieving (and demonstrating) muscular strength, comparing the strength of one person to another is of questionable value. A more logical approach would be to compare the results of your clients' strength testing to their previous performances. Even accounting for the occasional glitch in testing results that might be attributed to either emotional or mental factors, comparing the results of their assessment efforts with their previous test scores should, over time, provide a reasonable basis for measuring the relative progress of their training efforts.

MEASURING STRENGTH SAFELY

In view of the inherent problems in assessing strength (e.g., genetic differences, safety limitations), what measures should you use to assess this variable? Two of the better approaches are the strength-to-weight ratio and the one-rep predicted max from reps-to-fatigue.

The strength-to-weight ratio is a relative method of determining how much is lifted on a given exercise compared to the listed values. This approach uses body weight (BW) and gender to categorize performance on a scale ranging from excellent to poor. Tables 7-1 through 7-4 present the 1-RM/BW values for both the leg press and the bench press exercises. To use either table, you divide the amount lifted by body weight and then compare the result to the values listed in the table. For example, if a male client is 35 years old, weighs 200 pounds, and can bench press 250 pounds, his 1-RM/BW ratio of 1.25 (250 divided by 200) would categorize his performance as "excellent."

The one-rep predicted max from the reps-to-fatigue method is an approach based on the precept that a direct relationship exists between anaerobic endurance and strength. Given this relationship, it follows that you can determine your clients' level of strength by assessing their level of anaerobic endurance (and vice versa). Unquestionably, the most positive

Table 7-1. Leg Strength (men)*
1 Repetition Maximum Leg Press
Leg press weight ratio = weight pushed ÷ body weight

Percentile Rank	Age						
	<20	20-29	30-39	40-49	50-59	60+	
99	>2.82	>2.40	>2.20	>2.02	>1.90	>1.80	
95	2.82	2.40	2.20	2.02	1.90	1.80	S
90	2.53	2.27	2.07	1.92	1.80	1.73	
85	2.40	2.18	1.99	1.86	1.75	1.68	
80	2.28	2.13	1.93	1.82	1.71	1.62	E
75	2.18	2.09	1.89	1.78	1.68	1.58	
70	2.15	2.05	1.85	1.74	1.64	1.56	
65	2.10	2.01	1.81	1.71	1.61	1.52	
60	2.04	1.97	1.77	1.68	1.58	1.49	G
55	2.01	1.94	1.74	1.65	1.55	1.46	
50	1.95	1.91	1.71	1.62	1.52	1.43	
45	1.93	1.87	1.68	1.59	1.50	1.40	
40	1.90	1.83	1.65	1.57	1.46	1.38	F
35	1.89	1.78	1.62	1.54	1.42	1.34	
30	1.82	1.74	1.59	1.51	1.39	1.30	
25	1.80	1.68	1.56	1.48	1.36	1.27	
20	1.70	1.63	1.52	1.44	1.32	1.25	P
15	1.61	1.58	1.48	1.40	1.28	1.21	
10	1.57	1.51	1.43	1.35	1.22	1.16	
5	1.46	1.42	1.34	1.27	1.15	1.08	VP
1	<1.46	<1.42	<1.34	<1.27	<1.15	<1.08	
N =	60	424	1909	2089	1286	347	
Total N = 6115							

* Data provided by the Institute for Aerobics Research, Dallas, TX, (1994). S, superior; E, excellent; G, good; F, fair; P, poor; VP, very poor. (Reprinted with permission from American College of Sports Medicine. *ACSM's Guidelines for Exercise Testing and Prescription*, 5th ed. Baltimore, MD: Williams & Wilkins, 1995.)

aspect of this approach is that measuring anaerobic endurance is a much safer procedure than directly determining a 1-RM because it involves repetitive lifting of submaximal loads.

Despite being a much more safety-oriented approach for measuring a 1-RM, identifying a practical and relatively accurate method for assessing anaerobic endurance has traditionally been a challenging task for the exercise science community. However, research conducted in the early 1990s by Matt Brzycki, the health/fitness coordinator and strength coach at Princeton University, demonstrated that a nearly linear relationship exists between the number of reps that can be performed before reaching a fatigue state and the percentage of maximum load

Table 7-2. Leg Strength (women)*
1 Repetition Maximum Leg Press
Leg press weight ratio = weight pushed ÷ body weight

Percentile Rank	Age						
	<20	20-29	30-39	40-49	50-59	60+	
99	>1.88	>1.98	>1.68	>1.57	>1.43	>1.43	
95	1.88	1.98	1.68	1.57	1.43	1.43	S
90	1.85	1.82	1.61	1.48	1.37	1.32	
85	1.81	1.76	1.52	1.40	1.31	1.32	
80	1.71	1.68	1.47	1.37	1.25	1.18	E
75	1.69	1.65	1.42	1.33	1.20	1.16	
70	1.65	1.58	1.39	1.29	1.17	1.13	
65	1.62	1.53	1.36	1.27	1.12	1.08	
60	1.59	1.50	1.33	1.23	1.10	1.04	G
55	1.51	1.47	1.31	1.20	1.08	1.01	
50	1.45	1.44	1.27	1.18	1.05	.99	
45	1.42	1.40	1.24	1.15	1.02	.97	
40	1.38	1.37	1.21	1.13	.99	.93	F
35	1.33	1.32	1.18	1.11	.97	.90	
30	1.29	1.27	1.15	1.08	.95	.88	
25	1.25	1.26	1.12	1.06	.92	.86	
20	1.22	1.22	1.09	1.02	.88	.85	P
15	1.19	1.18	1.05	.97	.84	.80	
10	1.09	1.14	1.00	.94	.78	.72	
5	1.06	.99	.96	.85	.72	.63	VP
1	<1.06	<.99	<.96	<.85	<.72	<.63	
N =	20	192	281	337	192	44	
Total N = 1066							

* Data provided by the Institute for Aerobics Research, Dallas, TX, (1994). S, superior; E, excellent; G, good; F, fair; P, poor; VP, very poor. (Reprinted with permission from American College of Sports Medicine. *ACSM's Guidelines for Exercise Testing and Prescription*, 5th ed. Baltimore, MD: Williams & Wilkins, 1995.)

that can be lifted. Based upon his findings, Brzycki subsequently developed an equation for predicting 1-RM when the number of reps-to-fatigue performed is less than 10 (Box 7-1). If the number of reps-to-fatigue is exactly 10, the amount of weight lifted should be divided by 0.75 to get the predicted 1-RM. Thus, if 10 reps are performed with a weight load of 180 pounds, the estimated 1-RM would be 240 pounds. Because Brzycki's equation has been found to be less reliable if the number of successfully completed repetitions before reaching the point of fatigue exceeds 10, the reps-to-fatigue method for predicting 1-RM should not be used if the rep count exceeds 10. A user-friendly matrix for predicting 1-RM based on reps-to-fatigue with weights ranging from 45 to 310 pounds is presented in Table 7-5. For example, an individual

Table 7-3. Upper-Body Strength (men)*
1 Repetition Maximum Bench Press
Bench press weight ratio = weight pushed ÷ body weight

Percentile Rank	Age <20	20-29	30-39	40-49	50-59	60+	
99	>1.76	>1.63	>1.35	>1.20	>1.05	>.94	
95	1.76	1.63	1.35	1.20	1.05	.94	S
90	1.46	1.48	1.24	1.10	.97	.89	
85	1.38	1.37	1.17	1.04	.93	.84	
80	1.34	1.32	1.12	1.00	.90	.82	E
75	1.29	1.26	1.08	.96	.87	.79	
70	1.24	1.22	1.04	.93	.84	.77	
65	1.23	1.18	1.01	.90	.81	.74	
60	1.19	1.14	.98	.88	.79	.72	G
55	1.16	1.10	.96	.86	.77	.70	
50	1.13	1.06	.93	.84	.75	.68	
45	1.10	1.03	.90	.82	.73	.67	
40	1.06	.99	.88	.80	.71	.66	F
35	1.01	.96	.86	.78	.70	.65	
30	.96	.93	.83	.76	.68	.63	
25	.93	.90	.81	.74	.66	.60	
20	.89	.88	.78	.72	.63	.57	P
15	.86	.84	.75	.69	.60	.56	
10	.81	.80	.71	.65	.57	.53	
5	.76	.72	.65	.59	.53	.49	VP
1	<.76	<.72	<.65	<.59	<.53	<.49	
N =	60	425	1909	2090	1279	343	
Total N = 6106							

* Data provided by the Institute for Aerobics Research, Dallas, TX, (1994). S, superior; E, excellent; G, good; F, fair; P, poor; VP, very poor. Reprinted with permission from American College of Sports Medicine. *ACSM's Guidelines for Exercise Testing and Prescription*, 5th ed. Baltimore, MD: Williams & Wilkins, 1995.

Box 7-1.
Brzycki Equation
Equation for predicting 1-RM based on reps-to-fatigue

$$\text{PREDICTED 1-RM} = \frac{\text{Weight Lifted}}{1.0278 - .0278X}$$

where X = the number of reps performed

Table 7-4. Upper-Body Strength (women)*
1 Repetition Maximum Bench Press
Bench press weight ratio = weight pushed ÷ body weight

Percentile Rank	Age						
	<20	20-29	30-39	40-49	50-59	60+	
99	>.88	>1.01	>.82	>.77	>.68	>.72	
95	.88	1.01	.82	.77	.68	.72	S
90	.83	.90	.76	.71	.61	.64	
85	.81	.83	.72	.66	.57	.59	
80	.77	.80	.70	.62	.55	.54	E
75	.76	.77	.65	.60	.53	.53	
70	.74	.74	.63	.57	.52	.51	
65	.70	.72	.62	.55	.50	.48	
60	.65	.70	.60	.54	.48	.47	G
55	.64	.68	.58	.53	.47	.46	
50	.63	.65	.57	.52	.46	.45	
45	.60	.63	.55	.51	.45	.44	
40	.58	.59	.53	.50	.44	.43	F
35	.57	.58	.52	.48	.43	.41	
30	.56	.56	.51	.47	.42	.40	
25	.55	.53	.49	.45	.41	.39	
20	.53	.51	.47	.43	.39	.38	P
15	.52	.50	.45	.42	.38	.36	
10	.50	.480	.42	.38	.37	.33	
5	.41	.436	.39	.35	.305	.26	VP
1	<.41	<.436	<.39	<.35	<.305	<.26	
N =	20	191	379	333	189	42	
Total N = 1154							

* Data provided by the Institute for Aerobics Research, Dallas, TX, (1994). S, superior; E, excellent; G, good; F, fair; P, poor; VP, very poor. Reprinted with permission from American College of Sports Medicine. *ACSM's Guidelines for Exercise Testing and Prescription*, 5th ed. Baltimore, MD: Williams & Wilkins, 1995.

who can complete five repetitions before reaching the point of fatigue with a 100-pound weight has a predicted 1-rep max of 112 pounds. The reps-to-fatigue method of measuring muscular strength provides trainers with a safe, practical assessment tool.

CHECKING OUT THE FACTS

The need to check things out starts early in most people's lives. Check both ways before you cross the street. Check with your parents before you make plans. Check your appearance before you leave for school in the morning. Check your teeth before the big date. And, the need to check things out becomes continually more important as people grow older.

Table 7-5. Predicted 1-Rep Max Based on Reps-to-Fatigue

Weight	Repetitions									
	1	2	3	4	5	6	7	8	9	10
45	45	46	48	49	51	52	54	56	58	60
50	50	51	53	55	56	58	60	62	64	67
55	55	57	58	60	62	64	66	68	71	73
60	60	62	64	65	67	70	72	74	77	80
65	65	67	69	71	73	75	78	81	84	87
70	70	72	74	76	79	81	84	87	90	93
75	75	77	79	82	84	87	90	93	96	100
80	80	82	85	87	90	93	96	99	103	107
85	85	87	90	93	96	99	102	106	109	113
90	90	93	95	98	101	105	108	112	116	120
95	95	98	101	104	107	110	114	118	122	127
100	100	103	106	109	112	116	120	124	129	133
105	105	108	111	115	118	122	126	130	135	140
110	110	113	116	120	124	128	132	137	141	147
115	115	118	122	125	129	134	138	143	148	153
120	120	123	127	131	135	139	144	149	154	160
125	125	129	132	136	141	145	150	155	161	167
130	130	134	138	142	146	151	156	161	167	173
135	135	139	143	147	152	157	162	168	174	180
140	140	144	148	153	157	163	168	174	180	187
145	145	149	154	158	163	168	174	180	186	193
150	150	154	159	164	169	174	180	186	193	200
155	155	159	164	169	174	180	186	192	199	207
160	160	165	169	175	180	186	192	199	206	213
165	165	170	175	180	186	192	198	205	212	220
170	170	175	180	185	191	197	204	211	219	227
175	175	180	185	191	197	203	210	217	225	233
180	180	185	191	196	202	209	216	223	231	240
185	185	190	196	202	208	215	222	230	238	247
190	190	195	201	207	214	221	228	236	244	253
195	195	201	206	213	219	226	234	242	251	260
200	200	206	212	218	225	232	240	248	257	267
205	205	211	217	224	231	238	246	254	264	273
210	210	216	222	229	236	244	252	261	270	280
215	215	221	228	235	242	250	258	267	276	287
220	220	226	233	240	247	255	264	273	283	293
225	225	231	238	245	253	261	270	279	289	300
230	230	237	244	251	259	267	276	286	296	307
235	235	242	249	256	264	273	282	292	302	313
240	240	247	254	262	270	279	288	298	209	320
245	245	252	259	267	276	285	294	304	315	327
250	250	257	265	273	281	290	300	310	321	333
255	255	262	270	278	287	296	306	317	328	340
260	260	267	275	284	292	302	312	323	334	347
265	265	273	281	289	298	308	318	329	341	353
270	270	278	286	295	304	314	324	335	347	360
275	275	283	291	300	309	319	330	341	354	367
280	280	288	296	305	315	325	336	348	360	373
285	285	293	302	311	321	331	342	354	366	380
290	290	298	307	316	326	337	348	360	373	387
295	295	303	312	322	332	343	354	366	379	393
300	300	309	318	327	337	348	360	372	386	400
305	305	314	323	333	343	354	366	379	392	407
310	310	319	328	338	349	360	372	385	399	413

In a similar manner, it could be argued that if your clients want to maximize the capacity of their bodies to withstand daily demands and minimize musculoskeletal aches, pains, and injuries, they should periodically check their level of muscular fitness. Although they might have an intuitive feeling for how muscularly fit they are, a more structured evaluation can offer a quantified basis for deciding whether they need to take specific steps to remedy a functional deficiency.

The data they obtain from such an assessment can also serve as a subsequent benchmark for evaluating the effectiveness of their muscular conditioning programs. Individuals are never too old to be tested. If the test for evaluating their levels of muscular fitness is conducted safely and provides meaningful feedback, they have everything to gain and nothing to lose. The facts are irrefutable: Muscles do matter. Check it out.

Recommended Reading

American College of Sports Medicine. *ACSM's Guidelines for Exercise Testing and Prescription*, 6th ed. Philadelphia, PA: Lippincott Williams & Wilkins, 2000.

American College of Sports Medicine. *ACSM's Resource Manual for Guidelines for Exercise Testing and Prescription*, 4th ed. Philadelphia, PA: Lippincott Williams & Wilkins, 2001.

Brzycki, M. Strength testing – predicting a one-rep max from reps-to-fatigue. *Journal of Physical Education, Recreation and Dance* 64(1):88-90, 1993.

Golding, LA, Myers, CF, Sinning, WE. *The Y's Way to Physical Fitness, Revised*. Chicago, IL: National Board of YMCA, 1982.

Heyward, VH. *Advanced Fitness Assessment & Exercise Prescription*, 2nd ed. Champaign, IL: Human Kinetics Publishers, Inc., 1991.

Nieman, DC. *Fitness and Sports Medicine: An Introduction*, 3rd ed. Palo Alto, CA: Bull Publishing Company, 1995.

Peterson, JA, Bryant, CX (eds). *StairMaster Fitness Handbook*, 2nd ed. Champaign, IL: Sagamore Publishing Company, Inc., 1995.

Peterson, JA, Bryant, CX, Peterson, SL. *Strength Training for Women*. Champaign, IL: Human Kinetics Publishers, Inc., 1995.

CHAPTER 8

DEVELOPING A STRENGTH TRAINING PROGRAM

*U*ntil the early 1980s, resistance (strength) training was primarily performed by selected groups of athletes and body builders. However, today it has become an integral component of exercise programs for competitive athletes, children, older adults, cardiac rehabilitation patients, pregnant women, and individuals desiring to enhance physique and improve health.

Much of the increased popularity of resistance training can be attributed to successfully educating the fitness industry regarding the positive benefits associated with resistance training, which is highly effective in developing and maintaining:

- Muscular fitness (strength and endurance)
- Muscle mass
- Physical function (activities of daily living and athletic performance)
- Related health and fitness benefits

It is also of value in the treatment of low back pain, osteoporosis, diabetes, obesity, and orthopedic injuries and may be helpful in reducing falls in elderly persons. In addition, progressive resistance training may have favorable effects on resting blood pressure and lipid and lipoprotein levels and on cardiovascular function. Following a resistance-training program, heart rate and blood pressure responses are reduced when lifting any given load. Thus, resistance training can decrease stress on the heart during activities of daily living (e.g., carrying groceries or luggage).

Given the increasing body of knowledge concerning the benefits of resistance training, it is not surprising that the medical community and numerous professional organizations dedicated to exercise science now recommend that individuals of all ages and both genders participate in appropriately prescribed, resistance-training programs. This chapter addresses the basic principles and guidelines needed to develop safe and effective resistance-training programs for healthy adults and certain special populations.

RESISTANCE-TRAINING PROGRAM CONSIDERATIONS

Resistance training is considered an important component of a comprehensive fitness program. A proper resistance-training program should be based on several factors, including health and fitness status, goals, proper application of the basic principles of training, and the training environment.

HEALTH AND FITNESS STATUS

Prior to initiating resistance training, participants should take certain precautions. At a minimum, a health/medical questionnaire should be completed. One of the most widely used health/medical questionnaires is the Physical Activity Readiness Questionnaire (PAR-Q). The PAR-Q is a simple, yet valid query form used for screening individuals prior to beginning an exercise program (refer to Chapter 1).

A muscular fitness evaluation should be considered prior to initiating resistance training. Such information may serve several purposes. For example, the initial level of muscular fitness can affect the magnitude and rate of improvement from a resistance-training program. Generally, muscularly fit individuals do not improve as much or as quickly as untrained individuals, which should be considered when establishing goals or in evaluating the effectiveness of resistance training. It is important to note, however, that some individuals may be unable to tolerate muscular fitness testing, especially lifting heavy loads.

GOALS

Once pre-exercise screening and assessment is complete, it is important to develop realistic goals and objectives for the resistance-training program. Unrealistic expectations can lead to adverse outcomes, including discouragement, poor adherence, and injury. To enhance the likelihood that resistance training is based on appropriate expectations, an understanding of the physiological adaptations is important. Table 8-1 summarizes the effects of resistance training on selected health and fitness variables.

BASIC TRAINING PRINCIPLES

Overload and specificity are fundamental precepts of resistance training. Both relate to the ability of targeted muscle groups to adapt to progressive stress. Adherence to these principles elicits both structural and functional adaptations. A resistance-training program that does not incorporate these fundamentals cannot provide consistent improvement in muscular fitness.

Overload is accomplished when a greater than normal physical demand is placed on muscles or muscle groups. The amount of overload required is dependent upon the current level of muscular fitness. For example, a football player requires a different level of overload than a sedentary person. To produce strength and endurance gains, the muscular system must be progressively overloaded. By definition, overloading is dynamic (changing). As a muscle or muscle group adapts, a progressive overload is required to continue improvement. In the context of resistance training, overload can be achieved by one or more of the following variations:

- Increasing the resistance or weight
- Increasing the repetitions
- Increasing the sets
- Decreasing the rest period between sets or exercises

Table 8-1. The Effects of Resistance Training on Selected Health and Fitness Variables*

Variable	Training Adaptation
Bone Mineral Density	↑↑
Body Composition	
% fat	↓
Lean body mass	↑↑
Strength	↑↑↑
Glucose Metabolism	
Insulin response to glucose challenge	↓↓
Basal insulin levels	↓
Insulin sensitivity	↑↑
Serum Lipids	
HDL	↑↔
LDL	↓↔
Blood Pressure at Rest	
Systolic	↓↔
Diastolic	↓↔
$\dot{V}O_{2max}$	↑
Endurance Time	↑↑
Physical Function	↑↑↑
Basal Metabolism	↑↑

Legend: ↑ = increase; ↓ = decrease; ↔ = unchanged; ↑ or ↓ = small effect; ↑↑ or ↓↓ = moderate effect; ↑↑↑ or ↓↓↓ = large effect; HDL = high-density lipoprotein cholesterol; LDL = low-density lipoprotein cholesterol.

* Adapted from Pollock, ML, Vincent, KR. Resistance training for health. *The President's Council on Physical Fitness and Sports Research Digest,* 1996.

A training intensity of roughly 40 to 60 percent of one repetition maximum (1-RM) appears to be sufficient for the development of muscular strength in most normally active individuals. Intensities of 80 to 100 percent, however, have been shown to produce the most rapid gain in muscular strength. However, due to the possibility of overtraining or injury, such intensities are generally contraindicated, especially in previously sedentary middle-aged and older adults.

Specificity relates to the nature of changes (structural and functional, systemic and local) that occur in an individual as a result of training. These adaptations are specific, and occur only in the overloaded muscle groups or muscles.

The concept of specificity has other applications when applied to resistance training. Sports require specific movement patterns, which a properly designed program should consider. Although a comprehensive, resistance-training program should include exercises for all the major muscle groups, it can be modified to address the unique demands of a particular sport or activity. The resistance-training program for a baseball pitcher, for example, should emphasize the rotator cuff, the shoulder girdle, and the upper extremities more than resistance training for a soccer player, which focuses on the lower extremities and includes exercises to develop strength and endurance for the gluteals, quadriceps, hamstrings, abductors, adductors, and gastrocnemius.

One of the most controversial issues regarding specificity has been the debate over how to develop muscular strength versus muscular endurance. Based on the available literature, different programs should be employed. Muscular strength is the ability to generate force at a given speed (velocity) of movement, while muscular endurance is the ability to persist in physical activity or resist muscular fatigue. Generally, strength is developed with more resistance and fewer repetitions, while muscular endurance requires low-to-moderate resistance and more repetitions. Adaptations occur at both the cellular level (metabolic adaptation) and at the fiber level (selective hypertrophy and motor unit recruitment patterns). Both strength and endurance are developed, to some extent, regardless of the resistance-training prescription because both fitness components exist on a continuum. However, one component may be emphasized, depending upon the specific resistance-program prescription.

Strength gains also are dependent on the mode of resistance training (static, dynamic, isokinetic), the type of contraction (concentric, eccentric), the speed of contraction, and the joint position. How and the extent to which these factors should be incorporated into the design of a resistance-training program remains an ongoing topic of discussion.

THE TRAINING ENVIRONMENT

A wide variety of training methods and equipment exists for improving muscular fitness. Methods of resistance training are typically classified according to the type of muscular contraction (static, dynamic, or isokinetic).

Types of Muscular Contractions

During static (isometric) contractions, the muscle or muscle group involved maintains a constant length as resistance is applied and no change in joint position occurs. Research has demonstrated that static training produces improvements in muscular strength. The strength gains, however, are limited to the specific joint angles at which the static contractions are performed. As a result, static training may have limited value in enhancing functional strength. Static training has also been associated with acute elevations in blood pressure, perhaps due to increased intrathoracic pressure during the static contraction. Despite the limitations, static training appears to play a beneficial role in physical rehabilitation. For example, it is effective at maintenance of muscular strength and prevention of atrophy associated with the immobilization of a limb (e.g., application of a cast, splint, or brace).

Dynamic (isotonic) resistance training is another common method. If movement of the joint occurs during contraction, it is dynamic. If force is sufficient to overcome resistance and shortening of the muscle occurs (e.g., the lifting phase of a biceps curl), the contraction is concentric. When resistance is greater than force and the muscle lengthens during contraction, it is eccentric (e.g., the lowering phase of the biceps curl).

Most dynamic resistance training includes both concentric and eccentric action. Significantly heavier loads can be moved eccentrically. In nonfatigued muscle, the eccentric strength capabilities can be as high as 40 to 50 percent greater than the concentric strength capabilities. At the onset of fatigue, the relative level of eccentric strength and the eccentric:concentric ratio increase even more. Individuals who train eccentrically tend to experience increased levels of delayed-onset muscular soreness. Eccentric training can, however, play an important role in preventing and/or rehabilitating certain musculoskeletal injuries. For example, eccentric training, because it can affect deceleration capacity, has been shown to be effective for treating hamstring strains, tennis elbow, and patellofemoral pain syndrome.

Dynamic exercise can be further categorized into constant resistance and variable resistance. During constant resistance exercise, resistance applied does not change throughout the range of motion. Because force-production can vary significantly at different points in the range of motion, the potential gains are limited by inherent weak points on the strength curve of working muscle. During variable resistance exercise, leverage advantages and disadvantages are changed over the range of motion, resulting in potential gains that are, theoretically, not restricted by variations in the strength curve of a muscle.

The other major type of resistance training, isokinetic exercise, involves constant speed muscular contraction against accommodating resistance. The speed of movement is controlled and the amount of resistance is proportional to the amount of force produced throughout the full range of motion. The theoretical advantage of isokinetic exercise is the development of maximal muscle tension throughout the range of motion. Research documents the effectiveness of isokinetic training. Strength gains achieved during high-speed training (i.e., contraction velocities of 180 degrees per second or faster) appear to carry over to all speeds that are less than that specific speed. Improvement in strength at slow speeds of movement, however, has not been shown to carry over to faster speeds.

Types of Resistance-Training Equipment

A variety of equipment is available to accommodate different types of training and different resistance-training goals. Almost any type of resistance equipment enables individuals to meet training goals provided it allows an overload and appropriate exercise guidelines are followed. Individuals should select equipment that is accessible and is consistent with personal needs and interests. Table 8-2 compares three common types of equipment on selected criteria.

GUIDELINES FOR DEVELOPING MUSCULAR FITNESS

Specific guidelines for achieving muscular fitness are not as universally accepted as those for aerobic fitness. There is considerable controversy regarding the most appropriate prescription for developing muscular fitness, especially in novice exercisers and competitive athletes. However, there is growing acceptance that moderate-intensity resistance training should be an integral part of a comprehensive fitness program.

As with any exercise prescription, instructions regarding intensity, duration, and frequency, as well as guidelines for rate of progression and precautions, are important. This information should be based on health and fitness status and personal goals and interests.

Table 8-2. Comparative Overview of Various Types of Resistance-Training Equipment

	Free Weights (Barbells/ Dumbbells)	Multi-station Machines	Selectorized Machines
Cost	Low	Somewhat high	High
Functionality	Excellent	Limited	Limited
Learning curve	Limited	Excellent	Excellent
Muscle isolation	Variable	Excellent	Excellent
Rehabilitation	Excellent	Excellent	Excellent
Safety	Relatively safe	Very safe	Very safe
Space efficiency	Variable	Excellent	Variable
Time efficiency	Variable	Excellent	Excellent
Variety	Excellent	Limited	Limited
Versatility	Excellent	Limited	Limited

Muscular fitness can be developed through either static (isometric) or dynamic (isotonic and isokinetic) exercises. Dynamic resistance is recommended for most adults who wish to engage in basic resistance training. Because the primary objective of resistance training should be to develop total-body muscular fitness in a safe and time-efficient manner, individuals should be encouraged to perform 8 to 10 different exercises to condition major muscle groups.

Appropriate resistance training for healthy adults should be based on the following guidelines and principles:

- Use a brief warmup prior to performing resistance exercise.
- Adhere to proper techniques for performing each exercise.
- Perform at least 1 set of 8 to 12 repetitions of each exercise to the point of volitional fatigue. A recent review showed that 1 set of resistance-training exercises provides nearly the same improvement in muscular strength and endurance as multiple sets of resistance-training exercises. Consequently, for the average person beginning a resistance-training program, single-set programs are recommended over multiple-set programs because they are highly effective and less time-consuming.
- Increase the resistance when a predetermined number of repetitions (typically 8 to 12) can be completed using proper form. Increases in resistance should be made gradually (e.g., increments of approximately 2% to 5%).
- Exercise at least 2 days per week. Recovery time (rest) is an important component of muscular growth and strength development and most individuals require approximately 48 hours to recover from a typical resistance-training session. When training at very low loads (i.e., in certain therapeutic settings), more frequent training sessions may be tolerated.
- Perform both the lifting (concentric phase) and lowering (eccentric phase) portions

in a controlled manner. Using ballistic-type movements during resistance training can compromise safety and effectiveness.

- Perform each exercise through a functional range of motion. This helps ensure that joint mobility is maintained and, in some instances, enhanced.
- Maintain a normal breathing pattern; breath-holding may induce excessive elevations in blood pressure due to performance of a Valsalva maneuver.
- When possible, exercise with a training partner who provides feedback, assistance, and encouragement.

An understanding of resistance-training equipment and the most commonly used methods for developing strength (as well as advantages and limitations) is basic to effective modification of the prescription for resistance training for specific conditioning needs and interests. Such modification is necessary to maximize the benefits from resistance training and to avoid injury.

Recommended Reading

American College of Sports Medicine. *ACSM's Guidelines for Exercise Testing and Prescription*, 6th ed. Philadelphia, PA: Lippincott Williams & Wilkins, 2000.

American College of Sports Medicine. *ACSM's Resource Manual for Guidelines for Exercise Testing and Prescription*, 4th ed. Philadelphia, PA: Lippincott Williams & Wilkins, 2001.

Brzycki, M. *Maximize Your Training*. Chicago, IL: Masters Press, 2000.

Carpinelli, RN, Otto, RM. Strength training: Single versus multiple sets. *Sports Medicine* 26(2):73-84, August 1998.

Feigenbaum, MS, Pollock, ML. Strength training: Rationale for current guidelines for adult fitness programs. *The Physician and Sportsmedicine* 25(2):44-64, 1997.

Fleck, SJ, Kraemer, WJ. *Designing Resistance Training Programs*, 2nd ed. Champaign, IL: Human Kinetics Publishers, Inc., 1997.

Peterson, JA, Bryant, CX (eds). *StairMaster Fitness Handbook*, 2nd ed. Champaign, IL: Sagamore Publishing Company, Inc., 1995.

Pollock, ML, Franklin, BA, Balady, GJ, et al. Resistance exercise in individuals with and without cardiovascular disease: Benefits, rationale, safety, and prescription. *Circulation* 101:828-833, 2000.

Pollock, ML, Vincent, KR. *The President's Council on Physical Fitness and Sports Research Digest*. Series 2:No. 8, 1996.

CHAPTER 9

• •

DEVELOPING A
FLEXIBILITY PROGRAM

*F*exibility is an important, but frequently neglected, component of fitness. It can be defined as the ability to move muscles and joints through their full range of motion. As a personal trainer, you will undoubtedly encounter a number of clients who suffer from a variety of musculoskeletal conditions that can be linked to a lack of flexibility. It is important that you have an understanding of how to safely and effectively develop flexibility. Flexibility is developed by stretching. However, stretching is only effective when performed properly. Several reasons why active individuals should improve flexibility through stretching exercises are outlined in Table 9-1.

How Muscles Respond to Stretching

The human body has a few built-in protective mechanisms that help prevent too much stretch and excessive tension from occurring within the muscles. For the neuromuscular system to safely control skeletal movement, it must receive continuous sensory feedback information concerning the effects of its actions. This sensory information includes (a) muscle length, provided by the muscle spindle apparatus, and (b) the tension that the muscle exerts on its tendon, provided by the Golgi tendon organs (GTOs).

Neural receptors, called muscle spindles, lie parallel to the muscle fibers and are sensitive to the rate of change in muscle length. Stretching of a muscle stretches the muscle spindles. This action excites sensory endings in the spindle that send a signal to the spinal cord. If the stretch within the muscle is too extreme or occurs too fast, the spinal cord sends a reflex message back to the muscle, causing it to contract. This involuntary contraction, known as the stretch reflex or myotactic reflex, helps guard against overstretching and injury. It is for this reason that individuals should generally not perform ballistic or bouncing types of stretches. A ballistic stretch causes a counterproductive development of increased tension in the muscle being stretched, making it more difficult to stretch the muscle and surrounding tissues.

The GTOs continuously monitor tension in the tendons, produced by muscle contraction or passive stretching of a muscle. They serve as protection against the development of too much contractile force. When activated, the GTOs reflexively inhibit contraction and signal a muscle that is being stretched to immediately relax. This reaction, known as the inverse myotatic reflex, is possible only because the signals of the GTOs are strong enough to override

Table 9-1. Potential Benefits of Stretching
• Enhanced physical efficiency and performance
• Reduced risk of joint sprain or muscle strain
• Improved neuromuscular coordination
• Improved muscular balance and postural awareness
• Reduced muscular tension and soreness
• Improved circulation and nutrient transport to joint structures
• Decreased risk of low-back pain
• Reduced severity of painful menstruation in women

the excitatory impulses of the muscle spindle. The GTOs-mediated relaxation is an important protective mechanism that helps prevent muscles and tendons from being injured by tearing away from their points of attachment.

FACTORS INFLUENCING FLEXIBILITY

Range of motion (ROM) is highly specific to the joint and depends on the joint structure. For example, the ball-and-socket joints of the hips and shoulders allow for a greater degree of movement in more directions than the knee, which is designed to permit only hinge-like motion. The shape and positioning of bones also play a role in determining joint motion. It is anatomically impossible, for instance, to completely turn the ankle and lay the side of the foot on the ground because bone impinges on bone to prevent further motion.

Large, bulky muscles and excessive adipose (fat) tissue can limit range of motion due to the contact of adjacent body segments. The elasticity of soft tissue structures plays a critical role in determining flexibility. The joint capsule (i.e., the saclike structure that encloses the ends of bones) is the most significant factor of the total resistance encountered by a joint during movement (47 percent), followed by the muscle and its fascia (41 percent), the tendons and ligaments (10 percent), and the skin (2 percent). The joint capsule, tendons, and ligaments consist predominately of collagen — a nonelastic tissue, while the muscle and its fascia have more elastic tissue. Because the joint capsule, tendons, and ligaments have less elasticity than the muscle and its fascia, care must be taken not to overstretch these structures and, consequently, reduce the integrity of the joints. Efforts to enhance flexibility through stretching should be focused on the muscle and its fascia since they are the most modifiable structures in terms of reducing resistance to movement.

Flexibility is related to age, sex, and physical activity. Flexibility progressively declines with age due to changes in the elasticity of the soft tissues and decreases in physical activity. As a result, older individuals should be encouraged to perform flexibility exercises on a regular basis (preferably daily) to compensate for the age-related reductions in soft tissue elasticity and, concomitant, decreases in joint mobility.

Some evidence suggests that girls tend to be more flexible than boys of the same age. This sex difference continues throughout adult life, given that men typically have larger, bulkier muscles than women.

Physical inactivity is a major contributor to decreases in flexibility. It is well-documented that physically inactive individuals tend to be less flexible than active individuals and that regular exercise improves flexibility. Disuse as a result of physical inactivity or immobilization leads to contraction and shortening of the connective tissues, restricting joint mobility. Similarly, using the joints and muscles in repetitive activity patterns or maintaining habitual body postures can inhibit range of motion because of the shortening and tightening of the muscle tissue. Consequently, individuals, from runners to office workers, should stretch their hamstrings and low-back muscles to counteract any tightness that develops in these muscle groups.

The temperature surrounding a joint has also been observed to influence flexibility. It has been reported that warming a joint can produce an approximate 20 percent increase in ROM, whereas cooling a joint can result in a 10 to 20 percent reduction in flexibility. These results illustrate the importance of warming up prior to stretching.

TYPES OF STRETCHING

Stretches aimed at improving joint range of motion are designed to reduce the internal resistance of the muscles and connective tissues. Decreasing the resistance of the muscles is accomplished by either increasing connective tissue length or by achieving a greater degree of relaxation within the muscle. Several variations of stretching exercises exist, but most can be placed into three major categories: ballistic, static, and proprioceptive neuromuscular facilitation (PNF).

BALLISTIC STRETCHING

Commonly referred to as "bouncing" or "bobbing" stretches, ballistic methods use the momentum of the moving body segment to produce the stretch. This stretching method incorporates a high-force, short-duration stretch, stimulating the stretch reflex and, consequently, greater reflex muscular contraction. Excessive or uncontrolled movement can overload soft tissue structures beyond their normal elastic capabilities. As a result, many exercise professionals and sports medicine experts do not recommend ballistic stretching because attempting to stretch a muscle that is contracted is dangerous and contradictory to the goal of improving flexibility. However, individuals involved in ballistic sports activities may benefit from this stretching method. Ballistic stretching may promote the development of dynamic flexibility and reduce potential injury by preparing the musculoskeletal system for high-speed, dynamic movements.

STATIC STRETCHING

Static stretching involves slowly applying stretch to a muscle, and then holding it in a lengthened position for a period of 10 to 30 seconds. During this easy, held stretch, an individual should relax, focusing attention on the muscles being stretched. As they continue holding the stretch, the feeling of slight tension in the stretching muscles should slowly subside. Then, the individual stretches a bit farther, until mild tension (without pain) is felt again, as they continue to hold the stretch for another 10 to 30 seconds. The tension should again slowly subside, and the individual should be breathing easily and feeling relaxed. This is a low-intensity, long-duration stretching technique. Stretching in this manner physiologically inhibits the stretch reflex. Static stretching tends to be the *preferred* type of stretching because it is associated with less risk of overstretching the tissues and can result in less muscle soreness when compared to other methods.

PROPRIOCEPTIVE NEUROMUSCULAR FACILITATION

Research has shown that proprioceptive neuromuscular facilitation (PNF) stretch techniques may be more effective than conventional stretching methods for increasing joint range of motion. Muscle relaxation using PNF is first achieved by a contraction of the muscle to be stretched, followed by static stretching of the same muscle group. Two ways exist for performing PNF:

- *Contract-relax:* The right muscle group is first gently stretched. This is followed by an isometric contraction of the same muscle group held for approximately 6 to 15 seconds. The muscles are then relaxed and immediately stretched a little farther. The rationale behind the contract-relax technique is that the isometric contraction of the muscles being stretched induces a reflex relaxation of those same muscles.
- *Contract-relax with agonist contraction:* This is the same as the contract-relax technique except that at the same time the muscle is stretched, the opposing muscle (i.e., agonist) is submaximally contracted. This action is believed to facilitate greater relaxation in the stretched muscles.

PNF sequences are typically performed with a training partner and repeated several times. The most significant improvements in flexibility have been linked to PNF. Unfortunately, PNF techniques have several disadvantages. This stretching method is associated with more pain and muscle stiffness, requires a partner, and is more time-consuming.

AN EXERCISE PRESCRIPTION FOR FLEXIBILITY

The overload principle can be applied to flexibility exercises. For flexibility to improve, connective tissues and muscles must be elongated through regular, proper stretching. If regularly stimulated by increasingly intense stretching, the body will respond with an increased ability to stretch. Hooke's law states that the amount of stretch is proportional to the applied force. The type of stretching performed will depend on each client and his or her individual goals, and must be specifically tailored to the needs of your clients and their sports. Some of the contraindications for flexibility training include an unhealed fracture, infection, and/or acute inflammation that affects the joints or surrounding tissues, sharp pain associated with a stretch or uncontrolled muscle cramping that occurs during a stretch, and a local hematoma as a result of an overstretch injury. The F.I.T.T. Principle (Frequency, Intensity, Type, and Time or Duration) can be applied to help design your clients' flexibility training.

Before stretching, it is recommended that individuals take a few minutes to warm up because stretching cold muscles can lead to injury. They should begin with a simple, low-intensity warmup, such as walking while swinging the arms in wide circles. Individuals should spend at least 5 to 10 minutes warming up prior to stretching. According to the American College of Sports Medicine, an exercise prescription for a flexibility program can be outlined as follows:

Type:	A general stretching routine for the major muscle groups using static or PNF techniques

Frequency: A minimum of 2 to 3 days per week
Intensity: To a position of mild discomfort
Duration: 10 to 30 seconds for static; 6-second contractions followed
                  by 10 to 30 seconds of assisted stretch for PNF
Repetitions: At least 4 repetitions per muscle group

Please refer to the recommended reading list for excellent references illustrating safe, appropriate stretches for all the major muscle groups.

A FEW MINUTES CAN GO A LONG WAY

Few health and fitness professionals would argue that flexibility is an important component of fitness and a critical factor for achieving optimum physical conditioning. Although the rationale for flexibility training may not be as well-supported as those for aerobic conditioning and strength training, it is important to include flexibility training in any properly designed fitness program. Flexibility training may help prevent the injuries and/or impaired physical performance that can occur as a result of tight or stiff muscles. More benefits exist from stretching than disadvantages. Stretching programs should be individualized according to physical status, level of conditioning, and special needs. Just a few minutes of stretching can help to maintain flexibility, which in turn can improve athletic performance, make daily activities easier, and prevent injury.

Recommended Reading

Alter, MJ. *Science of Flexibility*, 2nd ed. Champaign, IL: Human Kinetics Publishers, Inc., 1996.

Alter, MJ. *Sport Stretch*, 2nd ed. Champaign, IL: Human Kinetics Publishers, Inc., 1998.

American College of Sports Medicine. *ACSM Fitness Book*, 2nd ed. Champaign, IL: Human Kinetics Publishers, Inc., 1998.

American College of Sports Medicine. *ACSM's Guidelines for Exercise Testing and Prescription*, 6th ed. Philadelphia, PA: Lippincott Williams & Wilkins, 2000.

American College of Sports Medicine. *ACSM's Resource Manual for Guidelines for Exercise Testing and Prescription*, 4th ed. Philadelphia, PA: Lippincott Williams & Wilkins, 2001.

Brzycki, M. *Maximize Your Training*. Chicago, IL: Masters Press, 2000.

Golding, LA. Flexibility, stretching, and flexibility testing: Recommendations for testing and standards. *ACSM's Health & Fitness Journal* 1(2):17-20, 1997.

Knudson, D. Stretching: From science to practice. *Journal of Physical Education, Recreation and Dance* 69(3):38-42, 1998.

Peterson, JA, Bryant, CX (eds). *StairMaster Fitness Handbook*, 2nd ed. Champaign, IL: Sagamore Publishing Company, Inc., 1995.

Pope, RP, Herbert, RD, Kirwan, JD, et al. A randomized trial of pre-exercise stretching for prevention of lower-limb injury. *Medicine & Science in Sports & Exercise* 32(2):271-277, 2000.

Shrier, I, Gossal, K. Myths and truths of stretching: Individualized recommendations for healthy muscles. *The Physician and Sportsmedicine* 28(8):57-63, 2000.

CHAPTER 10

* *

STRENGTH TRAINING
FOR CHILDREN

*U*ntil recently, the prevailing attitude among members of the medical community was that children (i.e., preteens) should not participate in strength-training programs because of safety concerns. These concerns focused on three issues: 1) whether strength training places undue stress on the musculoskeletal systems of adolescents; 2) whether strength-training programs provide any physiologic benefits for young participants; and, if so, 3) how should strength-training programs for children be designed to maximize possible benefits and minimize possible risks.

Due to interest in the benefits and consequences of resistance training, researchers have attempted to address these concerns. The results of these investigations have led three major organizations — the American Orthopedic Society for Sports Medicine, the American Academy of Pediatrics, and the National Strength and Conditioning Association — to develop position papers that make formal recommendations regarding children and strength training. In turn, these position papers have served to heighten interest in getting preteens involved in medically endorsed, resistance-training programs.

Another growing concern is the increase in the prevalence of juvenile obesity and obesity due to sedentary lifestyles of our youth. The key issue for health/fitness professionals and parents is making certain everything is done to make strength training a positive experience for children.

MAXIMIZING THE BENEFITS

Research has demonstrated that strength training for children, when properly performed, can be a positive experience. Adolescents participating in a comprehensive, supervised strength-training program have shown an improved level of muscle strength, better local muscle endurance (i.e., the ability of a muscle or muscle group to perform multiple repetitions or to resist fatigue), stronger connective tissue (resulting in increased resistance to injury during recreational and sports activities), enhanced motor performance in certain sports activities, increased bone strength, improved body composition, and greatly improved self-esteem. Unfortunately, despite its many beneficial aspects, strength training for children is not without some degree of risk. Of greatest concern is the potential to cause damage to a child's developing skeletal system and supportive tissues.

MINIMIZING THE RISKS

All exercise programs expose participants of any age to some degree of health risk. Straining a muscle, dropping a weight on the participant's foot, and hyperextending the back are a few examples of mishaps that sometimes occur in a weight room.

Unfortunately, the risks involved in strength training can be considerably more serious for children. For example, lifting excessively heavy weights (i.e., a resistance level that can be lifted fewer than six repetitions) may significantly increase a child's risk of injuring his or her growth cartilage. Growth cartilage is a type of connective tissue that is located at three primary sites in an individual's body: 1) the epiphyseal, or growth plate of long bones; 2) the apophyseal insertion (i.e., the point of tendon insertion onto bone); and 3) the articular cartilage that acts as a shock absorber between the bones of a joint.

The long bones of a child's body grow in length from the epiphyseal plates, which are located at each end of the bone. An excessively high level of load stress applied to the epiphyseal plates (e.g., from lifting too much weight while strength training) before they mature can inhibit further growth in the length of the bone(s) involved. As a result, a child's growth can be stunted.

The growth cartilage located at the apophyseal insertions ensures that a solid connection exists between the tendon and the bone. Placing excessive stress on this growth cartilage can increase the likelihood that the tendon may separate from the bone. When that occurs, the individual suffers pain when that bone is forced to move (e.g., during physical activity). Finally, damage to the articular cartilage can cause the surfaces between the bones of a joint to become rough, eliciting pain during movement.

The key point to remember is that all three sites of growth cartilage can sustain damage as the result of either a single bout of acute trauma or several repeated episodes of microtrauma. The most common acute injury to growth cartilage is to the epiphyseal plate. Epiphyseal plate fractures, for example, have been reported to occur when performing exercises involving overhead lifts (e.g., the clean-and-jerk, overhead press) with maximal or near-maximal loads while strength training. To minimize the risk of epiphyseal plate fractures, children should be encouraged to use light-to-moderate loads (i.e., a resistance level that can be lifted at least 10 times) when performing overhead lifts.

Specific guidelines and limits should be established for strength-training programs to reduce the risk of damaging a child's growth cartilage. In fact, growth cartilage injuries resulting from a properly designed and supervised strength-training program are very rare. The risk of injury associated with strength training in children is quite low, provided a proper lifting technique is used and appropriate demands are placed on the child.

DESIGNING A STRENGTH-TRAINING PROGRAM

Deciding at what age a child should start a strength-training program can be challenging, since each child grows and develops at an individual rate. Not surprisingly, no acceptable minimum age standard exists for getting involved in resistance training. As a consequence, several factors should be considered before allowing children to participate in a strength-training program, including:

- Is the child mature enough to accept and follow instructions?
- Does the child want to participate in such a program?
- Does the child possess the basic motor skills to safely perform the various exercises?

Depending upon how the aforementioned factors are weighed, strength training may appear to be more appropriate for some children than others (Table 10-1). For example, young people who participate in organized sports programs are probably more ready for some form of strength training than their inactive counterparts. Once the decision has been made that a child can engage in strength training, the key to remember is that all strength programs for children must adhere to basic guidelines and considerations, including:

- Pre-exercise physical exams should be conducted for children with existing or suspected medical conditions.

Table 10-1. Basic Guidelines for Resistance Exercise Progression in Children*

Age	Considerations
7 or younger	Introduce child to the basic exercises, using little or no resistance; develop the concept of a training session; teach exercise techniques; progress from body-weight calisthenics, partner exercises, and lightly resisted exercises; keep the volume of required effort relatively low.
8-10	Gradually increase the number of exercises; practice exercise technique in all lifts; start gradual progressive loading of exercises; keep exercises simple; gradually increase training volume; carefully monitor toleration of the exercise stress.
11-13	Teach all basic exercise techniques, including appropriate breathing; continue progressive loading of each exercise; emphasize exercise techniques; introduce more advanced exercises with little or no resistance.
14-15	Progress to more advanced developmental programs in resistance exercise for adolescents; add sport-specific components; emphasize exercise techniques; increase volume.
16 or older	Move adolescents to entry-level adult programs after all background knowledge has been mastered and a basic level of training experience has been gained.

Note: If a child with no previous experience begins a training program, start him or her at low levels and move to more advanced levels as exercise toleration, skill, amount of training time, and understanding of program requirements permit.

* Adapted from Kraemer, WJ, Fleck, SJ. *Strength Training for Young Athletes.* Champaign, IL: Human Kinetics Publishers, Inc., 1993.

Table 10-2. Example of Suggested Exercise Order

	Push	Pull
Legs	Leg Press	Leg Curl
Chest and back	Bench Press	Seated Row
Shoulders and back	Military Press	Lat Pulldown
Arms	Triceps Extension	Biceps Curl
Trunk	Back Extension	Abdominal Curl

- Children are physiologically immature, no matter how big or strong they may appear to be.
- Make sure that every child is taught and uses proper training techniques and procedures for all of the exercise movements involved in the strength-training program.
- All exercises should be performed in a controlled manner. To prevent orthopedic trauma to the joint structures, all fast or jerky movements should be strictly avoided while performing strength-training exercises.
- Select a weight that is appropriate to the needs and structural limitations of a child's body. Under no circumstances should a weight be used that allows less than 8 repetitions to be completed per set. Excessively heavy weights, in particular, can be damaging to developing skeletal and joint structures. Each set of an exercise should consist of 8 to 12 repetitions. Although adolescents should be encouraged to train hard and be challenged, they should not exercise to the point of exhaustion. Discourage any competitive lifting.
- As a training effect occurs, achieve an overload first by increasing the number of repetitions, and then by increasing the amount of weight lifted.
- Perform 1 or 2 sets of 8 to 10 exercises. The program selected should include at least 1 exercise for each of the major muscle groups.
- Initially perform 2 strength-training sessions per week with at least 1 day off between workouts (i.e., strength training on Mondays and Thursdays or Tuesdays and Fridays). In addition to protecting a child's body against excessive overload, such a schedule is sufficient because children need, and should also engage in, other forms of physical activity.
- Perform full-range, multi-joint exercises (e.g., leg press and lat pulldown), as opposed to single-joint exercises (e.g., leg extensions and biceps curls), whenever possible, because such exercises tend to develop functional strength.
- Balance a strength workout by alternating "pairs" of muscle groups, which is to perform a "pull" exercise for each "push" exercise (Table 10-2).
- Don't overload the skeletal and joint structures of children with excessively high weights. Too much resistance is particularly dangerous to the preteen whose skeletal system is highly prone to orthopedic trauma, due to the presence of active growth plates (areas where cartilaginous tissue is being converted to hard, bony tissue).

- Finally, and perhaps most importantly, closely supervise all strength-training activities with appropriately trained personnel.

A SAFE INVESTMENT

Strength training can be beneficial for children, and should be included as part of an overall fitness program. Perhaps the two most important factors for strength training to be a safe, effective, and enjoyable activity for children are quality instruction and supervision, and adherence to the concept of minimum effective dosage. First, children who strength train should receive proper instruction from an exercise professional. Second, the training program should be designed using only the minimum effective dosage of resistance exercise needed to produce a training effect. Recent research has shown that higher-repetition (13 to 15) and moderate weight training is more beneficial for youths than lower-repetition (6 to 8), heavier-weight training. Strict adherence to these two fundamental guidelines will help ensure that every young person who lifts weights will safely achieve training results that more than justify the efforts expended. A resolute commitment to both guidelines will provide substantial dividends.

Recommended Reading

Brzycki, M. *Maximize Your Training*. Chicago, IL: Masters Press, 2000.

Brzycki, M. *Strength Training for Kids*. Indianapolis, IN: Masters Press, 1995.

Cahill, B (ed). *Proceedings of the Conference on Strength Training and the Prepubescent*. Chicago, IL: American Orthopaedic Society for Sports Medicine, 1988.

Duda, M. Prepubescent strength training gains support. *The Physician and Sportsmedicine* 14(2):157-161, 1986.

Faigenbaum, A, Westcott, W. *Strength & Power for Young Athletes*. Champaign, IL: Human Kinetics Publishers, Inc., 2000.

Kraemer, WJ, Fry, AC, Frykman, PN, Conroy, B, Hoffman, J. Resistance training and youth. *Pediatric Exercise Science* 1:336-350, 1989.

Kraemer, WJ, Fleck, SJ. *Strength Training for Young Athletes*. Champaign, IL: Human Kinetics Publishers, Inc., 1993.

National Strength and Conditioning Association. Position statement on prepubescent strength training. *National Strength and Conditioning Association Journal* 7:27-31, 1985.

Peterson, JA, Bryant, CX, Peterson, SL. *Strength Training for Women*. Champaign, IL: Human Kinetics Publishers, Inc., 1995.

Risser, W, Risser, J, Preston, D. Weight-training injuries in adolescents. *American Journal of Diseases in Children* 144:1015-1017, 1990.

Sale, DG. Strength training in children. In: Gisolfi, CV, Lamb, DR (eds), *Perspectives in Exercise Science and Sports Medicine* (pp. 165-216). Carmel, IN: Bench Press, 1989.

Sewall, L, Micheli, LJ. Strength training for children. *Journal of Pediatric Orthopedics* 6:143-146, 1986.

Tanner, SM. Weighing the risks: Strength training for children and adolescents. *The Physician and Sportsmedicine* 21(6):105-116, 1993.

Westcott, W, Faigenbaum, A. Sensible strength training for preadolescents. *Fitness Management* 17(5):28-30, 2001.

CHAPTER 11

• •

STRENGTH TRAINING
FOR WOMEN

*A*s strength training continues to grow in popularity, especially among women, it is important to note that particular subgroups require special care and consideration when developing strength-training programs. The older woman, the adolescent woman, the pregnant woman, and the postpartum woman may need some adjustments in their strength programs to ensure both safety and effectiveness. While information on the impact of strength training for "special" groups of women is lacking, a limited number of appropriate guidelines and recommendations have been developed.

OLDER WOMEN

Exercise scientists and gerontologists now emphasize the importance of muscular fitness for older individuals. Impaired muscular functioning has been linked to many medical conditions and chronic diseases found in older adults, especially women. Indeed, the Framingham Heart Study, which discovered many links between lifestyle and cardiovascular disease, found that about half of women over age 65 cannot lift 10 pounds. Moreover, the typical 75-year-old woman often does not have sufficient lower-extremity muscular strength to rise effectively and efficiently from a seated position, to move from place to place, or to maintain balance. Such deficiencies can make independent living an unrealistic option.

A properly prescribed strength-training regimen can dramatically improve the overall functional abilities and well-being of older women. Participation in strength-training programs aimed at enhancing lower-extremity muscular fitness can lead to significant improvements in both balance and gait mechanics, and reduce a woman's potential for falling.

In addition, many experts believe that strength training can help women effectively manage osteoarthritis. A woman's ability to live with osteoarthritis is largely dependent upon how the stresses occurring around the joints are shared by the surrounding muscles and the unaffected joint structures. Generally speaking, stronger muscles are able to absorb a greater amount of the stress on a joint.

Osteoporosis, the age-related disorder that is characterized by a decreased bone mineral content, is also influenced by strength training in a positive manner. A growing body of evidence suggests that resistance exercise retards bone loss and can even increase bone density. When muscle-movement stress is applied to a bone, the pressure produces an adaptive

Table 11-1. Basic Guidelines and Principles for Strength Training for Older Women

- The major goal of a resistance-training program should be developing sufficient muscular strength and endurance to enhance the ability to live a physically independent lifestyle.
- Learn the proper training techniques for all of the exercises to be used in the program.
- Maintain normal breathing patterns while exercising, since breath-holding can transiently increase blood pressure.
- Perform all of the exercises in a slow and controlled manner. To prevent orthopedic trauma to joint structures, avoid ballistic (fast and jerky) movements.
- Never participate in strength-training exercises during active periods of arthritic pain, because exercise could exacerbate the condition.
- Control the range of motion so that the exercises are performed through a "pain-free arc" (i.e., the maximum range of motion that does not elicit pain or discomfort).
- Never use a resistance that is so heavy it cannot be lifted at least 8 repetitions per set. Heavy resistance can be dangerous and damage the skeletal and joint structures. It is recommended that every set consist of 8 to 12 repetitions.
- As a training effect occurs, achieve an overload initially by increasing the number of repetitions, and then by increasing the absolute resistance lifted.
- Limit each workout to 1 to 2 sets of 8 to 10 different exercises. Ensure that all the major muscle groups are included in the training session.
- Don't overtrain. A minimum of 2 strength-training sessions per week is required to elicit beneficial physiological adaptations. Depending on the circumstances, more sessions may neither be desirable nor productive.
- Perform multi-joint exercises (as opposed to single-joint exercises) since they tend to aid in the development of functional strength.
- Given a choice, use machines to strength train, as opposed to free weights. Machines tend to require less skill, and allow individuals to start with lower resistances, increase by smaller increments (this is not true for all strength-training machines), and more easily control the exercise range of motion.
- Understand that the first several strength-training sessions should be closely supervised and monitored by a trained professional who is sensitive to the special needs and capabilities of the older adult.

response by the bone (the piezoelectric effect). Furthermore, training-induced improvements in muscle strength and balance can prevent the falls that cause fractures in elderly women with osteoporosis.

Strength training can also help preserve muscle tissue as women age. Muscle tissue is more metabolically active than fat tissue (i.e., it will burn more calories). By retaining a higher amount of muscle tissue, women will maintain higher metabolic rates and, therefore, their optimal body weight.

Perhaps the most important benefit of strength training for older women is its impact on factors related to daily living. Most activities of daily living require some measurable involvement of muscular fitness. By engaging in a well-designed program of strength training, an older woman will be more likely to maintain an appropriate level of muscular fitness and, therefore, a higher level of function. As a consequence, she will be more likely to maintain an independent lifestyle.

Available research suggests that strength training will also enhance self-confidence and self-efficacy. While the thought of "pumping iron" may seem strange to many older women, an appropriate level of muscular fitness is critical to ensuring that women are able to spend their later years in an independent, dignified manner. The key to attaining such a level of muscular fitness lies in adhering to a sound strength-training program. An appropriate program for an older woman should include strict adherence to the guidelines and principles detailed in Table 11-1.

ADOLESCENT WOMEN

Until recently, the medical community was convinced that adolescents, both boys and girls, should refrain from participating in strength-training programs. Common concerns

---

Table 11-2. Basic Guidelines and Principles for Strength Training for Adolescent Women

- No matter how big, strong, or mature a young woman appears, recognize that she may be physiologically immature.
- Ensure that every young woman is taught and uses both proper training and breathing techniques (no breath-holding) for all of the exercise movements.
- All exercises should be performed with controlled speed. To prevent orthopedic trauma to the joint structures, no ballistic (fast and jerky) movements should be allowed while exercising.
- Under no circumstances should a weight be used that allows fewer than 8 repetitions to be completed per set. Heavy weights can be potentially dangerous and damaging to the developing skeletal and joint structures. Each set should consist of 8 to 12 repetitions, to volitional fatigue. While adolescents can be encouraged to train hard, it is not recommended that they exercise to the point of exhaustion.
- As a training effect occurs, achieve an overload initially by increasing the number of repetitions, and then by increasing the resistance.
- Perform 1 to 2 sets of 8 to 10 different exercises. Include all major muscle groups.
- Perform 2 strength-training sessions per week. Such a schedule is more than sufficient since young women need and should seek other forms of physical activity.
- Perform full range, multi-joint exercises since they facilitate the development of functional strength.
- Do not overload the skeletal and joint structures of adolescents with maximal weights. This practice is particularly dangerous to the preteen since the young skeletal system is highly prone to the effects of orthopedic trauma, largely due to the presence of active growth plates (areas where cartilaginous tissue is in the process of being converted to hard, bony tissue).
- Closely supervise and monitor all strength-training activities with appropriately trained personnel.

---

regarded safety and three basic issues: whether strength gains were actually possible, whether young people benefited from participation in strength-training programs, and how strength-training programs for adolescents should be designed. Fortunately, these questions stimulated research that led three major health organizations (see Chapter 10, page 76) to develop position papers providing recommendations for adolescents (for females, adolescents are defined as young women between the ages of 11 and 13). The efforts of these professional groups have prompted further research on the subject.

To date, research has shown that strength training, when properly performed, can elicit favorable adaptation and improvement in adolescents (i.e., the benefits far outweigh the risks). Young women can derive numerous benefits from participating in a comprehensive, supervised strength-training program. Some of the more desirable adaptations are improved muscle strength, better local muscular endurance, stronger connective tissue resulting in increased resistance to injury, enhanced motor performance in certain sport activities, and a greater appreciation of the value of fitness. Despite the numerous benefits, strength training for adolescent women is not without risks. It is imperative that certain precautions be taken to guarantee the safety of a young woman's developing musculoskeletal system. Perhaps the two most important factors are quality instruction and supervision, and adherence to a minimum effective dosage. That is, design the training program so that it employs only the minimum or threshold resistance required to produce a training effect.

The guidelines and principles in Table 11-2 should be followed when developing a strength-training program for adolescent women. In many instances, these guidelines are similar to those recommended for the elderly because the need for adhering to safe and effective practices while exercising transcends age.

PREGNANT WOMEN

Many women would like to continue strength training during pregnancy, but are hesitant due to varying opinions on the subject. In recent years, however, a growing number of professionals from the medical and exercise science communities have tendered specific advice for pregnant women interested in strength training. Most experts agree that, based on the limited data available, proper strength training poses little risk to either the mother or the developing fetus. In fact, it may be very beneficial for a pregnant woman. Strength training can provide the enhanced muscular fitness necessary to compensate for the postural adjustments that typically occur during pregnancy. Accordingly, improved posture should help lessen a pregnant woman's likelihood of experiencing low-back pain. The performance of activities of daily living should also be easier for a pregnant woman with an improved level of muscular fitness. Recent studies have shown that the benefits of exercise during pregnancy can reduce the level of fat deposition and retention, lead to shorter and less complicated labors, improve musculoskeletal function, and provide a faster postpartum recovery.

Authorities on the subject, however, are quick to point out that strength training is not advisable for all pregnant women. Available research suggests that the recommendations outlined in Table 11-3 are appropriate. Until more data are available, each pregnant woman should consult her physician for advice. In addition, training prescriptions for pregnant women who choose to strength train should be individualized. As a general rule, pregnant women should be conservative in their approach to manipulating the various strength-training variables.

Table 11-3. Basic Guidelines and Principles for Strength Training for Pregnant Women

- Women possessing any of the American College of Obstetricians and Gynecologists (ACOG) contraindications for aerobic exercise during pregnancy should not participate in strength training (Table 11-4).
- Women who have never participated in a strength-training program should not initiate one during pregnancy.
- No ballistic movements should be employed during pregnancy, and supine positions should be avoided after the first trimester. Pregnant women experience joint and connective tissue laxity, raising their susceptibility for injury while performing resistance exercises. Emphasize proper form and good posture.
- An adequate warmup is strongly recommended.
- Women should be encouraged to breathe normally during strength training. Oxygen delivery to the placenta may be reduced during breath-holding (i.e., the performance of a Valsalva maneuver).
- Maximal lifts and heavy resistances should be avoided, especially after the first trimester when increasing amounts of the hormone relaxin are present. Because relaxin increases tissue laxity, the performance of heavy lifts later in pregnancy may increase the risk of injury to the joints, connective tissue, and skeletal structures. An exercise set consisting of at least 12 to 15 repetitions without undue fatigue should ensure that the resistance level is not too great during any particular strength exercise.
- A strength-training workout consisting of a single set of a series of exercises, collectively involving all of the major muscle groups, should be performed 2 times per week.
- As a training effect occurs, it is recommended that overload be achieved initially by increasing the number of repetitions and, subsequently, by increasing the amount of resistance. Use slow progression.
- Strength training on machines is generally preferred to using free weights since machines tend to require less skill and can be more easily controlled. Choose activities that limit risk of abdominal trauma.
- If a particular strength exercise produces pain or discomfort, it should be discontinued and an alternative exercise should be performed. Recognize that body changes can affect balance and coordination.
- Avoid hot and humid exercise environments and hydrate well.
- A pregnant woman should listen to her body and modify exercises appropriately. She should immediately consult her physician if any of the following warning signs or complications appear: vaginal bleeding, abdominal pain or cramping, ruptured membranes, elevated blood pressure or heart rate, or lack of fetal movement.

Strength-training programs should be an integral part of a comprehensive fitness program. Health and fitness status, individual goals and basic principles of training should be considered when designing resistance-training programs. Strength training is generally safe for many special populations, including pregnant women, as long as appropriate precautions are observed. Exercise professionals should be aware of both the health status and the contraindications to exercise in all clients for whom strength training is recommended.

Table 11-4. Contraindications for Exercise During Pregnancy*

ABSOLUTE CONTRAINDICATIONS	RELATIVE CONTRAINDICATIONS
During a healthy pregnancy, exercise should be an important part of your life. If, however, any of the following Absolute Contraindications are present, the American College of Obstetricians and Gynecologists (ACOG) recommends NO exercise program should be performed: • Preterm rupture of membranes • Premature labor during a prior or current pregnancy, or both • Pregnancy-induced hypertension (high blood pressure) • Persistent second or third trimester bleeding • Incompetent cervix • Intrauterine growth retardation	If any of the following Relative Contraindications are present, consult your physician to determine the appropriate exercise program for you: • High blood pressure • Thyroid disease • Irregular heart beat • Obesity • History of precipitous labor • History of bleeding during pregnancy • Heart or pulmonary disease • History of spontaneous abortion or miscarriage • Vascular disease • Anemia • Diabetes • Breech in last trimester • Extremely underweight • History of intrauterine growth retardation • Extremely sedentary • Placenta previa • Multiple births • Excessive weight gain during the second or third trimester

* Adapted from American College of Obstetricians and Gynecologists. *Exercise During Pregnancy and the Postpartum Period (Technical Bulletin #189)*. Washington, D.C.: ACOG, 1994.

POSTPARTUM WOMEN

Not too long ago, women were instructed to stay in bed for up to two weeks following an uncomplicated delivery. Fortunately, medical professionals now know better. It is generally accepted that the sooner a woman gets moving after delivery, the better off she will be. Exercise, particularly specific strength activities, can help tone the abdominal region, improve posture, and help a woman regain her prepregnancy shape.

Several significant physical changes occur in a woman's body shortly after giving birth. Hormonal levels change in an effort to help the uterus, cervix, and birth canal contract and prepare her body for lactation. A woman's body also undergoes certain metabolic adjustments to meet the demands of pregnancy and birth.

Certain exercises should be started soon after delivery. Most physicians will instruct their patients to perform Kegel exercises almost immediately after the birth. Kegel exercises, named after the physician who devised them, help to keep the vagina elastic and to prevent a woman from developing bladder control problems. To perform Kegel exercises, a woman should simply pretend that she is stopping and starting her urine flow (for more detailed information, refer to Chapter 18). In addition to the role that Kegel exercises play in controlling bladder function, they are also important because they support the contents of the abdomen.

The day after an uncomplicated delivery, the attending physician may also recommend that the postpartum woman perform pelvic tilts so that she may begin to strengthen and tone her abdominal muscles. During the course of a woman's pregnancy, these muscles can become greatly stretched to accommodate the growing and developing fetus. Pelvic tilts will also help combat the low-back strain often associated with carrying the baby. To properly perform a pelvic tilt, a woman should engage in the following actions:

- Lie on her back with knees bent and hands relaxed by the side of her head.
- Tighten the muscles in the lower region of the abdomen by tilting the pelvis rearward and flattening the lower back against the floor.
- Hold this position for 5 to 10 seconds, relax, and repeat 8 to 12 times.

A woman should consult her physician before engaging in more vigorous strength-training activities during the postpartum period. As a general rule, a woman's body will take several weeks to heal following labor and delivery. Episiotomies, vaginal tears, and the point of attachment between the placenta and the uterus also require time to heal. Recovery rates differ from woman to woman, birth to birth, and typically take between six weeks to three months. A woman's physician is the best judge of when she can safely resume vigorous exercise.

AN "IRON" SUPPLEMENT FOR ALL TYPES OF WOMEN

The rise in the popularity of strength training has led to a point where it is now becoming an integral part of a well-balanced fitness program for healthy women. Research has also shown that a sound strength-training regimen can be useful in a wide variety of ways for women with special needs. Fortunately, the existing body of knowledge on the application of strength training to women will continue to grow. Given the emerging recognition of the value of strength training, it seems that many women may benefit from taking regular "iron" supplements.

Recommended Reading

Ebben, WP, Jensen, RL. Strength training for women: Debunking myths that block opportunity. *The Physician and Sportsmedicine* 26(5):86-97, 1998.

Fleck, SJ, Kraemer, WJ. *Designing Resistance Training Programs*, 2nd ed. Champaign, IL: Human Kinetics Publishers, Inc., 1997.

Kraemer, WJ, Fleck, SJ. *Resistance Training for Young Athletes*. Champaign, IL: Human Kinetics Publishers, Inc., 1993.

National Strength and Conditioning Association. Strength training for female athletes: A position paper, Part I. *National Strength and Conditioning Association Journal* 11(4):43-55, 1989.

National Strength and Conditioning Association. Strength training for female athletes: A position paper, Part II. *National Strength and Conditioning Association Journal* 11(5):29-36, 1989.

Peterson, JA, Bryant, CX, Peterson, SL. *Strength Training for Women*. Champaign, IL: Human Kinetics Publishers, Inc., 1995.

Petranick, K, Berg, K. The effects of weight training on bone density of premenopausal, postmenopausal, and elderly women: A review. *Journal of Strength and Conditioning Research* 11(3):200-208, 1997.

CHAPTER 12

STRENGTH TRAINING
FOR SENIORS

*O*ver time, all of the physiological systems of the body lose some of their capacity to function normally. As a result, an individual's ability to handle the physiological demands and stresses of illness or injury may be impaired. One of the most noticeable systems of the body that can be affected by age is the muscular system.

While a degree of muscular atrophy (a reduction in muscle size) is a normal consequence of aging, the loss of muscle mass in older adults accelerates with physical inactivity. Individuals typically begin to experience a pronounced loss of muscle mass in their mid-40s at a rate of approximately 1 to 2 percent each year. Over a 20-year period, roughly 20 to 40 percent of an individual's original level of muscle mass will be lost through inactivity-induced atrophy. Unfortunately, this is often camouflaged by a simultaneous increase in body fat.

The gradual loss of muscle mass and the accompanying strength decline usually do not prevent individuals from performing daily activities at a reasonable level; however, performing recreational-type activities becomes more and more challenging. Eventually, an individual's level of muscular strength can reach a point where activities of daily living (e.g., getting out of a car or bath tub, climbing stairs, or walking without assistance) require 100 percent of maximal strength capacity (Figure 12-1). If an individual then becomes ill or sustains an injury that results in a period of prolonged bed rest, they will lose muscle strength at an even more accelerated rate, possibly becoming so weak that they lose the ability to accomplish self-care activities.

Fortunately, the loss of muscle mass and strength that occurs with age can be prevented or minimized by strength training. A growing body of evidence has shown that older adults – even those over the age of 90 – can increase muscle mass and strength by participating in a sound strength-training program. As a result, age-related physiological declines of the muscular system can be minimized, and an individual's ability to maintain optimal health, rebound from an illness or injury, and live independently can be enhanced.

Possibly the most striking example was a study done by Dr. Maria A. Fiatarone and colleagues. The researchers studied a group of 10 frail, elderly men and women who ranged in age from 87 to 96 at the Hebrew Rehabilitation Center for the Aged, a chronic-care nursing facility near Boston. The subjects participated in an eight-week program of high-intensity strength training of the lower body. All but one subject completed the program. The nine

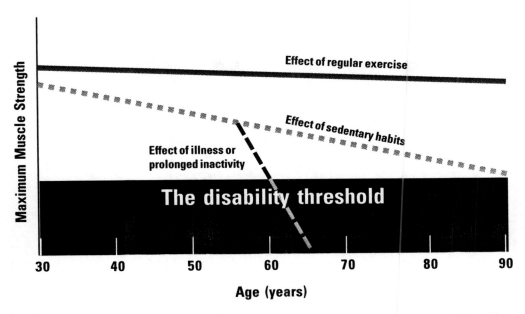

Figure 12-1. Muscle strength gradually declines after age 30 and markedly decreases with inactivity or illness. Individuals' muscles can become so weak that they may lose their ability to move and function (disability threshold).

remaining participants made improvements in (1) increased muscle strength by an average of 174 percent, (2) increased walking speed by an average of 48 percent, and (3) increased size of mid-thigh muscles by an average of 9 percent. The researchers concluded that exercise enables dramatic strength gains even in very old and frail people.

Resistance training may also assist in the effective management of osteoarthritis. Functional ability can be improved if surrounding muscles and unaffected joints share stress with affected joints. Stronger muscles absorb more of the attendant stress on a joint, thereby reducing stress on affected joint surfaces.

Evidence indicates that osteoporosis, which is characterized by decreased bone mineral content (decreased density), may be improved by resistance training, which slows bone loss and can increase bone density. Training-induced improvements in muscular strength and balance may prevent falls that cause fractures among elderly women with osteoporosis.

Resistance preserves muscle tissue during aging and may contribute to weight control by maintaining an increased metabolic rate. Improved muscle strength can also result in reduced heart rate and blood pressure responses when lifting. This means that strength training can decrease stress on the heart during daily activities like carrying groceries or lifting moderate-to-heavy objects. With appropriate resistance training, older adults can maintain appropriate levels of muscular fitness and improved daily function.

SLOWING DOWN THE BIOLOGICAL CLOCK

Although the ability of older adults to realize significant strength gains has been documented, strength-training protocols for older adults have not been adequately addressed.

Figure 12-2. Strength training wards off disability and helps keep "life in your years." Resistance training is an integral component of the Optimal Aging Program conducted at the Beaumont Rehabilitation and Health Center, Birmingham, Michigan.

For example, research has shown that achieving an appropriate training effect for muscular fitness does not have to involve spending extended periods in the weight room, lifting heavy weights, or engaging in complex lifting programs. On the contrary, calisthenics using body weight to stimulate an overload of the muscle, weighted and non-weighted stair climbing, and weight machines have all been found to produce substantial increases in muscular strength and endurance in older adults (Figure 12-2).

The key to ensuring that older adults receive maximum benefits from strength training is to design a resistance-training program that not only meets their needs, but also addresses the physiological factors of this "special" population. Fortunately, the American College of Sports Medicine (ACSM) has developed recommendations for an appropriate strength-training protocol. Similar to the guidelines for other types of training programs, such as aerobic fitness, ACSM's recommended strength-training protocol addresses three main training variables: intensity, frequency, and duration.

INTENSITY

The ACSM recommends that, at the minimum, an individual should perform one set of 8 to 10 exercises that train the major muscle groups of the body. Each set should involve 8 to 12 repetitions that elicit a perceived exertion rating of three to five (Table 12-1). However, for older and more frail persons (50 to 60 years of age and older), 10 to 15 repetitions may be more appropriate, using lighter weights (Figure 12-3). The selection of exercises should ensure that

Table 12-1. The Borg 17-Point Scale*

SCALE	INTENSITY	RESULTS
0	Nothing at all	No Intensity
0.3		
0.5	Extremely weak	Just noticeable
0.7		
1	Very weak	
1.5		
2	Weak	Light
2.5		
3	Moderate	
4		
5	Strong	Heavy
6		
7	Very strong	
8		
9		
10	Extremely strong	Strongest Intensity
11		
*	Absolute maximum	Highest possible

▨ Recommended training zone for resistance exercise

* Copyright Gunnar A. Borg. Reproduced with permission. For correct usage of the Borg scales, it is necessary to follow the administration and instructions given in Borg, G, *Borg's Perceived Exertion and Pain Scales*. Champaign, IL: Human Kinetics Publishers, Inc., 1998. Copies of the scale(s) with instructions can be obtained directly from Dr. Borg: www.borgperception.com.

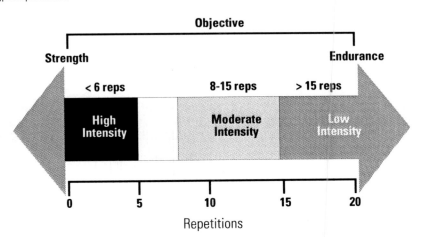

Figure 12-3. Using weight loads that permit 8 to 15 repetitions will generally facilitate improvements in muscular strength and endurance, regardless of age or health status. (Reprinted with permission from American College of Sports Medicine. *ACSM's Guidelines for Exercise Testing and Prescription*, 6th ed. Philadelphia, PA: Lippincott Williams & Wilkins, 2000.)

all the major muscle groups are included. Depending on an individual's personal philosophy, additional sets can be performed. Research conducted at the University of Florida by the late Dr. Michael Pollock and previous investigations at the United States Military Academy suggest that additional sets may have limited value, particularly for nonathletic populations.

Table 12-2. Health Screening Survey for Older Adults*

Questions to ask adults over the age of 65 who are beginning a training program:

1. Do you get chest pains while at rest and/or during exertion?
2. If the answer to Question 1 is "yes": Is it true that you have not had a physician diagnose those pains yet?
3. Have you ever had a heart attack?
4. If the answer to Question 3 is "yes": Was your heart attack within the last year?
5. Do you have high blood pressure?
6. If you don't know the answer to Question 5, answer this: Was your last blood pressure reading more than 150/100?
7. Do you have diabetes?
8. If the answer to Question 7 is "yes": Are you presently being treated for diabetes?
9. Are you short of breath after extremely mild exertion, at rest, or at night in bed?
10. Do you have any ulcerated wounds or cuts on your feet that don't seem to heal?
11. Have you experienced an unexplained loss of 10 lbs or more in the past 6 months?
12. Do you get pain in your buttocks, thighs (front or back), or calves when you walk?
13. While at rest, do you frequently experience fast, irregular heartbeats. Or, at the other extreme, very slow beats? (While a low heart rate can be a sign of an efficient and well-conditioned heart, a very low rate can also indicate a cardiac problem.)
14. Are you currently being treated for any heart or circulatory condition, such as vascular disease, stroke, angina, hypertension, congestive heart failure, poor circulation to the legs, valvular disease, blood clots, or pulmonary disease?
15. Have you previously undergone either coronary angioplasty or heart bypass surgery, or both.
16. As an adult, have you ever had a fracture of the hip, spine, or wrist?
17. Have you fallen more than twice in the past year (no matter what the reason)?

If you answered "yes" to any of the above questions, you should discuss exercise goals with your physician before starting a resistance-training program.

---

* Adapted from Evans, W, Ph.D., FACSM, a 1994 presentation titled "Exercise & Aging."

FREQUENCY

ACSM recommends that strength training be performed at least twice a week, with at least 48 hours of rest between workouts. Research indicates that older individuals require increased time for sufficient recovery from resistance stress imposed upon the body.

DURATION

It has been suggested that strength-training sessions lasting longer than 60 minutes may have a detrimental effect on exercise adherence. ACSM's guidelines suggest individuals complete total-body strength-training sessions within 20 to 25 minutes.

Table 12-3. Functional Capacity Questionnaire*

- Do you have difficulty picking up a small child?
- Do you have difficulty carrying a 10-lb bag of groceries?
- Do you have difficulty performing household chores (vacuuming, mopping, washing windows, etc.).
- Do you have difficulty climbing a flight of stairs?
- Do you have difficulty getting in and out of a car or the bathtub?
- Do you have difficulty rising from a sofa or a low chair without using your arms for assistance?
- Do you have difficulty opening a jar of food?

If you answered "yes" to any of these questions, it may be an indication that you have already experienced significant losses of muscular strength. The decline in your level of muscle strength can be partially countered or offset by participation in a well-designed strength-training program.

---

* Adapted from Evans, W, Ph.D., FACSM, a 1994 presentation titled "Exercise & Aging."

Special Considerations

Regardless of the protocol adopted, several common-sense guidelines pertaining to resistance training for older adults should be followed:

- Have potential participants complete a health status questionnaire prior to starting a program (Table 12-2).
- Assess relative muscular fitness by having clients complete a functional capacity questionnaire (Table 12-3).
- Set a goal to develop sufficient muscular strength and endurance to enhance an individual's ability to live a physically independent lifestyle.
- Closely supervise and monitor the first several training sessions, being sensitive to the special needs and capabilities of the elderly.
- Start out (the first 8 weeks) with very minimal levels of resistance to allow for adaptations of the connective tissue elements.
- Teach the older participant the proper training techniques for all of the exercises in the program.
- Instruct older participants to maintain normal breathing patterns while exercising, since breath-holding (performance of a Valsalva maneuver) can induce acute, excessive blood pressure elevations.
- As a training effect occurs, achieve an overload initially by increasing the number of repetitions, and then by increasing the amount of resistance lifted.
- Never use a resistance so heavy that the exerciser cannot perform at least 8 repetitions per set. Heavy weights can be dangerous and can damage the skeletal and joint structures of an older individual.
- Perform all exercises in a slow, controlled manner. To prevent orthopedic trauma to joint structures, no ballistic (fast and jerky) movements should be allowed.

- Perform the exercises in a range of motion that is within a "pain-free arc" (the maximum range of motion that does not elicit pain or discomfort). As favorable adaptation and improvement occur, gradually increase exercise range of motion to enhance flexibility.
- Perform multi-joint exercises (as opposed to single-joint exercises), because they tend to develop overall muscular fitness.
- Given a choice, use machines rather than free weights to resistance train. Machines require less skill, protect the back by stabilizing the body position, allow the user to start with lower resistance and increase it by smaller increments (not true for all strength-training machines), and allow for easier control of the exercise range of motion.

Table 12-4. Comparison of the Effects of Aging and Exercise on Selected Physiologic and Psychosocial Variables

	Aging	**Exercise**
Aerobic fitness	↓	↑
Resting metabolism	↓	↑
Blood fats	↓	↑
Blood pressure	↓	↑
Body fatness	↓	↑
Muscle mass	↓	↑
Insulin sensitivity	↓	↑
Joint mobility	↓	↑
Bone density	↓	↑
Psychological well-being	↓	↑
↓ (Deterioration) ↑ (Improvement)		

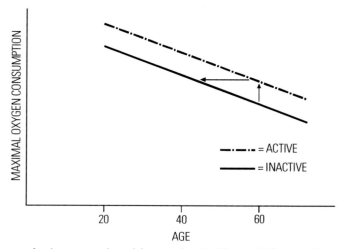

Figure 12-4. Influence of endurance exercise training on an inactive 60-year-old. The typical increase in maximal oxygen consumption (~20%) transforms the individual's aerobic fitness to what it was at the age of 40, corresponding to a 20-year functional rejuvenation.

- Don't allow individuals to overtrain. A minimum of 2 strength-training sessions per week is required to produce beneficial physiological adaptations. Depending on the circumstances, more sessions may be neither desirable nor productive.
- Never permit arthritic individuals to participate in strength-training during active periods of pain or inflammation, since exercise could exacerbate the condition.
- Engage in a year-round resistance-training program, since the cessation of resistance training can result in a rapid, significant loss of strength. When returning from a break in training, individuals should start with weights that are ≤50% of the intensity at which they had been training, and gradually increase the resistance over time.

ADDING LIFE TO YOUR YEARS

The number of Americans 50 years of age or older is currently growing at a pace far greater than the national birth rate. The "over 85 age group" is the fastest growing subset of our population today. The escalating number of older adults has resulted in increased attention on the physiological changes commonly attributed to the "aging process." The inescapable fact, however, is that many individuals age more rapidly than they need to – not because of what they do, but because of what they don't do. Fortunately, regular exercise can and does retard many of the debilitating effects of advancing years (Table 12-4). For example, an aerobic exercise program can typically result in a 20 percent improvement in aerobic fitness, corresponding to a 20-year functional rejuvenation (Figure 12-4). With respect to the effects of the aging process, individuals can control their own destiny. Irrefutable evidence exists to support the fact that consistent participation in a strength-training exercise program is the ideal recipe for improving and sustaining an independent lifestyle for older adults. As the adage goes, aerobic exercise, when combined with strength training, can "add years to your life, as well as life to your years."

Recommended Reading

American College of Sports Medicine. *ACSM's Guidelines for Exercise Testing and Prescription*, 6th ed. Philadelphia, PA: Lippincott Williams & Wilkins, 2000.

American College of Sports Medicine. *ACSM's Resource Manual for Guidelines for Exercise Testing and Prescription*, 4th ed. Philadelphia, PA: Lippincott Williams & Wilkins, 2001.

American College of Sports Medicine. Position stand: The recommended quantity and quality of exercise for developing and maintaining cardiorespiratory and muscular fitness and flexibility in healthy adults. *Medicine & Science in Sports & Exercise* 30(6):975-991, 1998.

Brandon, LJ, Gaasch, D, Boyette, L, Lloyd, A. Strength training for older adults: Benefits, guidelines, and adherence. *ACSM's Health & Fitness Journal* 4(6):12-16, 2000.

Fiatarone, MA, Marks, EC, Ryan, ND, et al. High-intensity training in nonagenarians: Effects on skeletal muscle. *JAMA* 263(22):3029-3034, 1990.

Franklin, BA. Pumping iron: Rationale, benefits, safety, and prescription. *ACSM's Health & Fitness Journal* 2(5):12-15, 1998.

McCartney, N, McKelvie, RS, Martin, J, et al. Weight-training-induced attenuation of the circulatory response of older males to weight lifting. *Journal of Applied Physiology* 74:1056-1060, 1993.

CHAPTER 13

STRENGTH TRAINING
WITHOUT WEIGHTS

*I*n these times of tight budgets and fierce competition for clients, the question facing fitness professionals who own their facilities is whether considerable financial outlay for new strength-training equipment is justified. The question does not lend itself to an easy answer. On the one hand, strength training serves as a fundamental component of any program to develop total (overall) fitness. On the other hand, the relatively high cost of most strength-training equipment can make such an expense prohibitive.

Fortunately, fitness professionals are not forced to choose between making a substantial capital investment in strength-training equipment and offering strength-training activities in their programs. Positive alternatives exist for developing muscular fitness that do not require much — if any — equipment.

MUSCLE IS NOT SMART

Considerable research indicates that, to develop muscular fitness, one basic step has to be undertaken: regularly place a *demand* on the muscle or muscle group to be improved, which involves applying *resistance* against a muscle at a level that is greater than the muscle is accustomed to handling. This process is referred to as placing an *overload* on a muscle. Depending on the type of response required of the muscle, stressing the muscles can elicit improvement in either muscular strength (the ability of a muscle or a muscle group to exert maximal force) or muscular endurance (the capacity of a muscle or muscle group to resist fatigue and/or make repeated submaximal contractions).

The type of resistance employed is not the key to improving muscular fitness. Muscles have neither eyes nor brains. They don't know if rocks, free weights, or sandbags are the source of resistance. Regardless of the exact type of resistance, the critical factors influencing the level of improvement in muscular fitness are how well the resistance is applied and what relative load (demand) is placed on the muscles.

Two of the most innovative actions involving strength training since World War II are the invention of the multi-station machine and the subsequent development of strength-training machines that employ variable resistance. Since the early 1970s when the introduction of Nautilus machines served as a catalyst for an explosion of interest in strength training, the equipment for developing muscular fitness has changed dramatically: new designs, new capabilities, new types of machines, and new (higher) prices.

LOW-COST STRENGTH TECHNIQUES

Four of the most effective low-cost techniques for developing muscular fitness are negative-only exercises, buddy exercises, stick exercises, and resistance-cord exercises.

NEGATIVE-ONLY EXERCISES

Negative-only exercises are based on the fact that the muscles used to raise a weight are the same muscles used to lower (under control) the weight. When lifting a weight, the muscles are shortening. This part of an exercise is referred to as the concentric or positive phase. When the weight is lowered, the muscles are lengthening, which is referred to as the eccentric or negative phase of the lift.

Negative-only exercises are calisthenic-type exercises involving only the negative phase of the exercise performed. The most common ones are push-ups, dips, chin-ups, pull-ups, and sit-ups. For example, in a negative-only push-up, exercisers would only perform that part of the exercise where the body is slowly lowered to the ground. They would not push back up to the front-leaning rest position (the starting position for a push-up performed in normal fashion). In a negative-only push-up, an all-fours position is initially assumed. Next, the legs are straightened (extended) to assume a front-leaning rest position. Keeping the back straight, an exerciser should slowly lower his or her body to the ground, taking three to four seconds. The difficulty of the exercise can be increased by taking longer (five to six seconds) or by wearing a weighted vest. To do another repetition, the process should be repeated.

BUDDY EXERCISES

Buddy exercises are exercises in which an exerciser performs a movement against force exerted by a buddy (partner). Also referred to as manual-resistance exercises and partner-resistance exercises, buddy exercises have been used since early in the 20th century to develop strength. In recent years, buddy exercises have been employed extensively by the military and a number of athletic teams as a viable means for developing muscular fitness.

Buddy exercises can be used to develop most of the muscles in the body. For example, a buddy exercise for developing abductor muscles (e.g., gluteus medius and minimus) would involve an exerciser lying on his or her side and slowly raising the upper leg (not the one next to the floor) against resistance applied by the "buddy." The partner would apply force sufficient to enable the exerciser to complete the movement in two to three seconds.

STICK EXERCISES

Stick exercises are buddy exercises, designed to develop upper-body musculature, that employ a wooden dowel or some other cylindrical device (e.g., a broomstick, a baseball bat, etc.) The wooden dowel used in stick exercises provides an added degree of comfort and control. The conditioning program at the United States Military Academy uses a 30-inch wooden dowel to perform stick exercises. At the minimum, the dowel should be as long as the width of the exerciser's shoulders.

Stick exercises usually involve combining two movements into one collective exercise. Among the more popular stick exercises are the lat pulldown/shoulder press; the chest press/ lat row; the biceps curl/negative curl; and the triceps extension/negative extension. For example, to perform a lat pulldown/shoulder press stick exercise, an individual would begin by assuming a seated position with arms raised, shoulder width apart over his or her head. The partner stands behind the exerciser and places a knee against their back to support them. The partner then places the dowel in the exerciser's outstretched hands and holds the dowel adjacent to their hands. On command, the exerciser pulls the dowel downward to the base of his or her neck against resistance provided by the partner (this movement is a lat pulldown). At that point, the exerciser pauses momentarily and pushes the dowel back to the starting position, again against force exerted by the buddy (this phase of the exercise involves doing a shoulder press). To perform another repetition, the process is repeated.

RESISTANCE-CORD EXERCISES

Resistance-cord exercises involve performing exercises (movements) against either the force required to stretch a cord or the muscular fitness necessary to permit a cord that has been stretched to return to its natural state gradually under control. Such cords must be made of materials that have a sufficient degree of elasticity (e.g., rubber). A resistance cord can be either a commercial product (e.g., the Sport Cord) or a homemade device (e.g., a length of surgical tubing). Resistance-cord exercises can be performed for both the lower body and the upper body. An individual should begin by either attaching one end of the cord to a fixed object or holding on to one end with each hand. Then, stretch the cord by moving an arm or leg in the movement pattern appropriate to whatever muscle or muscle group that is to be developed.

TO PAY OR NOT TO PAY

Any decision whether to incorporate low-cost strength-training exercises into a facility's basic program offerings can best be made after a thorough examination of the possible advantages and disadvantages of such exercises and reflecting on how these considerations would impact the facility. In addition to requiring a minimal capital investment, exercises for developing strength, which involve little or no equipment, offer the following advantages:

- They can add variety to a strength-training program.
- A large number of individuals can be trained simultaneously.
- An individual can perform a greater number of different exercises for developing strength.
- In some instances, these techniques allow exercises to be performed that may be even more effective (for a specific muscle) than a traditional exercise (with costly equipment).
- In most instances, these techniques permit better control of how fast an exercise is performed.
- Properly performed, they permit muscles to be worked at a very high level of intensity (the point of momentary muscle fatigue).
- These exercise techniques tend to rechannel the focus of the exerciser away from how much work is being performed (quantity) to the more critical issue – how well the work is being done (quality).

However, the results achieved by using these low-cost strength-training techniques may also have a few potential disadvantages, including:

- Both buddy exercises and stick exercises require two people: an exerciser and a partner (or a trainer). A client may not always have access to a training partner at a time that is convenient.
- For some clients, strength-training techniques that use little or no equipment may involve a more difficult learning curve than simply doing exercises on a machine designed to control the required movement pattern.
- For a small number of individuals, strength-training techniques involving little or no equipment may require a greater degree of coordination than what is typically required with traditional strength equipment.
- Buddy exercises and stick exercises are not as effective when one partner (or the trainer) is significantly stronger than the other or when a substantial height difference exists. The ability of the weaker and/or shorter individual to apply a sufficient amount of resistance is limited due to strength or leverage deficiencies.
- Strength-training techniques involving little or no equipment do not have participant feedback relating to how much work (quantity-wise) is being performed. Some individuals greatly prefer the satisfaction of being able to lift "X" number of lbs, "X" number of times.

MORE ($) IS NOT NECESSARILY BETTER

Just as "more exercise" does not necessarily result in a greater level of fitness, spending "more money" than other facilities will not ensure a better exercise offering. Wisely investing money in capital expenditures will have a critical impact on the degree to which an investment enables a fitness professional or fitness facility to accomplish their objectives. Invest money wisely. Successful people always do. The bottom line of a facility's profit-and-loss statement, as well as the ability of a facility to continue offering comprehensive fitness programming, may well be affected to a substantial degree by whether you can identify positive ways to accomplish "more with less."

Recommended Reading

Brzycki, M (ed). *Maximize Your Training.* Chicago, IL: Masters Press, 2000.

Fleck, SJ, Kraemer, WJ. *Designing Resistance Training Programs,* 2nd ed. Champaign, IL: Human Kinetics Publishers, Inc., 1997.

Mikesky, AE, Topp, R, Wigglesworth, JK, Edwards, JE. Resistance training using elastic tubing in older adults. *Medicine & Science in Sports & Exercise* 24(5 Suppl.):S138, 1992.

Peterson, JA, Bryant, CX, Peterson, SL. *Strength Training for Women.* Champaign, IL: Human Kinetics Publishers, Inc., 1995.

Riley, DP. *Maximum Muscular Fitness: Strength Training Without Equipment.* Champaign, IL: Human Kinetics Publishers, Inc., 1982.

• • •

SECTION III

SPECIAL EXERCISE CONSIDERATIONS AND POPULATIONS

CHAPTER 14

• •

EXERCISE AND
ENVIRONMENTAL ISSUES

*A*s a fitness professional, it is vital that you know how each of your clients will be influenced by an exercise environment. Clients with asthma will be affected by air quality. Clients with allergies can be affected by certain smells, pollen, and a variety of other air particulates. Clients with hypertension or diabetes can be affected by high heat and humidity. Understanding how the body responds and adapts to environmental conditions during exercise is critical to ensuring safe and profitable activities for your clients. This chapter focuses on specific responses and adaptations of the body to several common environmental stressors (high heat and humidity, cold, altitude, and air pollution) that affect exercise performance.

HIGH HEAT AND HUMIDITY

Of the many environmental factors that can impact exercise, none are as potentially life — and health — threatening as heat stress. Preventing heat-related problems by properly adjusting your exercise program to account for the effects of hot ambient temperatures involves a common-sense approach based on an understanding of how the body physiologically responds to heat. While few documented heat-related standards exist for recreational or clinical exercise environments, industry's experience in dealing with heat stress issues can provide important insight.

In industrial settings, heat stress has received considerable attention worldwide because of its potential impact on worker productivity, health, and safety. While no universally accepted standards exist for heat stress evaluation and decision making, several proposed standards in the United States and around the world provide quantitative information that can be directly applied to an exercise setting. In the U.S., the National Institute for Occupational Safety and Health (NIOSH), the American Conference of Governmental Industrial Hygienists (ACGIH), the American Industrial Hygiene Association (AIHA), and the U.S. Armed Forces have promulgated standards for heat stress. These organizations have proposed standards aimed at preventing body temperature from rising excessively during physical exertion and at mitigating the deleterious effects of dehydration. Based upon accurate assessments of the environmental conditions and the intensity of the physical activity, these standards can be easily adapted to an exercise setting (both indoor and outdoor). Although various standards differ slightly in their approach, these typically provide two cutoff points: "action limits" (above which specific actions should be taken during/prior to exercise) and "ceiling limits" (above which exercise should not be attempted without somehow changing the environment).

EVALUATION OF THE ENVIRONMENT

When trying to make decisions about the appropriateness of a thermal environment, it is important to evaluate all aspects of the environment that could impact an individual's ability to exercise safely. Not only are temperature and humidity important, but air movement and (when exercising outdoors) solar radiation should also be considered. One single temperature that takes all the environmental effects into account is the "wet-bulb globe temperature" or "WBGT." WBGT is a single temperature index that is dependent upon air temperature, humidity, solar radiation, and wind velocity. Consequently, it represents a composite measure of the impact of the environment on exercise participants.

WBGT can be measured using simple, low-cost instrumentation or calculated from data available from local weather services. Three measurements are combined into the WBGT calculation: air temperature, natural wet-bulb temperature (measured by placing a wetted wick over the thermometer bulb), and globe temperature (the temperature inside a copper globe painted flat black). Indoors, WBGT is calculated as WBGT = (0.7 times natural wet-bulb temperature) + (0.3 times globe temperature) and can be expressed as either Celsius or Fahrenheit. Outdoors, WBGT is calculated as (0.7 times natural wet-bulb temperature) + (0.2 times globe temperature) + (0.1 times air temperature).

BASING EXERCISE RECOMMENDATIONS ON WBGT

It is important to remember that no universally accepted standards exist concerning heat stress. Accordingly, the recommended cutoff points presented in this section serve only as guidelines in deciding such issues as "when it is too hot to exercise," "how long exercise should last under certain conditions," and related concerns. For exercise programs and individual exercise prescriptions, the criteria document proposed by NIOSH (under the Occupational Safety and Health Act of 1970 [Public Law 91-596]) in 1972 and revised in 1986 can be easily adopted.

Figures 14-1 and 14-2 graphically illustrate the NIOSH theory regarding what constitutes an appropriate approach to evaluating heat stress. Both figures define several distinct limits concerning when it is safe to exercise, using exercise intensity (expressed here as energy expenditure per hour) and ambient WBGT (in both Celsius and Fahrenheit) as modulating parameters. Two sets of limits are proposed, including one set for heat-unacclimatized persons (the Recommended Alert Limit or RAL) and one for heat-acclimatized persons (the Recommended Exposure Limit or REL). Each figure also reflects a proposed "ceiling limit" (C) – a level above which probably no one should exercise unless the environment can be changed. Several action limit lines are included on each graph for intermittent exercise of varying durations.

While it takes practice to use such guidelines, they do provide a numerical index for making appropriate decisions about the exercise environment. The most important question you may be confronted with is how to deal with an environment that is below the ceiling limit but above the RAL or REL (whichever applies). This area represents environmental conditions in which exercise can still be performed, but with an increased risk to the participant. In such cases, the following actions are recommended:

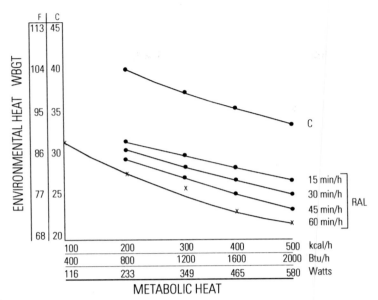

C = Ceiling Limit
RAL = Recommended Alert Limit
* For the "standard individual" of 70 kg (154 lbs) body weight and 1.8 m² (19.4 ft²) body surface.

Figure 14-1. Recommended heat stress alert limits for heat-unacclimatized individuals, based on information from DHHS NIOSH Publication No. 86-113.

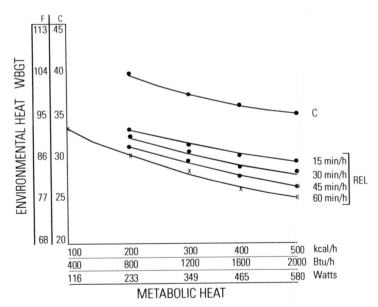

C = Ceiling Limit
REL = Recommended Exposure Limit
* For the "standard individual" of 70 kg (154 lbs) body weight and 1.8 m² (19.4 ft²) body surface.

Figure 14-2. Recommended heat stress alert limits for heat-acclimatized individuals, based on information from DHHS NIOSH Publication No. 86-113.

- *Change the environment.* If the exercise area cannot be cooled to an appropriate WBGT by means of fans or air conditioning, change the exercise site to one with an environment that meets the WBGT requirements; for example, move to a shaded area or an area with greater air movement.
- *Decrease the exercise intensity.* Similar to cooling the environment, lowering the intensity represents another way of staying within an acceptable temperature/ intensity zone. The way to accomplish this, while maintaining a sufficient training stimulus, is to slow the pace of the exercise bout and add rest cycles to a routine. Perhaps the most useful technique for achieving a safe and appropriate exercise intensity involves the proper use of target heart rate (unchanged from cool conditions). Exercise heart rate is increased approximately 1 bpm for every degree Celsius above 24°C or 75°F (Figure 14-3) and 2 bpm for every mm Hg above 20 mm Hg water vapor pressure. Strict adherence to a scientifically determined target heart rate will prevent excessive cardiac demands during exercise. Rating of perceived exertion can be used to modulate exercise intensity for individuals on medications that may influence the heart rate response.

HEAT ACCLIMATION

One of the best methods for decreasing the risk of developing heat illness or injury is to gradually acclimate to exercising in hot environments. Through acclimation, heart rate and body temperature (at a given exercise intensity) decrease, sweating rate increases, and sweat becomes more dilute. It has been estimated that as much as 25 percent of the apparently healthy population may be heat intolerant in an unacclimated state, with that number decreasing to about 2 percent after acclimation. The best method of heat acclimation is to exercise aerobically over time, in a hotter environment than normal. For safety reasons, the first session should be limited to 10 to 15 minutes and gradually increased to 20 to 60 minutes as the individual acclimates to the heat. It takes most healthy people 10 to 14 days to fully acclimate to hot environments, although illness and alcohol consumption have been shown to slow this process.

It should also be noted that the benefits of heat acclimation are lost quite rapidly when an individual stops exercising in the heat. For every two days of abstaining from heat exposure, one day of acclimation is lost. Thus, after three to four weeks, an individual should be considered unacclimated. After even short periods of de-acclimation (weekends, short periods of illness), the risk of exercising in the heat can be substantial.

FLUID INTAKE

Adequate hydration is another critical factor in preventing the adverse effects of exercise when the temperature and/or humidity are high. Progressive dehydration occurs during exercise when sweating is profuse. A reduction of as little as 2 percent in body weight during exercise can result in impaired temperature regulation. Furthermore, a 4 percent decrease in body weight translates into a 6 percent decrease in maximal aerobic capacity and a 12 percent reduction in exercise time to exhaustion.

As a fitness professional, you should take steps to ensure that fluids are readily available for your clients before, during, and after exercise. All individuals should be encouraged

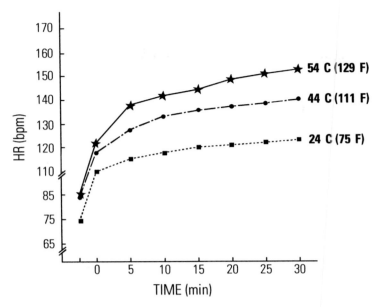

Figure 14-3. Influence of environmental temperature on heart rate (HR) responses at a fixed, submaximal work rate over time. Adapted from Pandolf, KB, Cafarelli, E, Nobel, BJ, et al. Hyperthermia: Effect on exercise prescription. *Archives of Physical Medicine and Rehabilitation* 56:524-526, 1975. (Reprinted with permission from American College of Sports Medicine. *ACSM's Guidelines for Exercise Testing and Prescription*, 6th ed. Philadelphia, PA: Lippincott Williams & Wilkins, 2000.)

to drink as much water as is physically comfortable 15 to 30 minutes prior to exercise, a cupful (6 to 8 ounces) of water at 15-minute intervals during exercise, and more water than their sense of thirst dictates after exercise. This latter point is especially applicable to clients over the age of 60, since research has shown decreased thirst sensitivity to body-hydration status in elderly persons.

The fluid should be cold (18° to 22°C/59° to 72°F) and palatable; moreover, with a few exceptions, water is the replacement fluid of choice. Little need exists to replace electrolytes lost during most exercise sessions, since any decremental loss is typically replenished when the next meal is eaten. For participants on a restricted salt diet, care should be taken with regard to salt balance. Unless the exercise bout lasts more than 90 minutes, little or no advantage can be attained by consuming commercially marketed sports drinks.

INDIVIDUALS AT RISK

The guidelines presented in this chapter are based on the assumption that the exercise participant does not have any overt disease or condition that may increase the likelihood of heat illness or injury. Among the factors that can raise the risk of incurring heat-related problems are hypertension (alters the control of skin blood flow), diabetes (neuropathies may affect sweating and/or skin blood flow), aging (alters peripheral cardiovascular and sweating responses), various drug regimens (including diuretics, beta-blockers, alpha-agonists, and vasodilators), alcohol use (causes vasodilation and enhances dehydration), obesity, and a prior history of heat illness or difficulty acclimating to heat. It is important to counsel your clients about the potential effects of these factors on temperature regulation.

MANAGEMENT PLAN FOR FACILITIES

To be prepared to deal with threatening or anticipated periods of hot weather, exercise professionals should develop and implement a standardized management plan for handling heat stress. Among the topics that should be included are:

1. An increase in the level of health/medical screening and surveillance of exercise participants.
2. An evaluation of all aspects of a facility's thermal environment, preferably using WBGT as a criterion measure.
3. An approved decision-making flow chart, concerning heat stress issues, that is based on proposed standards such as NIOSH, ACGIH, AIHA, etc., and tailored to your clients and the exercise setting.
4. A policy of strongly encouraging exercise participants to gradually acclimate to heat stress.
5. Counseling clients to wear light clothing and shorts to facilitate cooling by evaporation and to decrease the exercise dosage (e.g., speed, duration, resistance) at temperatures >27°C (81°F) and/or >75% relative humidity.
6. Making cold, palatable fluids readily available, and instituting a plan for increasing the fluid intake level of exercise participants before, during, and after exercise (schedule drink breaks for the entire exercise group).
7. Taking steps to make exercise participants more knowledgeable about heat stress, including early signs and symptoms of heat illness (chills, lightheadedness, dizziness, goose bumps, nausea, etc.).
8. Emergency procedures, for handling heat illness, that have been incorporated into the overall emergency plan for the facility.

COLD

The winter months signal the advent of cold weather for most areas. Cold temperatures, however, are not necessarily a reason for individuals to dramatically curtail their aerobic training efforts, even if they prefer to exercise outdoors. Similar to exercising in extreme heat, your clients can generally exercise safely in the cold, provided that they adhere to a few common-sense guidelines. These guidelines are applicable to all alternatives for exercising aerobically outdoors in the cold, including jogging, cross-country skiing, hiking, mountain climbing, and ice-skating.

HOW DOES THE BODY RESPOND TO THE COLD?

Before identifying your clients' personal needs for adapting to cold weather conditions, you should first consider how the body responds to the cold. Essentially, it responds physiologically to cold weather in two primary ways: increased metabolic rate and increased tissue insulation.

Changes in metabolic rate can be elicited either voluntarily (by exercising) or involuntarily (shivering). Thermogenesis involves the production of heat in the body by means of shivering (and to a smaller degree, sympathetic chemical excitation). Shivering results from "cold" signals to the hypothalamus, which in turn sends nonrhythmic impulses to the motor neurons of the skeletal muscles throughout the body. Contrary to most individuals' perception of the process of shivering, these impulses do not cause the muscles to actually shake. Rather, they prompt the muscle spindle stretch reflex mechanism to oscillate. At a certain point, shivering begins and heat production rises. During maximal shivering, the body can increase the amount of heat it produces to as high as four to five times normal.

Before the body alters its metabolic rate, however, its initial response to the cold is to constrict blood vessels. Except for the head, this constriction occurs in the peripheral blood vessels that supply the skin and subcutaneous tissues. When blood is literally sidetracked from the surface areas of the body into the deeper blood vessels (i.e., to the core), the net effect of the process of vasoconstriction is to increase the relative insulative level of surface tissues. When blood is shunted away from a person's skin, the "insulative thickness" of the surface tissues is increased. In turn, the rate of heat loss decreases.

EXERCISE RESPONSES TO THE COLD

Under most circumstances, cold weather should not present a significant problem for anyone who wants to exercise outdoors. Cold ambient air, for example, does not pose a particular danger to the respiratory passages. By the time inspired air reaches the bronchi in the lungs, the air is warmed to a temperature sufficiently high to be safe. Humans can breathe air at temperatures as low as -35°C (-31°F) without a detrimental effect. However, for individuals who have angina, breathing cold air may precipitate anginal pain. Using a scarf to cover the nose and mouth will prewarm and prehumidify the air.

As long as the body core temperature is kept close to normal, and sufficient clothing is worn to keep the surface areas of the body warm, the capacity to exercise will not be impaired. The maximal ability to take in, transport, and utilize oxygen (maximal oxygen uptake) and the oxygen cost of submaximal exercise are generally unaffected by the cold. The heart rate may be slightly lower while exercising in the cold, but this is not a consistent finding. Stroke volume (the amount of blood pumped by the heart per beat) may be higher at low exercise intensities, but is unaffected by cold at higher work loads. Cardiac output (the amount of blood pumped by the heart on a per minute basis) at submaximal and maximal exercise is largely unchanged.

If the core temperature and muscle temperature fall below normal, the maximal aerobic capacity and cardiovascular endurance may be reduced. A cool muscle has a decreased ability to generate force for a given cross-sectional area of muscle fibers. Therefore, to maintain force, more fast-twitch fibers must be recruited, resulting in a greater reliance on anaerobic glycolysis and, perhaps, more lactic acid production. Thus, the ability to perform activities that require dynamic muscle strength and power may be negatively affected by cold weather.

Fortunately, the process of maintaining the body core temperature at normal levels and of insulating the exterior surface area of the body against the cold elements is not particularly difficult. As was discussed previously, under almost all conditions the body produces sufficient heat to maintain core temperature. Aerobic exercise makes it easier for the body to regulate core temperature on a more voluntary basis. During exercise, more than 75 percent of the energy produced by the working muscles is converted to heat, which elevates core temperature. During moderate and vigorous exercise, sufficient heat is generated to maintain core temperature. At low intensities of exercise, however, core temperature could begin to fall after one hour of exercise in cold weather were it not for the onset of involuntary thermogenesis (shivering).

Insulating the body against the cold by wearing sufficient clothes involves common sense. Clothing maintains body heat best when worn in multiple layers, allowing easy adaptation to fluctuating environmental conditions. Simply remove or subtract layers one by one to keep pace with the current environment. The layer next to the skin (long underwear) should ventilate to allow the body to cool itself. This layer also transports perspiration away from the skin without absorbing the moisture. Wet or damp clothing transfers heat away from the body up to 25 times faster than dry clothing. The insulating layers (shirts, fleece, etc.) trap warm air next to the body. The outer protective layer is critical for minimizing skin conduction and convection heat loss from wind and rain. In recent years, significant progress has been made in the development and manufacture of cold weather exercise clothing. Clothing made of GORE-TEX fabric, for example, is lightweight and provides adequate protection from the environmental stressors, yet still permits water (perspiration) to evaporate.

The following guidelines are recommended with regard to clothing:

- Avoid heavy, bulky garments.
- Use up to 4 layers of clothing in extremely cold weather; a ventilation layer next to the skin, 1 or 2 insulating layers, and an outer protective layer.
- Wear 2 layers of socks – a ventilation layer and an insulating layer.
- Wear fleece or wool gloves to protect the hands.
- Wear a hat. Large amounts of heat can be lost from an uncovered head.
- If necessary, keep the facial area warm – preferably with a wool scarf.

How COLD IS TOO COLD?

Under most conditions, it will not be too cold to exercise outdoors provided proper clothing is worn. In some circumstances, however, the temperature will be such that exercising outdoors would be ill-advised. The most common way to express relative temperature is the wind chill index. Ambient temperature alone is not always a valid indication of "coldness." Because wind exacerbates heat loss by increasing the degree to which the warmer insulating layer of air that surrounds the body is continually replaced by the cooler ambient air, it can have a substantial cooling effect on the body. As an example, the combination of a -9.4°C (15°F) temperature with 30-mph winds yields an equivalent temperature of -32.2°C (-26°F). The measure used to quantify these equivalent temperatures is the wind chill index. Individuals who plan to exercise in cold weather should consult a wind chill index (Table 14-1) to ensure that the cooling effect of the wind, along with the ambient air temperature, does not produce a potentially unsafe environment for working out. As a rule of thumb, any wind chill temperature of less than -20°F should be viewed with caution and less than -70°F is potentially dangerous.

The key to safely exercising outdoors is to be prepared. Dress in layers. Use common sense. Unless the wind chill index dictates otherwise, don't let the elements interfere with the benefits and joys of exercising.

Table 14-1. Wind Chill Index

Wind Speed (mph)	Thermometer Reading (°F)										
	50	40	30	20	10	0	-10	-20	-30	-40	-50
	(Equivalent Temperature [°F])										
5	48	37	27	16	6	-5	-15	-26	-36	-47	-57
10	40	28	16	4	-9	-21	-33	-46	-58	-70	-83
15	36	22	9	-5	-18	-36	-45	-58	-72	-85	-99
20	32	18	4	-10	-25	-39	-53	-67	-82	-96	-110
25	30	16	0	-15	-29	-44	-59	-74	-88	-104	-118
30	28	13	-2	-18	-33	-48	-63	-79	-94	-109	-125
35	27	11	-4	-20	-35	-49	-67	-83	-98	-113	-129
*40	26	10	-6	-21	-37	-53	-69	-85	-100	-116	-132
	Minimal Risk			Increasing Risk				Great Risk			

* Wind speeds greater than 40 mph have little additional effect.

HYPOTHERMIA DURING WATER SPORTS

The risk of hypothermia is present even at higher ambient temperatures, when people are active in water-related sports (e.g., swimming or surfing). Water exposure results in an increase in heat loss of up to 25 times more than that in air environments. During the swimming portion of triathlons, when water temperatures are 18° to 19°C (64° to 66°F), 10 to 30 percent of the contestants will have body core temperatures below 35°C (95°F). At such temperatures, both physiological and psychological effects of the cooling can be expected. Similar problems may also occur during the cycling period, due to an "after drop" in body core temperature during the first 10 minutes of cycling. The risk of hypothermia for novice windsurfers is relatively high. Regular dips in cool water, with the subsequent evaporation of moisture when standing on the board, in combination with physical exhaustion, may create a substantial risk of hypothermia.

ALTITUDE

Altitude also has effects on the body that can impair physical and cognitive function. As altitude increases, barometric pressure decreases and the air becomes less dense. The percentage of oxygen in the air stays fairly constant (20.93%) with increasing altitude, but the partial pressure of oxygen (pO_2) declines, due to the declining barometric pressure. At sea level, pO_2 is 159 mm Hg; at 5,300 feet (Denver, Colorado), it is reduced to 132 mm Hg; and at 14,100 feet (Pikes Peak), it is as low as 94 mm Hg. A consequence of the reduction in pO_2 is that hemoglobin saturation is decreased (i.e., less oxygen is carried by the arterial blood) and the amount of oxygen available at the cellular level is diminished. This reduces maximal oxygen uptake ($\dot{V}O_{2max}$) and limits physical working capacity (PWC). These reductions are directly proportional to the increase in altitude. At very low pO_2's (<100 mm Hg), mental and motor performance may also be impaired. Problems with judgment result in a higher risk of injury.

Changes in performance capabilities begin to occur at approximately 5,000 feet (1,524 meters). For example, activities such as sprinting or long jumping tend to be enhanced at altitude – a performance improvement resulting from the fact that the body has to overcome less resistance (since the air is less dense) while it is in flight. It appears, however, that the more aerobic an activity is, the more it will be negatively affected by altitude. As a rule, the higher the altitude, the larger the decrement in aerobic performance. Because less oxygen is present in the blood at high altitude, the heart beats more frequently to deliver a sufficient amount of oxygen to the working muscles. As a result, when exercising at a high altitude, the intensity of an exercise bout must be reduced to stay within a prescribed training heart rate range.

When an individual remains at high altitude for extended periods, acclimatization occurs. This is partially due to an increase in red blood cell production, thereby increasing oxygen transport capacity. Improved muscle vascularization and increased cellular oxidative capacity may also occur. Nevertheless, $\dot{V}O_{2max}$ and PWC typically do not reach levels seen at sea level.

Many people experience some form of acute mountain sickness (AMS) after about six hours at high altitude. Symptoms such as severe headache, lassitude, nausea, indigestion, and sleep disturbances occur in some individuals at levels of 7,000 feet, and are quite common above 10,000 feet. At these higher altitudes, more severe symptoms such as brain or lung edema can occur. As a result of modern transportation (airplanes, cable cars, or mountain ascents by automobile), ascent times have decreased and incidences of mountain sickness have increased. A rule of thumb for the prevention of AMS is to rest one day at 7,500 feet and another day for each additional 2,000-foot increase in altitude. In addition, it is advisable to sleep at an altitude that is lower than a daytime altitude – "climb high, sleep low." If an individual experiences AMS, the rule is as follows: mild symptoms, stop ascent until the symptoms disappear; more severe symptoms, descend to a lower altitude immediately.

An additional factor that coincides with an increase in altitude is a change of climate. In general, with every 1,000 feet, ambient temperature decreases 2°C. Thus, additional risks of cooling (wind chill and hypothermia) are present and the risk of dehydration increases with altitude. Water loss is increased and water intake is often reduced due to limited availability. The former is due to both the decrease in the amount of water vapor in the air with altitude (increased evaporation) and increased diuresis (urine production). Thus, individuals should drink more than normal (>2.5 liters/day) when at altitude. Finally, at altitude the amount of UV radiation is much stronger than at sea level. As a result, precautions should be taken with respect to sunburn and snow blindness.

AIR POLLUTION

Many athletes and exercise enthusiasts live in densely populated urban areas where they are increasingly confronted with challenges related to air pollution caused by traffic and industry. During times of temperature inversion or when air movement is low, air pollutants can reach concentrations that can severely impede physical performance. The most common air pollutants are carbon monoxide, sulfur oxides, nitrogen oxides, ozone, peroxyacetyl nitrate, aerosols, soot, dust, and smoke. The effect of these pollutants is, in part, related to their penetration into the body.

As they are inhaled, the main effects of air pollutants are on the respiratory tract. The nose hairs remove large particles and highly soluble gases very effectively (e.g., 99.9 percent of inhaled sulfur dioxide is removed in the nose), but smaller particles and agents with low solubility pass easily. During exercise, where mouth breathing plays an important role, this air filtration process is much less efficient, and more pollutants reach the lungs. With respect to the short-term effects of pollutants on exercise performance, the main problems are irritation of the upper respiratory tract, respiratory discomfort, and reductions in the oxygen transport capacity of the blood.

Carbon monoxide (CO) emissions in urban areas are greater than emissions of all other pollutants combined. CO primarily affects exercise performance through its strong (200 times stronger than that of oxygen) capacity to bind to hemoglobin (COHb) in the blood, thereby reducing the blood's capacity to transport oxygen to the tissues. Very high levels of COHb are needed to produce reductions in submaximal exercise performance. Therefore, under realistic outdoor conditions, the effects of CO only become evident when maximal exercise performance is an issue. For example, maximal oxygen uptake is reduced at COHb concentrations above 4.3 percent. During prolonged exposure to heavy traffic, COHb concentrations of 5 percent have been observed. In persons with cardiovascular impairment, problems may occur during submaximal exercise at lower concentrations of COHb (2.5 to 3 percent).

Sulfur oxides (SOx), mainly in the form of sulfur dioxide, exert their influence through irritation of the upper respiratory tract, which can cause reflexive bronchoconstriction and increased airway resistance. Nose breathing strongly reduces this effect compared with mouth breathing. For submaximal exercise, the threshold level before pulmonary function is compromised is between one and three parts per million (ppm). For maximal exercise, no cutoffs are as yet available. For asthmatics, the threshold values for eliciting a bronchoconstrictor response are lower (0.2 to 0.5 ppm of SO_2).

Of the nitrogen oxides (NOx), only the effect of nitrogen dioxide (NO_2) has been studied in humans. Acute exposure to high concentrations of NO_2 (200 to 4,000 ppm) is extremely dangerous and has resulted in several reported deaths. During submaximal exercise, no effect of NO_2 levels up to 1 to 2 ppm has been observed, but effects of higher concentrations and/or its effects during maximal exercise have not been studied.

Another pollutant that may create a health risk is ozone (O_3). During light-to-moderate submaximal exercise lasting several hours, exposures to 0.3 to 0.45 ppm O_3 have resulted in decrements in pulmonary function and increased subjective discomfort. For more intense levels of exercise, the respiratory discomfort can become severe and thereby limit performance. Ozone has also been associated with eye irritation, general respiratory discomfort, and nausea.

Effects of aerosols on physiological function are usually caused by their effect as airway irritants. The most common aerosols are sulfates (minimal adverse effects), sulfuric acids (minimal effect, unless prolonged exposure, larger particles, and/or high ambient humidity are present), nitrate aerosols (minimal effect), and saturated and unsaturated aldehydes (e.g., formaldehyde, acrolein, and crotonaldehyde), which are also irritants with minimal effect.

The effects of minute particles of soot, dust, and smoke on exercising humans have not been evaluated. Generally, particulate inhalation results in bronchoconstriction. The penetration of these particulates in the respiratory system is related to the size of the particle.

Below three microns, they can reach the alveoli, between three and five microns they usually settle in the upper respiratory tract and above five microns they are not able to enter the respiratory tract. Thus, particles smaller than five microns can cause pulmonary inflammation, congestion, or ulceration. Exercise, by increasing respiratory rate, may aggravate the contamination of the lungs.

The presence of more than one pollutant, which is generally the case in most smog conditions, usually has a more powerful effect on the body. Also, an interaction of air pollution with other environmental stressors (e.g., heat, cold, and altitude) may occur. Additive effects have been observed for heat stress and carbon monoxide, peroxyacetyl nitrate, and ozone. Low relative humidity increases the adverse health effects of ozone, whereas high humidity can increase the untoward effects of sulfur dioxide and nitrogen dioxide. Low ambient temperature can, through breathing of cold air, result in reflexive bronchoconstriction, especially in asthmatic individuals. For asthmatics, the presence of a pollutant in the air has an even stronger effect than the sum of the two separate effects – cold plus pollution. Finally, high altitude interacts with carbon monoxide. Both stressors limit the oxygen transport capacity of the blood and, thus, create cumulative adverse effects on exercise performance. Because the pollutants present in cigarette smoke have been shown to have a deleterious effect on exercise performance, they should also be avoided prior to and during exercise. When combined with smog, the effects of cigarette smoke are obviously compounded.

When exercise is to be performed in a high pollution area, valuable information may be acquired from local meteorologists. To minimize potential problems, activities should be carefully planned, taking into consideration daily and seasonal fluctuations in pollution:

- Avoid exercising during rush hours (the CO level peaks during rush hours).
- Avoid high cigarette smoking areas prior to and during exercise.
- Avoid combinations of high temperature, humidity, and air pollution.
- Limit the amount of time spent in high pollution areas to a minimum (physiological effects of air pollution are both time and dose dependent).
- Be aware of seasonal variations in ozone levels. The ozone level is usually low in winter, increases during summer with a daily peak around 3 p.m., and reaches maximal values in early autumn.

Recommended Reading

Adams, WC. Effects of ozone exposure at ambient air pollution episode levels on exercise performance. *Sports Medicine* 4:395-424, 1987.

American Conference of Governmental Industrial Hygienists. Threshold limit values for chemical substances and physical agents in the workroom environment with intended changes. ACGIH, Cincinnati, 1979.

American Industrial Hygiene Association. *Heating and Cooling for Man in Industry*, 2nd ed. Akron, OH: AIHA, 1975.

Balke, B. Variations in altitude and its effects on exercise performance. In: Falls, H. (ed), *Exercise Physiology*. New York, NY: Academic Press, 1968.

Bernard, TE. Environmental considerations: Heat and cold. In: American College of Sports Medicine, *ACSM's Resource Manual for Guidelines for Exercise Testing and Prescription*, 4th ed. Philadelphia, PA: Lippincott Williams & Wilkins, 2001.

Brooks, GA, Fahey, TD. *Exercise Physiology: Human Bioenergetics and Its Applications*. New York, NY: John Wiley & Sons, 1984.

Hage, P. Air pollution: Adverse effects on athletic performance. *The Physician and Sportsmedicine* 10:126-132, 1982.

Havenith, G, Holewijn, M. Exercise and the environment: Altitude and Air Pollution. In: American College of Sports Medicine, *ACSM's Resource Manual for Guidelines for Exercise Testing and Prescription*, 4th ed. Philadelphia, PA: Lippincott Williams & Wilkins, 2001.

Horvath, SM. Exercise in a cold environment. *Exercise in Sport Sciences Reviews* 9:221-263, 1981.

Kenney, WL. Physiological correlates of heat intolerance. *Sports Medicine* 2:279-286, 1985.

Kenney, WL. Considerations for preventive and rehabilitative exercise programs during periods of high heat and humidity. *The Exercise and Malpractice Reporter* 3(1):1-7, 1989.

National Institute for Occupational Safety and Health. Criteria for a recommended standard ... occupational exposure to hot environments (DHHS NIOSH Publ. No. 86-113). U.S. Department of Health and Human Services, Washington D.C., 1986.

Pandolf, KB, Cafarelli, E, Nobel, BJ, et al. Hyperthermia: Effect on exercise prescription. *Archives of Physical Medicine and Rehabilitation* 56:524-526, 1975.

Pierson, WE, Covert, DS, Koenig, JQ, et al. Implications of air pollution effects on athletic performance. *Medicine & Science in Sports & Exercise* 18:322-327, 1986.

Powers, SK, Howley, ET. *Exercise Physiology: Theory and Application to Fitness and Performance*. Dubuque, IA: Wm. C. Brown Publishers, 1990.

Sawka, MN, et al. Hydration and vascular fluid shifts during exercise in the heat. *Journal of Applied Physiology* 56:91-96, 1984.

Sutton, JR, Jones, NL. Exercise at altitude. *Annual Review of Physiology* 45:427-437, 1983.

Triservices Document. Prevention, treatment, and control of heat injury. *US Army TB Medicine* 507, 1980.

CHAPTER 15

EXERCISE AND HYPERTENSION

*T*he force created by the pumping action of the heart provides the constant movement of blood through the body. Every cell in the body requires an ongoing supply of blood to deliver oxygen and nutrients and to remove waste products. A complex system of nerve signals, hormones, and other physiological factors serves to regulate exactly how much blood flows to each area of the body by affecting the expansion and contraction of the vascular walls. This flow of blood causes pressure to be exerted on the walls of the arteries. Depending on how much blood is flowing through the arteries, the rate of blood flow, and the relative resiliency of the walls of the arteries, the pressure on the walls will vary.

TAKING HIGH BLOOD PRESSURE SERIOUSLY

More than 60 million adults have high blood pressure (a condition that is commonly referred to as hypertension). Individuals are classified as hypertensive when their blood pressure level equals or exceeds 140 mm Hg (millimeters of mercury) systolic (as the heart beats and blood surges into the arteries) and/or equals or exceeds 90 mm Hg diastolic (as the heart rests and blood flows back into the heart) on two or more consecutive measurements.

The primary effect of high blood pressure is that it makes the heart work harder and causes the arteries to be under added strain. As a result, the heart may become enlarged (left ventricular hypertrophy) and less efficient. The artery walls may also become damaged. Fatty plaque may be deposited on the walls, increasing the possibility that these vessels may be scarred and hardened. This leads to a condition known as atherosclerosis. Such damage can reduce the flow of blood and oxygen to the kidneys, heart, brain, and eyes, or can lead to a blood clot being formed in a narrowed artery.

As Table 15-1 indicates, degrees of high blood pressure exist. Regardless of the degree of hypertension an individual has, the condition warrants serious attention. As a person's blood pressure rises, the risk of developing complications also rises. It is hardly surprising, then, that hypertension ranks as the most common risk factor for diseases of the heart, blood vessels, and kidneys, including congestive heart failure, stroke, kidney failure, and atherosclerosis. In fact, high blood pressure has been estimated to contribute to over 250,000 deaths per year in the United States. This statistic is particularly discouraging since hypertension can be controlled and even prevented.

Table 15-1. Classification of Blood Pressure (BP) for Adults*†

Category	Systolic BP (mm Hg)	Diastolic BP (mm Hg)
Optimal	<120	<80
Normal	120-129	80-84
High normal	130-139	85-89
Hypertension		
Mild	140-159	90-99
Moderate	160-179	100-109
Severe	≥180	≥110

* An adult is defined as an individual 18 years of age or older.

† When systolic and diastolic blood pressures fall into different categories, the higher category should be selected to classify the individual's blood pressure status.

Note: Adapted from the Sixth Report of the Joint National Committee on Prevention, Detection, Evaluation, and Treatment of High Blood Pressure (JNC VI). Archives of Internal Medicine 157:2413-2446, 1997.

RISK FACTORS FOR HYPERTENSION

Because little conclusive evidence exists regarding the precise causal factors for hypertension, very few individuals can be certain why they are afflicted with this potentially dangerous medical condition. Even though physicians can pinpoint the cause of high blood pressure only 10 percent of the time, individuals can examine their backgrounds and lifestyles to determine their relative "exposure" to hypertension, and identify what steps they can take to reduce their risk.

The risk factors for high blood pressure can be grouped into two basic categories: those factors that cannot be changed and those that can be eliminated or favorably modified. Obviously, individuals who have unalterable risk factors for hypertension should aggressively modify risk factors that they can control.

Among the risk factors for high blood pressure that an individual cannot change are heredity, race, and pregnancy. A person with a family history of hypertension is approximately twice as likely to develop this condition as those who do not. Moreover, black Americans are 33 percent more likely to have high blood pressure than white Americans, and a pregnant woman – even one who has never had high blood pressure – has a heightened risk of developing hypertension.

Factors that can help prevent (or at least reduce or postpone) hypertension include the following dietary and lifestyle steps: consuming less salt and other sources of sodium; maintaining weight at a proper level; drinking alcohol in moderation; stopping smoking; consuming caffeine in moderation; eating magnesium and potassium-rich foods (e.g., grains, low-fat dairy products); increasing calcium intake; reducing intake of dietary saturated fat and cholesterol for overall cardiovascular health; engaging in relaxation techniques (meditation, biofeedback, yoga, etc.); taking antihypertensive drugs (under the guidance of a physician); and becoming physically active. While the effect of such alterable factors is not entirely predictable, research suggests that each of these actions, individually and collectively, has a positive (lowering) effect on blood pressure.

DESIGNING AN EXERCISE PROGRAM TO TREAT HYPERTENSION

While drug therapy is traditionally considered to be the most effective form of treating high blood pressure, exercising on a regular basis has been found to be a valuable and safe adjunct therapy for many hypertensive individuals. In fact, a sound exercise program may serve as an effective non-drug alternative for some people.

Research shows that low-intensity (40 to 70 percent of $\dot{V}O_{2max}$) aerobic exercise can lower systolic blood pressure by approximately 11 mm Hg and diastolic blood pressure by approximately 9 mm Hg in mild-to-moderate hypertensives. It is theorized that exercise lowers resting blood pressure by decreasing sympathetic nervous system activity. A reduction in sympathetic nerve activity could lower one or both of the two principal determinants of blood pressure, since mean arterial blood pressure equals the product of cardiac output and total peripheral resistance.

In the past decade, substantial information has emerged concerning what constitutes an appropriate exercise prescription for hypertensive individuals. Key steps that should be considered when designing an exercise program include the following:

- Counsel clients to avoid exercise if their resting systolic blood pressure exceeds 200 mm Hg and/or diastolic blood pressure exceeds 115 mm Hg.
- Emphasize non-weight-bearing activities (e.g., swimming, stationary cycling) or low-impact aerobic activities (walking, stair climbing, cycling, swimming, etc.) since a significant number of hypertensives are obese or elderly – groups that frequently suffer from a variety of lower-extremity orthopedic problems.
- Keep the intensity level of the exercise bout at the low end of the intensity range (40% to 70% of $\dot{V}O_{2max}$ or 50% to 75% of maximum heart rate [MHR]). Evidence suggests that higher-intensity exercise (>70% of $\dot{V}O_{2max}$ or 80% of MHR) produces no greater reductions in blood pressure and that it may be less beneficial.
- Use ratings of perceived exertion (RPE) to monitor exercise intensity for individuals who are taking antihypertensive medications (e.g., beta-blockers) that influence heart rate response. The recommended RPE range for these individuals would be 2 to 4 (weak to moderate). Angiotensin-converting enzyme inhibitors are least likely to impair exercise performance, and are generally recommended as the first-line drugs for active individuals.
- Exercise should last 20 to 30 minutes per session and progress to 30 to 60 minutes as adaptation occurs. This time frame should help reduce blood pressure, as it is consistently associated with weight loss.
- Encourage individuals to exercise at least 4 times per week (although exercising on a daily basis is preferable). A single bout of aerobic exercise may temporarily reduce blood pressure for several hours.

- Require individuals to engage in a warmup period longer than 5 minutes to ensure that the cardiovascular system is prepared for the upcoming physical activity. In addition to the benefits typically attributed to a proper warmup before exercise, it reduces the hypertensive's chances of experiencing an abrupt, sudden rise in blood pressure.
- Encourage individuals to perform more than 5 minutes of cool-down exercises so that a gradual transition can be made from the conditioning activity to the resting state. Cooling down helps to prevent dizziness, lightheadedness, or fainting – all of which are frequently associated with an abrupt cessation of exercise, especially in hypertensive individuals taking certain medications such as vasodilating agents.
- Avoid prescribing isometric or high-tension, dynamic-resistance strength-training exercises. All strength-training exercises should be performed at a low-to-moderate level of intensity (i.e., a level that enables an exerciser to perform 12 to 20 repetitions per set).
- Require all participants to maintain normal breathing patterns while exercising (particularly while engaged in strength training), since breath-holding can induce a Valsalva effect, causing an excessive, transient rise in blood pressure.
- Caution hypertensive clients who wish to engage in competitive sports that involve a high-intensity, start-stop burst of activity (e.g., racquetball, tennis, basketball, handball), since these can induce an abrupt rise in blood pressure.

A LITTLE BIT OF EXERCISE CAN GO A LONG WAY

Encourage hypertensives to make a firm commitment to exercise, because even a small amount of regular activity (and the subsequent reduction in blood pressure) can help diminish the long-term consequences of high blood pressure. For example, lowering systolic blood pressure by a mere 2 millimeters of mercury has been shown to reduce deaths from stroke by 6 percent, heart disease by 4 percent, and all causes by 3 percent. Furthermore, a drop in diastolic pressure of as little as 1 to 3 mm Hg can lower the overall incidence of hypertension in the general public.

Recent research indicates that low-intensity aerobic training significantly lowers blood pressure in patients with advanced stages of hypertension complicated by left ventricular hypertrophy. This training effect appears to persist even after a reduction in antihypertensive medication. Effectively managing hypertension with reduced medication would have a profound impact on public health and medical economics in view of the high prevalence of hypertension in the United States. The widespread tendency to treat hypertension pharmacologically has markedly reduced stroke mortality, but has not significantly reduced the mortality from coronary heart disease (CHD). Proper use of a non-drug therapy, such as exercise, in conjunction with drug therapy can offer hypertensive patients added protection against CHD. Exercise has also been shown to favorably modify other CHD risk factors (e.g., obesity, lipid-lipoprotein profiles, and glucose tolerance). In short, a sound exercise program is an excellent strategy for helping to treat and prevent high blood pressure.

Recommended Reading

American College of Sports Medicine. *ACSM's Resource Manual for Guidelines for Exercise Testing and Prescription*, 4th ed. Philadelphia, PA: Lippincott Williams & Wilkins, 2001.

American College of Sports Medicine. Position Stand. Physical activity, physical fitness, and hypertension. *Medicine & Science in Sports & Exercise* 25:i-x, 1993.

American Council on Exercise. *Clinical Exercise Specialist Manual: ACE's Source for Training Special Populations.* San Diego, CA: American Council on Exercise, 1999.

Bove, AA, et al. Active control of hypertension. *The Physician and Sportsmedicine* 26(4):45-53, 1998.

Kokkinos, PF, Narayan, P, Colleran, JA, et al. Effects of regular exercise on blood pressure and left ventricular hypertrophy in African-American men with severe hypertension. *New England Journal of Medicine* 333:1462-1467, 1995.

Leutholtz, BC. Exercise can reduce incidence and severity of hypertension: Keep it up to keep it down. *ACSM's Health & Fitness Journal* 2(5):36-39, 1998.

Nieman, DC. *Fitness and Sports Medicine: An Introduction*, 3rd ed. Palo Alto, CA: Bull Publishing Company, 1995.

Peterson, JA, Bryant, CX (eds). *The StairMaster Fitness Handbook*, 2nd ed. Champaign, IL: Sagamore Publishing Company, Inc., 1995.

Pollock, ML, Franklin, BA, Balady, GJ, et al. Resistance exercise in individuals with and without cardiovascular disease: Benefits, rationale, safety, and prescription: An advisory from the Committee on Exercise, Rehabilitation, and Prevention, Council on Clinical Cardiology, American Heart Association. *Circulation* 101:828-833, 2000.

The Sixth Report of the Joint National Committee on Prevention, Detection, Evaluation, and Treatment of High Blood Pressure (JNC VI). *Archives of Internal Medicine* 157:2413-2446, 1997.

Wallace, JP. Exercise can reduce high blood pressure. *ACSM's Health & Fitness Journal* 2(1):29-36, 1998.

CHAPTER 16

• •

EXERCISE AND DIABETES

*T*he human body is a smoothly functioning food processor. It transforms sugars, starches, and other nutrients into energy — energy needed to sit, walk, lift, and perform tasks of daily living. The body's cells need glucose (a form of sugar) to produce energy. The hormone insulin normally helps glucose enter the cells, but when an individual has diabetes, that system goes awry. The precise cause of diabetes is unknown. What is known, however, is that either the cells don't respond to insulin, the pancreas doesn't produce enough insulin, or both. Rejected by the body's cells, glucose accumulates in the bloodstream.

Two major forms of diabetes exist — Type I (insulin-dependent) diabetes and Type II (non-insulin-dependent) diabetes. Approximately 90 percent of the more than 14 million Americans suffering from diabetes have Type II, the more easily controlled form of the disease. Formerly referred to as "adult-onset diabetes" because it is typically diagnosed after an individual reaches age 40, Type II diabetes is usually the result of the body's cells not responding to insulin. In some Type II diabetics, the pancreas simply does not produce enough insulin, while other individuals may suffer from both conditions. Obesity and family history appear to be the two most significant risk factors for Type II diabetes.

Type I diabetes is often referred to as "juvenile-onset diabetes" because it usually occurs in children and young adults. Because individuals who suffer from Type I diabetes produce little or no pancreatic insulin, they must receive insulin injections. While a family history of Type I diabetes affects an individual's risk of developing the disease, a genetic predisposition is not nearly as common as with Type II diabetes.

Regardless of which type of diabetes an individual has, the condition can have serious consequences. For example, an extremely elevated blood-sugar level (i.e., hyperglycemia) can cause fatigue, dehydration, and blurred vision. Left unchecked for a few days, particularly in individuals suffering from Type I diabetes, severe hyperglycemia can result in loss of consciousness, coma, or even death. Over an extended period, moderately elevated blood-sugar levels can affect the blood vessels feeding the brain, eyes, heart, and kidneys, causing damage to those vital organs. Moderately elevated blood-sugar levels can also lead to nerve damage.

EXERCISE TO THE RESCUE

Fortunately, exercise can help diabetics control their condition and reduce their risk of life-threatening complications. Exercise can greatly decrease an individual's chances of incurring the disease in the first place. In fact, research shows that regular exercise can reduce an individual's likelihood of developing diabetes by more than half, including people who either are obese or are genetically predisposed to the disease. For example, in a major study conducted at the University of California, Berkeley, researchers found that for every extra 500 Calories (kcal) a week an individual expends during exercise, the risk of developing diabetes is reduced by 6 percent.

Exercise also can help those individuals who have developed diabetes. Among the beneficial aspects of exercise that are either directly or indirectly related to diabetes are:

- *Regulates blood-sugar levels.* Exercise encourages the body to use more glucose – its primary fuel source. As a result, exercise has the effect of lowering elevated blood-sugar levels by helping transport glucose out of the bloodstream and into the cells where it can be used. By exercising on a regular basis, some diabetics who require medication to control their blood-sugar levels are able to reduce or, in the case of many Type II diabetics, even discontinue their glucose-regulating medications. When individuals stop working out for just 3 days in a row, however, the beneficial effects of exercise are almost completely lost. Of the various types of conditioning regimens, aerobic exercise appears to provide the greatest benefit in terms of blood-sugar control. Strength-training has also been shown to have a positive impact on blood-sugar levels.
- *Minimizes the health risk of diabetes.* In diabetics, the most common causes of illness and death are coronary heart disease (CHD), stroke, and various cardiovascular complications due to atherosclerosis (i.e., development of fatty deposits in the arteries). Regular exercise improves blood lipid profiles: it lowers triglycerides and low-density lipoprotein levels (the bad-type of cholesterol carrier) and raises high-density lipoprotein levels (the good type of cholesterol carrier). It also helps lower heart rate, blood pressure, and blood platelet adhesiveness levels (i.e., the stickiness of the blood), which makes the blood less likely to clot. Collectively, the net effect of exercise is that it helps reduce the risk of cardiovascular disease for individuals with diabetes.
- *Reduces body weight and fat stores.* Exercise helps individuals reduce excess weight and body fat – major contributing factors to the development of Type II diabetes in many individuals as they age. Insulin sensitivity (i.e., the responsiveness of cells to insulin) is significantly enhanced following exercise-induced reductions in weight and body-fat levels. As a result, the diabetic's need for insulin is reduced. The lower the insulin dosage, the closer the body's metabolic system is to its normal physiological level. As such, much less of a metabolic roller coaster occurs, allowing for more consistent blood-sugar regulation.
- *Enhances psychological well-being.* Although the physiological effects of exercise are most frequently examined, exercise also can have a positive psychological impact on diabetics. For example, regular exercise may effectively reduce emotional stress, increase feelings of well-being, and improve overall quality of life. While these psychological effects are more difficult to quantify, they are well-supported anecdotally and represent important benefits for individuals with diabetes.

CHOOSING THE RIGHT KIND OF EXERCISE

Regular exercise – particularly aerobic exercise – has proven to be effective in helping control diabetes. In general, exercise is the safest and most beneficial treatment for individuals with Type II diabetes. Any exercise program for a diabetic, however, should be designed in accordance with the type of diabetes and its level of severity. Although some disagreement exists regarding how exercise can best be incorporated into the "total" treatment program for diabetes, specific guidelines have been identified that will help ensure the potential hazards of exercise are minimized and the benefits are maximized. Among those guidelines are the following:

- Diabetic individuals should undergo a complete medical evaluation before starting an exercise program. Exercise is contraindicated for individuals with poor blood-sugar control, which means their fasting blood-sugar level exceeds 300 mg/dL or is >250 mg/dL with urinary ketone bodies. If the diabetic is over 35 years of age, the evaluation should include an exercise stress test to screen for the presence of "silent" coronary heart disease.
- Diabetics should keep a diary of their blood-glucose levels and record how they change under different conditions. They should be encouraged to monitor blood-sugar levels before, during, and after exercise. Monitoring will allow individuals, along with their physicians, to assess the effects of exercise on blood-sugar levels and make any necessary adjustments in diet or the dosage or timing of medication. Available clinical data suggest that it is safe to exercise if a diabetic's blood-sugar level is between 100 and 300 mg/dL.
- Unless limited by complications, diabetics can engage in the same types of aerobic activities as non-diabetics. Obese diabetics (common for Type II), or those with eye or nerve damage (typically seen in Type I), should avoid high-impact exercise and should select non-weight-bearing or low-impact alternatives such as cycling, walking, or machine-based stair climbing.
- The intensity of exercise may be slightly lower for diabetics than the intensity that is typically prescribed for healthy adults (50% to 85% of $\dot{V}O_{2max}$). The exercise prescription for individuals without medical problems often involves workouts that are either too long or too frequent for those with diabetes.
- Diabetics with autonomic neuropathy may not be able to use heart rate to accurately gauge exercise intensity. Instead, such individuals should use ratings of perceived exertion (RPE) and/or MET equivalents for modulating exercise intensity.
- Type I diabetics should be advised to exercise 20 to 40 minutes per session. Exercise performed for longer than 40 minutes increases the risk of hypoglycemia for Type I diabetics. Type II diabetics should be encouraged to exercise for a longer duration (40 to 60 minutes per session) to further enhance weight loss.
- Both types of diabetics should be encouraged to exercise daily – preferably at the same time each day. A regular, consistent exercise pattern helps diabetics to more effectively balance their training with diets and medications and, thus, maintain better control of their blood-sugar levels.

- Diabetics should be encouraged to exercise within 1 to 3 hours after a meal or snack, when blood-sugar levels are still relatively high. Because of the insulin-like effect of exercise, diabetics who engage in physical activity without adequate food ingestion (especially carbohydrates) are at high risk for experiencing hypoglycemia (low blood sugar).
- Type I diabetics should be instructed to (1) avoid exercising during periods of peak insulin activity or take special precautions (e.g., consume a light meal or carbohydrate snack), and (2) alter the insulin injection site to an area of the body that is not primarily involved in the exercise activity (the abdomen tends to be an effective location) to prevent exercise-induced hypoglycemia.
- Diabetics should be instructed to always carry a form of fast-acting carbohydrate (e.g., juice, soft drinks, candy, glucose tablets) in case of a hypoglycemic emergency.
- Diabetics should be encouraged to exercise with a partner. They and their partners should be aware of the signs of hypoglycemia (e.g., confusion, weakness, unconsciousness, convulsions) and should know how to effectively treat hypoglycemia (Table 16-1). If diabetic individuals choose to exercise alone, they should be instructed to wear a diabetic identification tag – a precaution that should help to ensure that they receive proper treatment in the event they become ill while exercising.
- Diabetics (especially Type I) should be advised to avoid exercising in extreme heat due to their increased susceptibility for anhidrosis (failure of the sweating mechanism). As a rule, diabetics should curtail exercise when the temperature is above 32°C (90°F), when the relative humidity is above 60%, or both.
- Diabetics should be instructed to check their feet carefully before and after exercise because they have an increased susceptibility to infection. They should watch for skin lesions, blisters, discoloration, or swelling, and consult their physician if any of these appear.
- Strength training at a low-to-moderate intensity (a range of 8 to 15 repetitions per set) level can be incorporated into the total fitness program. Strength training, like

---

Table 16-1. How to Treat Hypoglycemia

The following steps should be rapidly taken at the first sign of a hypoglycemic reaction:

- The individual should stop what he/she is doing and immediately consume any form of quick-acting sugar. If no quick-acting sugar can be found, the individual should consume any food that is available, preferably foodstuffs that are primarily carbohydrate or protein.
- The individual should sit down. If the hypoglycemic symptoms persist after 10 minutes, repeat the first step. If the symptoms do not subside within 10 minutes of the second treatment, seek appropriate medical attention.
- Before resuming activity, the individual should eat a snack containing protein and a longer-acting carbohydrate (e.g., milk and crackers). The individual should also eat all scheduled meals that day – including a bedtime snack.

aerobic training, can improve glucose uptake by exercising the skeletal muscles.
- Because exercise has an insulin-like effect that can persist, diabetics may need to eat more than usual or eat an extra carbohydrate-rich snack after working out. Otherwise, they can become hypoglycemic, even up to 4 to 6 hours after an exercise bout.

A DELICATE BALANCE

The role of exercise in treating diabetes involves a carefully considered balance. When properly combined with a sensible diet and appropriate medications, exercise can have a positive impact on the lives of diabetics. The challenge is to strike the proper balance between the three critical elements of an effective treatment program for diabetics: diet, medication, and exercise.

It is important to understand that a change in one of the three primary treatment factors usually requires a concurrent adjustment in the other two elements as well. For example, an increase in the level of physical activity by a diabetic often necessitates an increase in food intake and/or an alteration in the dosage or timing of medication.

Statistics indicate that the number of diabetics is growing rapidly. In fact, approximately 650,000 new cases of diabetes are diagnosed in the United States each year. During that same period, an estimated 650,000 new cases of diabetes will go undiagnosed. It would seem logical to assume, therefore, that over time the number of Type II diabetics joining health and fitness facilities would also rise. Accordingly, the more fully health/fitness professionals comprehend the nature of the delicate balance that exercise has in treating diabetes, the more prepared they will be to meet the unique needs of this group of individuals. Without question, exercise is sound medicine. Consequently, exercise must be an integral ingredient in a diabetic's recipe for a well-balanced, healthy life.

Recommended Reading

American College of Sports Medicine. *ACSM's Exercise Management for Persons with Chronic Disease and Disabilities.* Champaign, IL: Human Kinetics Publishers, Inc., 1997.

American College of Sports Medicine. *ACSM's Guidelines for Exercise Testing and Prescription,* 6th ed. Philadelphia, PA: Lippincott Williams & Wilkins, 2000.

American College of Sports Medicine. *ACSM's Resource Manual for Guidelines for Exercise Testing and Prescription,* 4th ed. Philadelphia, PA: Lippincott Williams & Wilkins, 2001.

American Council on Exercise. *Clinical Exercise Specialist Manual: ACE's Source for Training Special Populations.* San Diego, CA: American Council on Exercise, 1999.

Campaigne, BN. Exercise and type I diabetes. *ACSM's Health & Fitness Journal* 2(4):35-42, 1998.

Diabetes Mellitus and Exercise: A joint position statement of the American College of Sports Medicine and The American Diabetes Association. *Medicine & Science in Sports & Exercise* 29:1-5,1997.

Young, JC. Exercise for clients with type 2 diabetes: Facts and guidelines. *ACSM's Health & Fitness Journal* 2(3):24-29, 1998.

CHAPTER 17

* *

EXERCISE AND ASTHMA

*T*he term asthma is derived from the Greek word meaning "to pant." In literal terms, asthma is a tightening of the airways of the lungs that results from either inflammation or specific triggering factors. It is a somewhat common, but potentially serious problem in the United States for individuals of all ages. Approximately 5 percent of the adult population suffers from asthma.

Some of the most common triggers for asthma are respiratory infections, exercise (which causes cooling and drying of airways), allergies (which stimulate a hypersensitive immune system, thereby releasing chemicals that can cause swelling of the airways and the overproduction of mucus), emotional stress, cold air, sudden changes in either humidity or ambient temperature, air pollution (e.g., dust, tobacco smoke, paint, or the fumes from household cleaners, perfume), and certain medications (e.g., aspirin). Regardless of the cause, understanding what happens during an asthma attack, how to cope with an attack, and how to increase the likelihood of an asthma-free workout should prove useful for fitness professionals working with clients afflicted with asthma.

WHAT OCCURS DURING AN ASTHMA ATTACK?

One of the most common symptoms of asthma is recurring episodes of breathlessness. The cause of such breathlessness is apparent when the mechanisms underlying an asthma attack are understood.

While the cause of an asthma attack often varies from one person to another, the process is relatively straightforward. During an asthma attack, the bronchioles (small branches of the airways that distribute air throughout the lungs) transiently narrow because the muscles surrounding them have gone into spasm. In turn, this narrowing, collectively referred to as "bronchospasm," restricts the level of air flow to the alveoli (tiny air sacs deep in the lungs that serve as the terminal branches of the respiratory tract where oxygen and carbon dioxide are exchanged). When a bronchospasm occurs, individuals experience the symptoms of an asthma attack, which can take between 30 to 60 minutes to resolve without any treatment. In some instances, the asthmatic may have to be hospitalized. If properly managed, however, asthma sufferers can minimize any undue discomfort and/or adverse reactions.

COPING WITH AN ATTACK

Numerous treatment options are available for asthma sufferers. As a general rule, the primary method for controlling asthma is taking medication – inhaled and oral. Because inhaled drugs reach the airways directly and more quickly, they are the preferred option in most instances. The following four classes of medications are used to treat asthma and to prevent an attack of exercise-induced asthma:

- *Beta-agonists* (bronchodilators), such as albuterol (Proventil, Ventolin), alleviate asthma by relaxing the smooth muscles of the bronchioles and opening up the air passages in the lungs. Bronchodilators are usually most effective if they are inhaled in aerosol form a few minutes before an individual engages in vigorous physical activity or planned exercise.
- *Corticosteroids*, such as beclomethasone (Beclovent, Vanceril), work by preventing certain cells in the lungs and breathing passages from releasing substances that can cause inflammation. They can be inhaled, taken orally, or injected. When used regularly, inhaled corticosteroids decrease the frequency and severity of asthma attacks, but will not relieve an asthma attack in progress.
- *Cromolyn sodium* works by acting on specific inflammatory cells (mast cells) in the lungs to prevent the release of substances (e.g., histamine) that can cause asthma symptoms or bronchospasm. When used prophylactically (i.e., as a preventive measure), cromolyn sodium reduces the frequency and severity of asthma attacks by decreasing inflammation in the lungs. Cromolyn sodium, however, has little if any effect when used after exercise.
- *Theophylline* (available under various brand names) treats and/or prevents the symptoms of bronchial asthma by opening up the air passages of the lungs (bronchial tubes) to increase the flow of air through them. The oral liquid, tablet, and capsule dosage forms of theophylline can be used for either the treatment of an attack or for chronic (long-term) therapy. For best results, theophylline should be taken 30 to 60 minutes prior to initiating exercise. Theophylline is often given with a beta-agonist because the synergistic combination of these medications can be more effective than either drug taken alone.

Although drugs are often helpful, asthmatics should also take additional, specific steps to help alleviate their medical condition and try to avoid those factors that evoke asthmatic symptoms. Recommendations for reducing the incidence of complications include the following:

- *Use a peak flow meter.* A relatively inexpensive device, this apparatus measures how fast asthmatics are able to exhale air from their lungs. A precipitous drop in expired air (e.g., more than 10 percent) may herald an increased level of airflow resistance in the lungs.
- *Use over-the-counter medications, if necessary.* Over-the-counter, inhaled asthma medications should be used when a person does not have access to his or her regular medications during symptomatic situations.
- *Use a spacer.* Use of a spacer will ensure that the medicine inhaled will reach the lungs and not simply coat the roof of the mouth or the back of the throat. Attached to an inhaler, a spacer allows asthmatics to better inhale medicine by holding it in "suspension," allowing them to inhale several times to rapidly increase the efficiency of the medicine.
- *Adhere to recommended dosages.* Excessive medication can produce adverse side-effects (e.g., rapid heart rate, dizziness).
- *Drink water.* Consuming water after using inhalers helps clear the back of the

throat of medicine.

- *Stay hydrated.* Mucus plugging can result from an inadequate level of fluid intake (i.e., dehydration).
- *Monitor air quality.* Asthmatics should always be aware of what to do when confronted with various pollutants and pollens.
- *Use masks or scarves in cold weather.* Wherever necessary, asthmatics should reduce the impact of cold air on their air pathways by masking their noses and throats.
- *Be sensitive to asthma-related reactions.* Some foods may precipitate asthma attacks. For example, depending on the foodstuff (e.g., celery, carrots, peanuts, egg whites, bananas, shrimp) certain individuals may increase the likelihood and severity of an asthmatic attack because of what they eat.

ENJOYING ASTHMA-FREE WORKOUTS

In recent years, regular exercise has been shown to be a therapeutic asthma treatment. Unfortunately, asthmatics often mistakenly believe that exercise is not a viable option for them. Nevertheless, sensible exercise may actually help asthmatics to better cope with their sometimes debilitating medical condition.

The primary key to exercise effectiveness as a therapeutic option for asthma sufferers is that it makes breathing more efficient. Ample evidence suggests that proper exercise makes the airways of the lungs less sensitive to those factors that precipitate a bronchospasm.

Because vigorous exercise can, in some instances, trigger an asthma attack, it is extremely important that fitness professionals, asthmatics, and their physicians work together to develop a comprehensive exercise and medication plan. Keep in mind, however, that one individual's specific response to exercise may vary from another's. If exercise is approached in a sensible manner, asthmatics have much to gain from a program of regular physical activity, including an increase in exercise tolerance and overall feelings of well-being.

Most physicians suggest that the first step in formulating an exercise program is to evaluate how an asthmatic's body responds to a progressive-exercise to volitional-fatigue training program. The next step is to develop an exercise regimen that meets the individual's needs and interests. Among the guidelines you should follow to ensure that an asthmatic's exercise program is both safe and effective are:

- Select an exercise that raises the heart rate, increases the respiratory rate, and is relatively easy on the lungs, such as swimming.
- Avoid asthma triggers as much as possible. For example, asthmatics allergic to pollen should exercise indoors.
- Avoid exercising outdoors on either polluted or cold, dry days. Wear a mask or a scarf to warm and moisten the inspired air while exercising outdoors on a cold day. Whenever possible, exercise in warm, humid air.
- Perform specific breathing exercises to strengthen the lungs.
- Use ratings of perceived exertion (refer to page 36) in conjunction with target heart rate to regulate exercise intensity, since many of the above-referenced

medications can alter an asthmatic's heart rate response to exercise.
- Premedicate prior to exercising (within 30 minutes prior to engaging in activity).
- Keep an inhaler on hand while exercising.
- Perform warmup exercises for an extended period of time (more than 5 minutes) prior to working out.
- Avoid sudden, intense exercise for prolonged periods of time.
- Breathe through the nose as much as possible while exercising.
- Avoid hyperventilation by using a controlled breathing pattern.

BREATHING EASIER

Fortunately, the innumerable benefits of exercising on a regular basis are well within the reach of most persons with asthma. To gain the most from their exercise programs, you, as their fitness professionals, will need to have input from a personal physician, be sensitive to each individual's particular needs, and encourage them to embark on a reward-filled journey. By proceeding sensibly and purposefully in your quest to design and implement appropriate exercise regimens for your asthmatic clients, you can help them to get a much-needed "breath of fresh air."

Recommended Reading

Afrasiabi, R, Spector, SL. Exercise-induced asthma: It needn't sideline your patients. *The Physician and Sportsmedicine* 19(5):49-62, 1991.

American College of Sports Medicine. *ACSM's Exercise Management for Persons with Chronic Disease and Disabilities.* Champaign, IL: Human Kinetics Publishers, Inc., 1997.

American College of Sports Medicine. *ACSM's Guidelines for Exercise Testing and Prescription,* 6th ed. Philadelphia, PA: Lippincott Williams & Wilkins, 2000.

American College of Sports Medicine. *ACSM's Resource Manual for Guidelines for Exercise Testing and Prescription,* 4th ed. Philadelphia, PA: Lippincott Williams & Wilkins, 2001.

American Council on Exercise. *Clinical Exercise Specialist Manual: ACE's Source for Training Special Populations.* San Diego, CA: American Council on Exercise, 1999.

Cerny, FJ, Maxwell, PJ. Control of exercise-induced asthma: Triggers, medications, warm-ups. *ACSM's Health & Fitness Journal* 4(1):17-24, 2000.

Mahler, DA. Exercise-induced asthma. *Medicine & Science in Sports & Exercise* 25(5):554-561, 1993.

Rupp, NT. Diagnosis and management of exercise-induced asthma. *The Physician and Sportsmedicine* 24:77-87, 1996.

Skinner, JS (ed). *Exercise Testing and Exercise Prescription for Special Cases: Theoretical Basis and Clinical Application,* 2nd ed. Philadelphia, PA: Lea & Febiger, 1993.

CHAPTER 18

. . . .

EXERCISE AND WOMEN'S ISSUES

*O*pportunities for women have increased dramatically since 1972 – the year that Congressional legislation (Title IX) mandated equal opportunity for females in all areas of education, including athletics. A partial review of the achievements of women in the last 20-plus years illustrates how pervasive and far-reaching this growth has been. During the 1980s, two American women reached the summit of Mt. Everest. Recently, women have taken first place in national ultra-marathon races, beating both female and male competitors. Increasing numbers of women are now engaged in occupational activities that have been traditionally male-oriented, such as firefighters, police officers, and construction workers. The effects of Title IX have been far-reaching and significant.

As more women train and push their performance capacities to higher limits, however, several important health issues need to be addressed. Specific areas of concern are the female triad – disordered eating, amenorrhea, and osteoporosis; exercise and pregnancy; and exercise and menopause. This chapter is intended to provide information to help women and the individuals who train them to design medically sound physical conditioning programs.

THE FEMALE TRIAD

Unfortunately, some athletic women are at risk for developing one or more of three medical disorders collectively known as the female triad: disordered eating, amenorrhea, and osteoporosis. Young women, driven to excel in their chosen sports and pressured to fit a specific body image (e.g., leanness, low percent body fat, or lower weight) to attain their performance goals, place themselves at risk for developing disordered eating patterns. Such eating behavior may lead to menstrual dysfunction and, subsequently, premature osteoporosis. Alone, each disorder is a significant medical concern, but collectively they pose more serious health consequences and a higher risk of mortality.

EXERCISE AND EATING DISORDERS

Disordered eating refers to the spectrum of abnormal patterns of eating, including behaviors such as:

- Binging, purging, or both
- Food restriction
- Prolonged fasting
- Use of diet pills, diuretics, laxatives

- Inappropriate thought patterns, such as a preoccupation with food, dissatisfaction with one's body, fear of becoming fat, and a distorted body image

Anorexia nervosa and bulimia nervosa are at the extreme end of the disordered eating spectrum. Anorexia nervosa is the syndrome of self-imposed starvation and distorted body image. Of the general female population, 1 percent suffers from this disorder, as do nearly 7 percent of the population of ballet dancers and gymnasts. Some anorexic women are indistinguishable from high-performance athletes. It is absolutely essential that you encourage clients to seek professional help if you feel that they might have anorexia nervosa, since it can be fatal.

Bulimia nervosa is the syndrome of secretive binge-eating episodes followed by self-induced vomiting, fasting, and purging with laxatives and/or diuretics. It affects up to 10 percent of college-age students. It can lead to blood electrolyte abnormalities (hypokalemia, which is low potassium levels), erosion of the teeth, tears in the esophagus, and digestive problems. Again, clients who may be suffering from bulimia should be encouraged to seek professional help.

Other health consequences of disordered eating can include bradycardia, anemia, hormonal alterations, decreased immune function, gastrointestinal disease, reduced endurance and strength, and increased risk of injury.

Some of the contributing factors for disordered eating can include societal pressures; family climate; low self-esteem and/or depression; physical and/or sexual abuse; pressure from coaches and trainers to be thin; and sport-specific pressure, including scoring based on subjective appearance, weight categories for participation, and emphasis on the prepuberty body type. Although many athletes do not meet strict diagnostic criteria for anorexia nervosa or bulimia nervosa, they may exhibit similar behaviors and thought patterns, placing them at a significantly increased risk for the development of the serious endocrine, metabolic, skeletal, and psychiatric disorders that are often observed in these conditions.

EXERCISE AND AMENORRHEA

Menstruation is the cyclic discharge through the vagina of blood or tissue from the nonpregnant uterus. A normal menstrual cycle ranges from 21 to 36 days. Most women start their menstrual periods by age 12. Primary amenorrhea is when a woman has not started her menstrual period by age 16. If a woman's period has not started by that age, or her cycles are shorter than 21 days or longer than 36 days, she should consult a physician.

Women who engage in intense training (e.g., runners who run more than 50 miles per week) may stop having their periods altogether. Secondary amenorrhea is the absence of a menstrual period for three to six months once a woman has started menstruation. While the absence of a period may appear to be less problematic for the athlete, it is important to clarify why she is not having a cyclic menstrual period. Of the general female population, 2 to 5 percent, and up to 43 percent of athletic women, do not have menstrual periods. Amenorrhea, however, is not exclusive to athletes. Other factors have also been found to cause amenorrhea, including pregnancy, very early menopause, anorexia nervosa, and certain types of tumors.

The cause of exercise-induced amenorrhea is still not fully understood, but contributing factors include excessive weight loss/thinness, low body fat, psychological stress, fatigue, age, a previous history of menstrual abnormalities, and diet – plus the physical stress of exercise. The incidence of amenorrhea is particularly high in gymnasts, distance runners, ballet dancers, and figure skaters. Amenorrhea can, however, result from intense training for any sport.

Why all the concern about amenorrhea? Since the 1980s, research has linked amenorrhea to low estrogen levels. Because estrogen is essential for developing and maintaining normal bone health, low levels can reflect serious deficits. The basic human skeleton – calcium deposition in the bone – is laid down by age 35. Theoretically, if adequate levels of calcium are not deposited in the bones when women are young, they may develop osteoporosis (i.e., decreased bone mass and increased susceptibility to fractures) at an earlier age. In such cases, osteoporosis may be even more severe. Unfortunately, osteoporosis affects 25 million Americans annually. Amenorrhea can also lead to infertility, unfavorable changes in blood lipoprotein profiles, and increasing risk of fractures.

A more common form of menstrual dysfunction is oligomenorrhea, which is infrequent menstruation of two or more months between cycles, with no ovulation. The precise cause of menstrual irregularities is unknown. Amenorrhea and oligomenorrhea are not permanent conditions. In fact, in most highly active women, normal menstrual functioning returns one to two months after decreasing their levels of physical activity. If amenorrhea persists, a woman should undergo a thorough hormonal and gynecological evaluation and, if necessary, receive medical treatment.

Perhaps the most common type of menstrual problem is premenstrual syndrome (PMS). Premenstrual syndrome is believed to be caused by a hormonal imbalance – either an excess in estrogen or a deficiency in progesterone. An alternative theory concerning the etiology of PMS has identified the gradual withdrawal of endorphins (opiate-like proteins found in the nervous system) as contributing to PMS. Premenstrual syndrome encompasses a variety of emotional, behavioral, and physical symptoms.

Due to the large variability in onset during the menstrual cycle, duration of symptoms, and severity of symptoms, the identification of an appropriate treatment for PMS is often difficult. Non-pharmacologic treatments that have been shown to be effective include exercise, smoking cessation, weight loss, stress reduction/relaxation therapy, minimizing alcohol intake, and a diet high in protein but low in sodium and sugar. If these non-drug therapies are ineffective for a woman, she should consult her gynecologist for treatment.

EXERCISE AND OSTEOPOROSIS

Osteoporosis refers to premature bone loss and inadequate bone formation, resulting in low bone mass, microarchitectural deterioration, increased skeletal fragility, and an increased risk of fracture. The areas of the body commonly affected by osteoporosis are the hip, wrist, and vertebrae. Osteoporosis affects 5 million men and 20 million women in the United States. Research has found that, relatively speaking, women experience greater consequences from osteoporosis than men and, in general, are at high risk, especially older women, Caucasian women, and postmenopausal women. Other risk factors include genetics, cigarette smoking, excessive alcohol consumption, a diet low in calcium, anorexia, amenorrhea and menstrual history, infrequent weight-bearing exercise, diminished peak bone mass, and steroid use.

Any condition or action that reduces the level of calcium in the bones increases the risk of osteoporosis. Factors that have been shown to decrease calcium absorption include cigarette smoking, consuming caffeine or alcohol, lactose (milk) intolerance, and high fiber intake. Treatment includes calcium supplements: 1,000 mg per day in menstruating women, 1,500 mg in menopausal or nonmenstruating women. The best source of calcium, however, is food. Eight ounces of milk or four ounces of cheese provides 200 mg of calcium. Tums and oyster-based calcium (calcium carbonate) are also helpful. A practical guideline is that active women who eat less than 2,000 Calories daily should supplement their diets with calcium.

Amenorrheic and postmenopausal women may wish to consult their physicians regarding the possible benefits (and risks) of hormone replacement therapy. Sunlight and low-impact weight-bearing (e.g., walking, stair climbing) or weight-loading (e.g., resistance training) exercise also help keep bones healthy. However, recent evidence suggests that exercise alone is not a sufficient stimulus to prevent the loss of bone mass after menopause. Exercise in combination with estrogen replacement therapy and adequate calcium intake (1,500 mg/day), however, has been shown to effectively protect against postmenopausal-related bone loss. As a preventive measure, women should be encouraged to exercise and eat a nutritious diet during the critical years between adolescence and early middle-age (approximately 35 years) when bone mass is being laid down.

EXERCISE DURING PREGNANCY

Many women want to continue exercising during pregnancy. They are often perplexed, however, by warnings that exercise during pregnancy may be harmful, or by open-ended suggestions to simply "use common sense" when deciding whether to exercise during this critical period in their lives. Should pregnant women exercise? To answer this question, three critical issues need to be addressed: Is it safe for a woman who is pregnant to exercise? If so, what types of exercise modalities and exercise prescriptions are appropriate for a pregnant woman? Finally, what benefits does exercising offer a pregnant woman and the developing fetus?

Without question, the most important factor that must be considered when designing and implementing an exercise program for a pregnant woman is safety. An exercise program must not subject either the expectant mother or her fetus to undue harm or risk of injury. To ensure that a pregnant woman can safely engage in a medically sound exercise program, two steps are essential. First, she must be evaluated to determine whether any possible contraindications exist to her exercising. Second, if she is cleared to exercise, she should engage in an exercise program that places particular emphasis on precautionary measures that have been incorporated into the exercise regimen to ensure that the program addresses her special needs as an expectant mother.

CONTRAINDICATIONS FOR EXERCISE DURING PREGNANCY

Prior to initiating or maintaining an exercise program, a pregnant woman must be evaluated for contraindications or signs that she should not exercise. The American College of

Obstetricians and Gynecologists (ACOG) provides a list of absolute and relative contraindications for aerobic exercise during pregnancy. Absolute contraindications include coronary heart disease, ruptured membranes, premature labor, multiple gestation, vaginal bleeding, placenta previa, incompetent cervix, and a history of three or more spontaneous abortions or miscarriages. Relative contraindications include hypertension (high blood pressure), anemia or other blood disorders, thyroid disorders, diabetes, palpitations or irregular heart rhythms, breech presentation in the last trimester, excessive obesity, extreme underweight, history of precipitous labor, history of intrauterine growth retardation, history of bleeding during present pregnancy, and an extremely sedentary lifestyle. Women possessing absolute contraindications should not exercise, while those with relative contraindications may exercise with their physician's approval (these women, however, should be enrolled in appropriately supervised exercise programs). Physicians are the only individuals qualified to evaluate the aforementioned contraindications. A pregnant woman who does not have an obstetrician or physician should not be allowed to participate in an exercise program.

PRECAUTIONARY MEASURES

The numerous physiological changes that occur during pregnancy require special adjustments in an exercise program for the expectant mother. Exercise programs developed for pregnant women should always place particular design emphasis on precautionary measures to avoid placing the mother or her fetus at risk.

One potential threat (especially during the first trimester of pregnancy) to the safety of the developing baby is exercise-induced fetal hyperthermia (i.e., increased temperature in the uterus). Heat stress is known to cause fetal growth retardation in humans. Exercise is associated with a rise in both maternal and fetal body core temperature. The fetus usually maintains a body core temperature 0.5° to 1.0°C above that of the mother, and has no means of dissipating heat; therefore, the fetus must depend entirely on the mother's thermoregulatory abilities. By adhering to four relatively basic guidelines, a pregnant woman who exercises can ensure she does not place herself and her fetus at risk for heat injury. First, make sure that she is adequately hydrated. This objective can be accomplished by consuming copious amounts of fluid (just short of feeling bloated) thirty minutes before exercise, and drinking beyond the point of thirst cessation during the recovery period. (Note: Water is generally the best replacement fluid.) Second, keep the intensity of her exercise regimen at the low end of the intensity range (50 to 60 percent of maximal exercise capacity) since this precautionary measure will decrease the heat load generated by the exercise and reduce the strain placed on a pregnant woman's thermoregulatory mechanisms. Third, never wear clothing that is impermeable to water (e.g., the synthetic stretch fibers often worn during aerobic dance), because they prevent the evaporation of sweat from the skin (the body's chief heat loss mechanism), thereby increasing the risk of heat injury. Fourth, and perhaps most importantly, be particularly sensitive to the existing environmental conditions at the time of the exercise bout, since temperature and relative humidity can greatly influence both the degree of heat stress and the body's ability to effectively respond to the heat stress. As a general rule, a pregnant woman should refrain from exercising when the ambient temperature is greater than 80°F and, concurrently, the relative humidity exceeds 50 percent.

Another potential threat to the fetus of an exercising pregnant woman is an inadequate blood and oxygen supply. Exercise has been linked to a reduction in blood flow to the uterus since more blood is required by the working skeletal muscles. This condition could lead to a transient reduction in oxygen supply to the fetus. The mechanism responsible for the redistribution of blood flow away from the uterus and to the exercising muscles has not been clearly identified. The available evidence, however, suggests that the uterine vasculature is very sensitive to the effects of catecholamines (biochemicals that exert actions similar to those of the sympathetic nervous system). Catecholamine release into the circulation is dependent upon the intensity and duration of exercise (as intensity and duration increase plasma catecholamine levels rise). Low-to-moderate intensity exercise bouts lasting less than 30 minutes do not appear to impair uterine blood flow.

Prolonged (greater than five minutes) exercise performed in a supine (lying face-up) position, on the other hand, can be problematic for both the mother and the fetus. When an expectant mother is in a supine position, the excess weight of her fetus may obstruct venous return (the flow of blood back to the heart). Therefore, after the fourth month of pregnancy, the ACOG recommends that exercise not be performed in a supine position. Signs and symptoms of obstructed blood flow include lightheadedness, dizziness or syncope (fainting). Research has demonstrated that during exercise in a supine position, blood flow to the fetus is decreased. Although such a condition may not affect the mother, her fetus may experience negative side effects. Most experts, however, believe that in a normal uncomplicated pregnancy, the fetus can experience up to a 50 percent reduction of its blood supply for a short time without any adverse effects. Nonetheless, exercising in a supine position should be avoided and replaced with exercises that alternately require the expectant mother to assume a variety of different body positions.

Relaxin, a hormone that loosens all the joints, ligaments, and tendons within the body (particularly within the pelvic region), is present in high amounts during pregnancy. Thus, most women are generally more flexible during pregnancy than at any other time in their life. This increase in joint and connective tissue laxity concomitantly increases the potential for joint injury. Consequently, pregnant women must not overstretch or perform exercises in a ballistic (jerky, bouncy) manner. The aim of flexibility programs during pregnancy should not be to improve joint range of motion, but rather to relieve muscle cramping or soreness and relax the lower-back region to alleviate the pain generated from the lordosic pressure on the spine.

Finally, it is important that pregnant women carefully monitor their diets to make sure they consume adequate amounts of carbohydrates to meet the demands of both exercise and their fetus. Theoretically, exercise (especially vigorous activity performed late in pregnancy) could induce a maternal hypoglycemic (i.e., low blood sugar) response by increasing the glucose uptake by the skeletal muscle of a pregnant woman. In the extreme, this response could impair fetal development.

Once the decision has been made that it is safe for a pregnant woman to exercise, it is essential that every effort be taken to ensure that her exercise program adheres to medically sound guidelines. The two major components of physical fitness that must be considered for inclusion in a comprehensive exercise program are aerobic fitness and muscular fitness.

AEROBIC CONDITIONING

The ACOG has established guidelines (Table 18-1) for aerobic exercise during pregnancy and the postpartum period that are based on many of the aforementioned theoretical concerns. These advisory instructions are intended to be suitable for all pregnant women regardless of their basic level of physical fitness. Many leading authorities, however, believe that the ACOG guidelines are too conservative and that a more appropriate exercise prescription for a pregnant woman would be one that is more individualized. These experts feel that decisions related to the type, intensity, duration, and frequency of exercise should be made according to a woman's current fitness level, the stage of her pregnancy, and her personal interests.

It appears that some exercise activities are more suitable than others. Generally, the most suitable aerobic exercises for a pregnant woman are low-impact activities such as walking, swimming, cycling, and independent-action stair climbing. Women accustomed to running prior to pregnancy can safely continue to do so provided that they reduce the intensity (i.e., decrease their running speeds, run on level terrain, include relief bouts of walking, etc.) at which they run. All factors considered, the most appropriate form of aerobic exercise for a pregnant woman is the one that she most enjoys and can safely perform.

The fundamental purpose of exercise during pregnancy is to maintain and improve fitness. Thus, the intensity, frequency, and duration at which exercise is prescribed should be adjusted slightly downward. An appropriate level of exercise intensity for a pregnant woman is 50 to 60 percent of maximal oxygen uptake, or resting heart rate plus 50 to 60 percent of the difference between resting and maximal heart rate. If, however, a pregnant woman is unable to comfortably carry on a conversation while exercising (a.k.a. the "talk test"), she should reduce her exercise work rate. The "talk test" tends to err on the side of conservatism and can be very helpful in ensuring that the intensity of an exercise bout is not excessive for a particular individual at a particular moment in time. As far as exercise frequency and duration are concerned, it is suggested that a healthy pregnant woman exercise at least three times a week (nonconsecutive days) for 20 to 30 minutes per session. Although some women (e.g., Joan Benoit Samuelson) are able to engage in more intense, more frequent, and longer bouts of exercise without negative consequences, it is our opinion (along with many experts) that a moderate – yet individualized – exercise prescription is safer and more effective for the vast majority of pregnant women. For instance, utilizing the heart rate reserve method (a.k.a., Karvonen method) ensures that the level of exercise intensity decreases as her full term approaches because an expectant mother's resting heart rate progressively increases throughout her pregnancy. (*Note:* Information regarding strength-training guidelines for pregnant women can be found in Chapter 11.)

Growing evidence (both scientific and anecdotal) suggests that exercise can and will enhance the well-being of pregnant women. Among the more commonly cited benefits of exercising during pregnancy are the following: It reduces the severity and frequency of back pain associated with pregnancy by helping pregnant women maintain better body posture; it provides a psychological "lift" that helps counteract the feelings of stress, anxiety, and/or depression which frequently accompany pregnancy; it helps control weight gain; it improves digestion and reduces constipation; and it produces a greater energy reserve for meeting the requirements of daily life.

Table 18-1.	American College of Obstetricians and Gynecologists (ACOG) Recommendations for Exercise in Pregnancy and Postpartum

1. During pregnancy, women can continue to exercise and derive health benefits even from mild-to-moderate exercise routines. Regular exercise (at least 3 times per week) is preferable to intermittent activity.
2. Women should avoid exercise in the supine position after the first trimester. Such a position is associated with decreased cardiac output in most pregnant women; because the remaining cardiac output will be preferentially distributed away from splanchnic beds (including the uterus) during vigorous exercise, such regimens are best avoided during pregnancy. Prolonged periods of motionless standing should also be avoided.
3. Women should be aware of the decreased oxygen available for aerobic exercise during pregnancy. They should be encouraged to modify the intensity of their exercise according to maternal symptoms. Pregnant women should stop exercising when fatigued and not exercise to exhaustion. Weight-bearing exercises may, under some circumstances, be continued throughout pregnancy at intensities similar to those prior to pregnancy. Non-weight-bearing exercises, such as cycling or swimming, will minimize the risk of injury and facilitate the continuation of exercise during pregnancy.
4. Morphologic changes in pregnancy should serve as a relative contraindication to types of exercise in which loss of balance could be detrimental to maternal or fetal well-being, especially in the third trimester. Further, any type of exercise involving the potential for even mild abdominal trauma should be avoided.
5. Pregnancy requires an additional 300 kcal/day in order to maintain metabolic homeostasis. Thus, women who exercise during pregnancy should be particularly careful to ensure an adequate diet.
6. Pregnant women who exercise in the first trimester should augment heat dissipation by ensuring adequate hydration, appropriate clothing, and optimal environmental surroundings during exercise.
7. Many of the physiologic and morphologic changes of pregnancy persist 4 to 6 weeks postpartum. Thus, prepregnancy exercise routines should be resumed gradually, based upon a women's physical capability.

American College of Obstetricians and Gynecologists. *Exercise During Pregnancy and the Postpartum Period (Technical Bulletin #189)*. Washington, DC: ACOG, 1994.

In summary, an exercise program can be undertaken during pregnancy without undue risk to the mother or the fetus provided that basic exercise prescription guidelines are followed. Controversy still exists, however, regarding the safety and efficacy of vigorous exercise during pregnancy. A good indicator of an appropriate exercise prescription is that the woman be fully recovered within 15 to 20 minutes after the completion of the exercise bout. Table 18-2 provides a listing of signs and symptoms that should prompt a pregnant woman to stop exercising and consult the physician who is monitoring her pregnancy. A knowledgeable fitness professional, working closely with the woman's physician, can make exercise a safe (for both the mother and the fetus), productive, and enjoyable endeavor.

Table 18-2. Reasons to Discontinue Exercise and Seek Medical Advice
1. Any signs of vaginal discharge
2. Sudden swelling of the ankles, hands, and face
3. Persistent, severe headaches and/or visual disturbance; unexplained spells of faintness or dizziness
4. Swelling, pain, and redness in the calf of one leg (phlebitis)
5. Elevation of pulse rate or blood pressure that persists after exercise
6. Excessive fatigue, palpitations, chest pain
7. Persistent contractions (>6 to 8 hours) that may suggest onset of premature labor
8. Unexplained abdominal pain
9. Insufficient weight gain (<1.0 kg [2.2 lbs]/month during last 2 trimesters)

American College of Obstetricians and Gynecologists. *Exercise During Pregnancy and the Postpartum Period (Technical Bulletin #189).* Washington, DC: ACOG, 1994.

EXERCISE AND MENOPAUSE

Menopause, commonly referred to as the "change of life," represents the point in time when cessation of menstrual function occurs. Women typically stop menstruating between the ages of 45 and 55. A gradual decline in reproductive function tends to characterize the 10 to 15 years preceding the final menstrual period. Hot flashes are perhaps the earliest sign that a woman is going through menopause. Additional signs of menopause may include any or all of the following: vaginal dryness, a reduced sex drive, urinary incontinence (a problem with urine leakage), weight gain, anxiety, depression, hot flashes, and irritability. These alterations can be very unpleasant and disconcerting for many women.

Women in the postmenopausal stage undergo several important hormonal changes — most notably, a reduction in serum estrogen levels. The greatly reduced ability of the ovaries to produce estrogen during menopause results in significant physiological changes. The loss of estrogen, for example, causes a decrease in the absorption of minerals (e.g., calcium) by bone. Lower levels of calcium cause bone to become less dense and weakened, a condition collectively known as osteoporosis. Estrogen deficiency may also place postmenopausal women at a higher risk for heart disease because of its adverse effect on blood lipid-lipoprotein profiles. Specifically, low serum estrogen levels have been associated with elevated lipid levels (cholesterol and triglycerides) and reduced levels of high-density lipoprotein (the "good" cholesterol carrier that plays a cardio-protective role).

Exercise has been found to have positive effects on several menopausal symptoms. For example, it promotes bone mineralization, which helps retard the progression of osteoporosis. Anecdotal evidence and limited research suggest that exercise can decrease the number and severity of hot flashes. Exercise has also been shown to improve self-image and feelings of confidence, decrease anxiety and depression, and positively contribute to energy level, quality of sleep, and management of stress in menopausal women.

Postmenopausal women are often instructed to perform pelvic floor (Kegel) exercises. Kegel exercises are designed to improve the tone of the muscles, ligaments, and fascia known as the pelvic floor. The pelvic floor controls urination and defecation, enhances the sexual response to orgasm, and provides support to the pelvic organs. Many women are unaware that they have muscles in this area that can be strengthened just like their biceps or quadriceps.

Why should a woman pay attention to this small group of muscles? Millions of women are affected by stress urinary incontinence. Stress urinary incontinence is the involuntary loss of urine during physical exertion or activities such as laughing, sneezing, or coughing. Unfortunately, many women consider incontinence an inevitable consequence of childbirth and aging, which it is not. Active women of all ages report experiencing incontinence. This can be particularly bothersome when it occurs during physical exertion. In fact, some women stop exercising, change their choice of activity, or begin wearing a protective pad instead of seeking medical advice or beginning a program of Kegel exercises. Strengthening the pelvic floor muscles can provide these women with much needed support and control.

The following serve as basic guidelines for women who wish to perform Kegel exercises:

- Contract or tighten the pubococcygeus muscle (the same muscles used when stopping and starting the flow of urine). This can be done while standing, sitting, or lying down.
- Hold the contraction for a count of 4 seconds, and then relax for 4 seconds. Don't tighten the abdominal, quadricep, or gluteal muscles when performing this exercise.
- Perform the exercise continuously for a period of 5 minutes twice a day.

It typically takes approximately eight weeks for the Kegel exercises to result in a noticeable improvement in bladder control. Because no other exercise strengthens the pelvic floor muscles as effectively as these, many urinary incontinence experts recommend that all women athletes, including those without stress incontinence, perform five minutes of Kegel exercises daily as a preventive measure.

NOT FOR MEN ONLY

No one could reasonably argue against the fact that exercise can and should be an integral part of a woman's lifestyle. In some situations, the role of exercise is unduly limited by misplaced concern over several special health/medical considerations that exist for physically active women. These special considerations should not, however, discourage women from participating in sensible exercise programs.

Fortunately, a growing amount of information on the effects and applications of exercise is becoming available, which allows fitness professionals to be better equipped to design and supervise exercise programs for women. The key for women who want to increase the likelihood of living life to its fullest is to seek help from a qualified professional when they have questions regarding exercise and fitness. They should recognize that women reap as many, if not more, benefits from exercise as men. The substantial rewards of an active lifestyle can and should be enjoyed by men and women alike.

Recommended Reading

American College of Obstetricians and Gynecologists. *Exercise During Pregnancy and the Postpartum Period (Technical Bulletin #189)*. Washington, DC: ACOG, 1994.

Bachmann, G. Prevention of menopausal sequelae. *New England Journal of Medicine* 10(2):359-369, 1991.

Dembo, L, McCormick, KM. Exercise prescription to prevent osteoporosis. *ACSM's Health & Fitness Journal* 4(1):32-38, 2000.

Johnson, M. Disordered eating. In: Agostini, R (ed), *Medical & Orthopedic Issues of Active and Athletic Women*. Philadelphia, PA: Hanley & Belfus, 1994.

Lemcke, D. Osteoporosis and menopause. In: Agostini, R (ed), *Medical & Orthopedic Issues of Active and Athletic Women*. Philadelphia, PA: Hanley & Belfus, 1994.

Manore, MM. Running on empty: Health consequences of chronic dieting in active women. *ACSM's Health & Fitness Journal* 2(2):24-31, 1998.

Marshall, L. Clinical evaluation of amenorrhea in active and athletic women. *Clinical Sports Medicine* 13(2):405-418, 1994.

Nattiv, A, et al. The female athlete triad. *Clinical Sports Medicine* 13(2):405-418, 1994.

Otis, CL. Too slim, amenorrheic, fracture-prone: The female athlete triad. *ACSM's Health & Fitness Journal* 2(1):20-25, 1998.

Otis, CL, Drinkwater, B, Johnson, M, et al. ACSM Position Stand on the Female Athlete Triad. *Medicine & Science in Sports & Exercise* 29:i-ix, 1997.

Otis, CL, Goldingay, R. *The Athletic Woman's Survival Guide*. Champaign, IL: Human Kinetics Publishers, Inc., 2000.

Stuhr, RM. Strategies for beating the barriers to exercise for women. *ACSM's Health & Fitness Journal* 2(5):20-29, 1998.

Wolfe, LA, Brenner, I, Mottola, M. Maternal exercise, fetal well-being, and pregnancy outcome. In: Holloszy, JO (ed), *Exercise and Sport Sciences Reviews*. Baltimore, MD: Williams & Wilkins, 1994.

CHAPTER 19

• •

EXERCISE AND STRESS MANAGEMENT

*F*or decades, people have reported that exercising on a regular basis "makes them feel good." How and why exercise affects a vast array of psychological factors has been addressed by a number of studies. As a result, the field of exercise psychology has evolved to provide more accurate information on the relationship between exercise and the mind/body connection. Researchers have found that an inherent interaction exists between the mind and the body during all daily activities, including exercise. Not surprisingly, health/fitness professionals are interested in the possible benefits of exercise on both the mind and the body. In this chapter, we will explore the effects of exercise on three specific psychological states: anxiety, mood, and depression.

IS RELIEF SPELLED E-X-E-R-C-I-S-E?

People often report that they feel better after exercising. "Feeling better" may collectively represent several different effects of exercising, including physiological responses (increased energy), perceptual responses (enhanced self-esteem), and affective responses (reduction of negative thoughts and feelings). Exercise psychologists have been particularly interested in these responses as they may help to explain the individual motives for exercise involvement and adherence. And, they are specifically interested in the influence of exercise on anxiety, general mood, social isolation, and depression.

Anxiety is typically defined as a transitory emotional state arising from a threat to an individual's basic sense of personality, self-esteem, and self-worth. It is important to understand anxiety because it can manifest in a wide range of behaviors, from extreme excitement to a state of stupor. Even relatively minor occurrences of anxiety are often linked to personal unhappiness, increased health care costs, and decreased work productivity.

Mood is generally defined as a state of emotional arousal of varying (but not permanent) duration. As opposed to emotions, which are typically more intense and don't last as long, moods are frequently perceived as being dispositions or tendencies to respond in specific emotional ways. Obviously, the more likely a person is to respond in a positive way, the less likely he or she is to have negative feelings. This represents a highly desirable and frequent outcome of exercise.

Depression is a psychological state characterized by feelings of despair, hopelessness, low self-esteem, sadness, and pessimism. The possible symptoms of depression range from

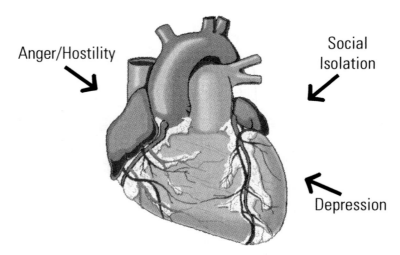

Anger/Hostility

Social
Isolation

Depression

Figure 19-1. Selected psychosocial variables, including anger/hostility, depression, and social isolation, are associated with atherosclerotic heart disease and its sequelae. (Reprinted with permission from American College of Sports Medicine. Franklin, BA, Emerging psychosocial risk factors, *ACSM's Health & Fitness Journal*, Vol. 4, No. 6, 2000. Baltimore, MD: Lippincott Williams & Wilkins, 2000.)

minor fatigue, indecisiveness, and irritability to social withdrawal and even suicidal feelings. Because depression, anger/hostility, and social isolation are among the major psychosocial problems in the United States (Figure 19-1) and have been linked to heart disease, it is important to explore the positive effect that exercise has on these emotional conditions.

EXERCISE, ANXIETY, AND GENERAL MOOD

Research has shown that exercise can improve both anxiety and mood over baseline levels. The findings of such studies suggest that the effects of exercising on anxiety are dependent on whether the anxiety is acute or short-term (state anxiety) or chronic (trait anxiety).

On one hand, research suggests that state anxiety is not reduced more through exercise than with other physical activities. Such results lend some support to the "time-out" hypothesis regarding why stress levels are reduced following exercise – a theory which suggests that exercise may serve simply as a useful distraction from daily worries.

On the other hand, exercising over a longer period appears to reduce trait anxiety to a greater extent than exercise performed for a relatively short period. This reduction is commonly linked to the "training" effect that accompanies long-term exercise participation. Many researchers have shown that exercise itself represents a physiological stressor. Accordingly, regular exposure to exercise reduces the body's negative response to exercise. In turn, exercise performed regularly elicits specific positive reactions which "toughen" the body, thereby enabling it to adapt and respond in a more appropriate manner to other subsequent stressors (e.g., physiological and/or psychological). Exercise has also been shown to increase the brain's emission of alpha waves – the brain waves associated with a relaxed meditation-like state of mind.

Two factors that have been found to have a substantial effect on anxiety and mood are the duration and the intensity of exercise. Exercise should be performed at least 20 minutes at an intensity of greater than 70 percent of maximum heart rate (MHR) to be associated with reduced anxiety and improved mood. Workouts lasting longer than 30 minutes have not been shown to produce greater benefits. Increasing exercise intensity up to as high as 90 percent of MHR, however, has been associated with a more positive mood and reduced anxiety. A few studies indicate that exercising at an extremely high intensity (above 90 percent of MHR) may have a negative effect on both anxiety and mood. Reductions in anxiety and mood improvements have been reported to last for at least 30 minutes, and perhaps as long as six hours, after a moderate exercise bout has ceased.

The type of exercise performed has been identified as yet another factor that appears to influence whether an anxiety reduction or mood improvement occurs. Most research in this area has focused on aerobic exercise, which has been shown to have the most positive effect on anxiety and mood levels. In contrast, relatively little is known about the effects of either resistance-type exercise or flexibility training on anxiety and mood.

THE IMPACT OF EXERCISE ON DEPRESSION

Exercise has long been advocated as a possible treatment for depression. Early research on the subject suggested that higher levels of depression were found primarily in sedentary and deconditioned individuals. As a result, it was erroneously believed that only unfit people could relieve feelings of depression by exercising. However, exercise has been reported to be effective in reducing depression across all age groups, for both men and women, and especially for those with major depressive disorders. Contrary to the earlier assumptions, this finding indicates that exercise has a positive effect on elevated levels of depression among most people, not just the deconditioned.

Finally, many studies show that both acute and chronic exercise significantly decrease depression. The results of these studies suggest that the antidepressant effects of exercise may begin in the first session of exercise. In addition, exercise appears to be a better antidepressant than relaxation or other "enjoyable" activities, and is as effective in decreasing depression as medications (i.e., Sertraline) or formal psychotherapy techniques. Nevertheless, considerable evidence suggests that exercise, when combined with psychotherapy, is a more effective therapeutic approach in reducing depression than exercise alone.

A variety of explanations have been advanced regarding the antidepressant effects of exercise. The reasons offered generally fall into one of two categories: psychological or physiological. The psychological factors that have been proposed include cognitive-behavioral changes, social interaction factors, and the "time-out" hypothesis.

The cognitive changes that may occur as a result of exercise include an increased level of both self-confidence and self-esteem that often results when an individual meets the challenges of a task that he/she perceives to be somewhat difficult (e.g., exercise). In turn, the ability to master one set of challenges often enables an individual to be better prepared to deal with a wider variety of life's challenges – all of which may lead to a reduction in depression.

The belief that social interaction can have a positive effect on depression levels implies that contact with others may lead to decreases in depression. Exercise psychologists suggest that the social aspects of exercise may be more influential at the onset of an exercise program, since the rewards of exercise are primarily external and have not been internalized at this point. This hypothesis, however, has not been universally supported by studies. Research indicates that exercise programs conducted in the home can lead to comparable or greater decreases in depression than those conducted in either health/fitness centers or university settings. On the other hand, the "time-out" hypothesis suggests that exercise may simply offer a distraction from daily worries and problems.

The physiological factors that have been advanced to explain the antidepressant effects of exercise include an increase in aerobic fitness, biochemical changes, the release of endorphins, or combinations thereof. It is highly unlikely, however, that the antidepressant effect of exercise that occurs during the first few weeks of exercising is due to training-induced improvements in aerobic fitness (which does not occur to any substantial degree for most individuals at this point in the training regimen).

While it is possible that subsequent increases in aerobic fitness may play some role in decreasing chronic depression, the acute antidepressant effects of exercise may be better explained by the release of specific biochemicals. Depressed individuals are thought to have decreased secretions of specific neurotransmitter metabolites (e.g., norepinephrine, dopamine, and serotonin), which are thought to increase during exercise. As a result, exercise is believed to stimulate the release of these substances, which, in turn, reduces depression.

The release of endorphins (endogenous opiates) is also frequently cited as the mechanism for the alteration of mood state. While increases in endorphin levels have been observed in the blood of humans, endorphins have not been found in the brain. And, although euphoric feelings have been linked to endorphin release, until research determines whether endorphins cross the blood-brain barrier, any hypothesis regarding their mood-altering properties remains speculative.

THE MIND/BODY CONNECTION

Exercise, particularly aerobic exercise, has been shown to have a positive effect on a person's state of mind. By the same token, psychological state has been found to greatly influence the results of exercise, including how an individual's body responds physiologically to the demands of the exercise, how much they enjoy the exercise activity, and how their attitude is shaped regarding the value of exercise (a very important component of exercise adherence).

As exercise professionals and personal trainers learn more about the mind/body relationship to exercise, the psychological benefits and behavioral adaptations resulting from a sound exercise program will become increasingly apparent. It seems obvious that exercise prescriptions will eventually address psychological objectives, as well as physiological concerns. At that point, fitness professionals will become true full-service professionals serving the mind, as well as the body.

Recommended Reading

American College of Sports Medicine. *ACSM's Resource Manual for Guidelines for Exercise Testing and Prescription*, 4th ed. Philadelphia, PA: Lippincott Williams & Wilkins, 2001.

American Council on Exercise. *Clinical Exercise Specialist Manual: ACE's Source for Training Special Populations.* San Diego, CA: American Council on Exercise, 1999.

Dienstbier, RA. Arousal and physiological toughness: Implications for mental and physical health. *Psychological Review* 96(1):84-100, 1989.

Nieman, DC. *Fitness and Sports Medicine: An Introduction,* 3rd ed. Palo Alto, CA: Bull Publishing Company, 1995.

North, TC, McCullagh, P, Tran, ZV. Effect of exercise on depression. *Exercise Sport Science Review* 18:379-415, 1990.

Peterson, JA, Bryant, CX (eds). *The StairMaster Fitness Handbook,* 2nd ed. Champaign, IL: Sagamore Publishing Company, Inc., 1995.

Petruzzello, SJ, Landers, DM, Hatfield, BD, et al. A meta analysis on the anxiety reducing effects of acute and chronic exercise: Outcomes and mechanisms. *Sports Medicine* 11:143-182, 1991.

Williams, TJ, Krahenbuhl, GS, Morgan, DW. Mood state and running economy in moderately trained male runners. *Medicine & Science in Sports & Exercise* 23:727-731, 1991.

Willis, JD, Campbell, LF. *Exercise Psychology.* Champaign, IL: Human Kinetics Publishers, Inc., 1992.

CHAPTER 20

EXERCISE AND FIBROMYALGIA

*I*magine constantly suffering from muscle aches, fatigue, and sleep deprivation. You wake up every morning stiff and tired, feeling like you've run a marathon. To compound your dilemma, physicians are unable to identify your condition. Is it chronic fatigue syndrome, lupus, or Lyme disease? Is it psychological?

Welcome to the world of fibromyalgia (FM), a relatively unknown disease that the National Association of Fibromyalgia states affects 10 to 12 million Americans annually (80 percent women and 20 percent men). Most of the individuals who get FM develop symptoms between the ages of 20 and 55. Affecting approximately 2 percent of the general population, FM is more common than rheumatoid arthritis.

Initially described in Europe in the mid-19th century, FM was officially recognized as a syndrome by the World Health Organization in 1993. Fibromyalgia remains controversial in nature, with many individuals enduring symptoms for several years before receiving an appropriate diagnosis.

CLINICAL FEATURES OF FIBROMYALGIA

In 1990, the American College of Rheumatology established diagnostic criteria for FM (Table 20-1). Individuals must satisfy two criteria before a diagnosis of FM can be made. One criterion is the presence of widespread pain for at least six months involving the upper and lower extremities, the left and right sides, and the axial skeleton (the portion of the skeleton comprising the skull, vertebral column, and thorax). The other criterion is the presence

---

Table 20-1. Diagnostic Features of Fibromyalgia

- Chronic, widespread pain
- Tender points
- Paresthesia (numbness or tingling), dysesthesia, headaches, fatigue, Raynaud's syndrome
- Pelvic pain, female urethral symptoms
- Presence of widespread pain for more than 6 months, plus 11 or more of 18 tender points (the pain should also be present in all 4 quadrants of the body)

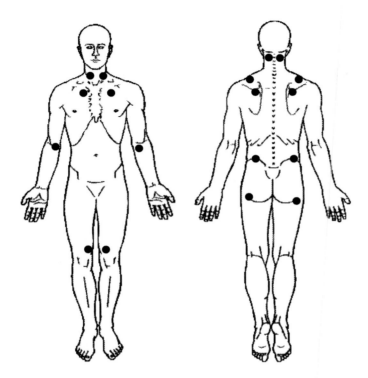

Figure 20-1. Location of the 18 tender point sites indicative of fibromyalgia.

of widespread tender points at 11 or more of 18 defined sites. The tender points refer to localized painful areas in a muscle, musculotendinous junction, fat pad, or bursal sac region (Figure 20-1).

The most frequently reported FM symptoms are aches and pains similar to flu-like exhaustion, multiple tender points (accompanied by muscle spasms clustered in the neck, shoulder, upper chest wall, and lower back), stiffness, decreased stamina and endurance, fatigue, and paresthesia (numbness or tingling). Other common symptoms include excessive tiredness, sleep disturbances, bowel and bladder irritability, numbness of the extremities, anxiety, and depression. Many FM sufferers wake up tired following a restful night's sleep – some report feeling as though they were run over by a freight train. Joint stiffness and pain frequently occur when individuals with FM stay in one position for an extended period.

USING EXERCISE TO MANAGE FIBROMYALGIA

Because of the wide array of symptoms, no single medication or therapeutic approach is completely effective in treating FM sufferers. Research suggests that, because FM is chronic, treatment should be focused on reducing symptoms instead of curing the underlying cause, which is presently unknown. A multidisciplinary approach that combines a variety of treatment methods may be most effective in relieving symptoms. The primary components of a multidisciplinary treatment program should include education about the diagnosis and prognosis of FM, sleep improvement, psychological tools (meditation, relaxation techniques, etc.), possibly medicine (antidepressants, antianxiety medicine, anti-inflammatories, supplements, etc.), and regular exercise.

Many individuals with FM significantly reduce their levels of physical activity, thereby decreasing functional capacity. Deconditioned muscles are more susceptible to microtrauma from even light activity. This microtrauma can result in greater pain, which leads to further reductions in physical activity, creating a hypokinetic lifestyle, deconditioning, microtrauma, pain, and more inactivity.

In light of this progression, regular exercise should be a critical part of an effective treatment program for FM. Exercise promotes improvements in muscular fitness (strength and endurance), balance, coordination, and range of motion, serving to reduce the functional disability associated with FM. In addition, exercise increases the concentration of mood-elevating endorphins within the central nervous system, and has a positive impact on anxiety and depression.

While exercise is important for managing FM and its related symptoms, proper instruction regarding the frequency, intensity, duration, and type of activity is essential to prevent exacerbation of symptoms. Acute stress from sudden, forceful, jarring movements, repetitive motions, improper exercise techniques or biomechanics, and inappropriate exercise dosages (frequency, intensity, and/or duration) can lead to increased pain, excessive fatigue, and, in some instances, musculoskeletal injuries. Many FM sufferers do not exercise because of prior painful experiences related to improper exercise programming. Accordingly, fitness professionals must carefully supervise the workouts of clients with FM, providing them with clear instructions regarding proper technique and exercise progression.

Fitness professionals first need to help FM clients understand that muscle is an active, living tissue which shortens, and then stiffens, and progressively loses function when not used. As a result, individuals with FM cannot afford to adopt a sedentary lifestyle, despite the musculoskeletal pain and severe fatigue that encourage inactivity. The focus of exercise programs is "active relaxation" not "sport conditioning." The "no pain, no gain" mantra and mentality should not be applied to individuals with FM.

FM clients must also be taught that the key to improvement is consistency, not how hard or how long they work out. Reducing exercise intensity and/or duration or even resting during periods of severe flare-ups is acceptable provided the long-range pattern includes moderate physical activity. Exercise should not be viewed as a quick fix, but as a permanent lifestyle change.

Finally, individuals with FM should be reminded that exercise does not necessarily require sophisticated or expensive equipment. An exercise program of walking, light strength training using resistance bands and tubing, and mild stretching will benefit most FM clients. Individuals with FM who are not currently exercising can benefit greatly by simply increasing their level of day-to-day activities.

Exercise programs for FM sufferers should be designed to promote health and wellness, not athleticism. Fitness professionals need to be able to modify the programs to safely meet their clients' current health and functional status. Guidelines for safe exercise for this population include the following:

- Encourage FM clients to avoid prolonged periods of inactivity and to adjust the intensity and/or duration of their exercise regimens according to their symptomatology. Physical activity is essential for preserving function.
- Train clients at light-to-moderate intensity levels – 35% to 69% of maximum heart rate or "weak/light" to "strong/heavy" on the Borg Rating of Perceived Exertion (RPE) Scale. Perceived exertion may be the best tool for determining and monitoring exercise intensity. Using RPE allows for day-to-day variations in symptoms that may not be reflected by heart rate. Remember, FM clients do not need to train hard.
- Encourage FM clients to participate in a variety of activities to avoid repeatedly stressing the same muscles and joints.
- Clients should use very light weights, elastic resistance bands or cords, and/or gravity for resistance training. Emphasize proper exercise technique, keeping resistance loads at a minimum.
- Encourage individuals who have been inactive to start with 5 to 10 minutes of activity 3 or more times per day. As conditioning improves, the duration of activity can be gradually increased, and the daily frequency reduced. The goal is for FM clients to be able to exercise for 30 minutes 3 to 4 times per week. Longer exercise sessions are not necessary to provide significant health benefits and may, in fact, produce diminishing returns.
- Instruct clients to gradually increase activity levels using activities of daily living and low-impact aerobic activities. Warm-water (84° to 90°F) exercise is generally well-tolerated by FM clients.
- Reduce exercise intensity and/or duration when clients are experiencing periods of increased pain or fatigue.
- Encourage participation in a static stretching program to enhance and/or maintain flexibility and joint mobility. Stretching exercises should be incorporated in the warmup and cool-down periods and throughout the day.
- Stress the importance of consistency. FM individuals should avoid sporadic and, especially, vigorous workouts.

CONSISTENCY IS THE KEY TO FUNCTIONALITY

Fibromyalgia is a complex syndrome that requires a multidisciplinary treatment approach. Given that the fundamental objective of treatment for FM sufferers is to enhance functional capacity, regular exercise is a critical part of the treatment program. Fitness professionals, however, must help their clients with FM exercise at the proper intensity, duration, and frequency. Exercising too hard or progressing too quickly can have detrimental effects, resulting in increased pain and fatigue, and chronic inactivity. In fact, individuals with FM do not need to train hard or push themselves to near maximal or maximal effort. Instead, they should focus on developing an active lifestyle characterized by consistent, comfortably paced aerobic workouts that are augmented by light strength training and mild stretching. Adopting such a lifestyle will significantly enhance the level of physical ability and functional independence of those who suffer from FM.

Suggested Fibromyalgia Resources

Associations:

National Chronic Fatigue Syndrome and Fibromyalgia Association
P. O. Box 184426, Suite 222
Kansas City, MO 64133

Fibromyalgia Alliance of America
P. O. Box 21990
Columbus, OH 43221

Fibromyalgia Network
P. O. Box 31750
Tucson, AZ 85751

American Sleep Disorders Association
1619 – 14th Street NW, Suite 300
Rochester, MN 55901

Internet Sites:

www.futureone.com/~hunter/resource.htm
www.cais.nel/cts-news/fibro.htm
www.studyweb.com/med/fibro.htm
www.my.webmd
www.members.aol.com/FMSwebpage/FMShome.html

Recommended Reading

American College of Sports Medicine. *ACSM's Guidelines for Exercise Testing and Prescription*, 6th ed. Philadelphia, PA: Lippincott Williams & Wilkins, 2000.
American Council on Exercise. *Clinical Exercise Specialist Manual: ACE's Source for Training Special Populations*. San Diego, CA: American Council on Exercise, 1999.
Bennett, RM, McCain, G. Coping successfully with fibromyalgia. *Patient Care* 29:29-39, 1995.
Deuster, PA. Exercise in the prevention and treatment of chronic disorders. *Women's Health Issues* 6(6):320-331, 1996.
Gowans, SE, et al. A randomized, controlled trial of exercise and education for individuals with fibromyalgia. *Arthritis Care & Research* 12(2):120-128, 1999.
Gremillion, RB. Fibromyalgia: Recognizing and treating an elusive syndrome. *The Physician and Sportsmedicine* 26(4):55-65, 1998.

CHAPTER 21

• •

EXERCISE AND WEIGHT CONTROL

*T*he proportion of U.S. adults who are classified as obese, which is defined as a body mass index greater than or equal to 30 kg/m^2, rose 49 percent over the last decade, with the greatest increases among young adults, college-educated, and those of Hispanic ethnicity. During this time period, obesity increased in every state, in both sexes, and each age group, race, educational level, and smoking status. Indeed, the latest figures show that more than half of all Americans are overweight or obese. A startling one out of five children ages 5 to 17 is obese!

Americans are barraged with a never-ending abundance of nutrition and weight-control information as new research, diets, and exercise programs emerge. At any given time, approximately 28 million adults are dieting to lose weight and another 23 million think they should be. It is estimated that more than 40 billion dollars is spent annually on diet books, products, and services. Unfortunately, this information is often confusing, complicated, and even fraudulent. The resulting chaos is leading many people to make serious, even life-threatening, mistakes in pursuit of the ultimate goal — weight loss.

HOW DID AMERICANS REACH THIS POINT?

Obesity can be caused by numerous factors, including genetics, hyperphagia (eating too many calories), eating a high-fat or high-sugar diet, having a sluggish metabolic rate, and leading a sedentary lifestyle. In the current obesity-conducive environment, food has become abundant and relatively inexpensive, portion sizes have expanded to dwarf those of past generations, and restaurant eating/carry-out have increasingly become the norm. Simultaneously, however, we've engineered physical activity out of our work environment, as cellular phones, dictaphones, and laptop computers have increasingly become part of our vocational armamentarium. Moreover, our leisure-time activities, which traditionally involved sports and recreational games, are now competing with more sedentary pastimes like watching television, playing video games, and computer interactions. These trends have resulted in a tendency toward positive energy balance by increasing energy intake and decreasing energy expenditure (Figure 21-1).

One of the most frequently cited types of obesity is hyperplastic obesity — a condition caused by an abnormal increase in the number of fat cells during the first year of life and during puberty. An individual of normal weight has about 25 to 30 billion fat cells, while a hyperplastic obese person can have as many as 42 to 106 billion fat cells. With so many reservoirs for fat, it is relatively easy for an individual to accumulate unwanted poundage.

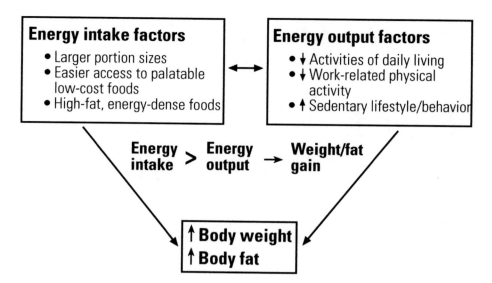

Figure 21-1. The effect of environmental factors on energy balance. When energy intake equals energy output, the system is in energy balance and body weight and body fat remain stable. In the current environment, factors on the left are driving energy intake up, whereas factors on the right are driving energy output down, creating a positive energy balance, resulting in weight/fat gain. (Adapted from Hill, JO, Melanson, EL. Overview of the determinants of overweight and obesity: Current evidence and research issues. *Medicine & Science in Sports & Exercise* 31(11 Suppl.):S515-S521, 1999.)

But, hyperplastic obesity is rare. Most Americans suffer from hypertrophic obesity, in which the number of fat cells is normal, but the size of the cells increases by up to 40 percent. Contrary to popular belief, obesity in this country appears to be primarily the result of a sedentary lifestyle, not overeating. Research shows that, oftentimes, obese people don't necessarily eat more than their leaner counterparts, they simply move less. As a result, they burn fewer calories and store more fat, which causes the size of their fat cells to expand (adipocyte hypertrophy).

Obsession with weight management is not restricted to those who are obese. People who are overfat struggle to lose weight as well. The high premium that the American culture places on thinness has made dieting a way of life for a large segment (up to 40 percent) of the adult population. The resultant demand for quick fixes has encouraged promises of immediate weight loss through nutritionally inane plans such as fasting, the semi-starvation diet, the all-grapefruit diet, the high-protein/low-carbohydrate diet, the high-fat/low-carbohydrate diet, or even the wood pulp regimen — several of which have been found to cause serious health problems. Weight conscious individuals are also confronted with an overwhelming number of gadgets, gimmicks, and supplements that are promoted as "miracle methods of weight reduction" — few of which are legitimate and many of which may be dangerous. Admittedly, it is challenging for the average person to know what is sound advice.

In reality, countless efforts to reduce body weight and fat stores haven't helped dieters shed pounds and keep them off. Dieting just doesn't work for most people. Ninety percent of all dieters regain lost weight within one year and 99 percent within five years. Many are trapped by the "yo-yo syndrome" in which they repeatedly lose and regain weight. As a consequence, the weight-loss industry is flourishing simply because no diet gimmick or special food is ultimately successful at promoting long-term weight control.

The only permanent way to effectively lose weight and keep it off is to swear off diets and exercise gimmicks forever. Instead, individuals should commit to a lifetime of sound nutritional practices and regular exercise, forget promises of instant weight loss, and accept the fact that successful weight control requires time, discipline, and perseverance. Although it sounds difficult, the benefits of this approach to weight management far outweigh the endless frustration of repeatedly losing and regaining pounds.

HEALTH CONSEQUENCES

The dramatic rise in the prevalence of overweight individuals and obesity in the U.S. has created a serious public health concern for a large percentage of the population, including children and adolescents. Being overweight has been directly or indirectly linked to several chronic health problems, including insulin resistance and Type II diabetes, coronary heart disease, certain types of cancer, hypertension, osteoarthritis, and gallbladder disease. In 1998, in response to an emerging body of scientific evidence, the American Heart Association reclassified obesity as a major modifiable risk factor for coronary heart disease. Consequently, weight reduction is often prescribed in the prevention and treatment of many chronic diseases and medical conditions.

CALORIES, METABOLISM, AND ENERGY BALANCE

To facilitate proper weight-control programs for your clients, you should understand the relationship between calories, metabolism, and energy balance. Calories are a measure of the energy value of food. When food is broken down through the process of digestion and used to create energy, the body produces heat. The more calories a particular food contains, the more heat that will be produced and the more energy that will be available for the body. However, if a person eats lots of high-calorie foods and doesn't use the energy, the body stores this energy for future use in the form of fat.

Metabolism is the process of breaking down food into fuel. Metabolic rate is a quantitative measure of how fast the body digests food and burns calories through activity and muscular work. Because the muscles use 90 percent of the calories a person consumes, the more muscular tissue individuals have and the more active they are, the higher their metabolism. The greater the level of metabolism, the greater the caloric needs. Understandably, highly active individuals can eat more food than sedentary individuals because they require more calories to fuel their muscles. Because athletes, for example, have a higher metabolism, they tend to burn calories faster than inactive people.

How do calories and metabolism apply to weight loss? When individuals eat and burn the same number of calories daily, their energy level is balanced and an existing level of weight is maintained. In contrast, individuals gain weight when they eat more calories than they use: Overindulgence plus inactivity equals fat gain. One approach to losing weight is to eat less by following sound nutritional practices; the other is to increase caloric expenditure through exercise. When individuals consume fewer calories than they use, their bodies will rely on stored fat and/or muscle to produce energy. Once they start using body fat or muscle for energy, they will begin to lose weight. For example, an energy deficit of 3,500 Calories (or, more appropriately, kilocalories) will result in the loss of one pound.

The Importance of Maintaining Blood Sugar

If weight loss is this simple, why do so many individuals fail in their efforts to "win the losing game"? Unfortunately, many individuals try to lose weight by limiting their intake of fluids so they don't retain water weight. Water weight loss, however, won't cause a lasting change in body composition (the ratio of muscle to fat) and any weight lost will be regained almost immediately when fluids are ingested.

Many dieters also reduce their caloric intake by either skipping meals or cutting back on their intake of carbohydrates, both of which can cause blood-sugar levels to plummet. When the blood-sugar level drops severely, the human body thinks it is starving and doesn't know when it will be fed again. To protect itself against starvation, the body actually conserves fat. The longer the blood-sugar level is low, the more efficient the body becomes at storing food as fat and holding on to existing fat.

If calorie intake is severely restricted, a person's body will burn muscle tissue to help supply energy. Because lean body mass (LBM) affects the metabolic rate, using muscle for energy (and thereby losing it) causes the resting energy expenditure to fall, which actually slows the rate of caloric expenditure. With a decreased metabolic rate, caloric needs decline proportionately, making the process of losing weight and keeping it off much more difficult. In addition, cutting calories without incorporating exercise into a weight-control program further depresses the metabolism. Without the "boost" that exercise provides to the metabolic rate, an individual will continue to burn calories more and more slowly, eventually resulting in plateaus.

After dieting for a while, what happens when individuals step on a scale? Often, they are lighter due, in large part, to the fact that they have lost water and muscle weight. They have, however, lost very little fat weight. It is important to remember that weight loss is not necessarily fat loss. Although individuals may appear to be lighter, they actually may be proportionally fatter.

This area of misplaced optimism is the point where many dieters go wrong. In their excitement about achieving a lower number on the scale, they immediately and incorrectly assume that they have lost fat. Instead, they may have set themselves up for failure (not being able to keep the weight off) by metabolizing LBM instead of fat. In the process, they have also lowered their resting metabolic rate. To lose weight and keep it off, the focus must be on losing fat – not muscle.

Losing the Right "Weigh"

Because restrictive diets don't produce long-lasting results and have been known to negatively affect health, they should be avoided. No matter how appealing, diets are destined to fail. Successful weight control begins with a lifetime commitment to nutritionally balanced eating habits and a physically active lifestyle.

Before trying to lose weight, individuals should realize that successful weight control will involve commitment, determination, and hard work. To lose weight and keep it off, permanent changes in eating and physical activity habits must be made. Although this approach may sound intimidating, the benefits of a lifestyle change (improved health, more energy, better self-esteem, a lower risk of developing a wide variety of medical conditions, an enhanced quality of life, etc.) far outweigh the costs.

Making a long-term commitment to weight control involves behavioral changes. While many theories exist about how to properly change personal behavior, the process essentially involves substituting unhealthy behaviors with healthy, well-established habits. This process takes time. The best way for you to help your clients approach the task is to help them determine what their long-term goals should be and then to break them down to short-term, attainable goals — one step at a time — by identifying eating and exercise habits that need to be changed. Experts say it takes approximately 30 days to "make" a new habit. You will need to motivate and encourage clients who may want to give up.

To develop habit awareness, most experts recommend keeping a diary to determine what specific behavior(s) contributed to the present weight problem. Individuals should keep a journal for a week to record all food and beverages consumed, every physical activity performed (e.g., walked up four flights of stairs, washed and folded three loads of laundry, stood on their feet seven hours at work, exercised for 20 minutes), and the times of day they ate and were physically active. It can also be helpful to record what moods/feelings were experienced before eating (bored, upset, nervous, sad, etc.) This information will be helpful in identifying how to expand the total amount of time spent on exercise and/or how to eliminate extracurricular eating (snacking).

After a week, you can help clients review the information in their diaries and help them determine if they should take that information to qualified professionals for help. A registered dietitian, for example, can help analyze nutrient and caloric intake, identify triggers that may stimulate eating (e.g., coffee breaks, television, and restaurants), and evaluate overall levels of energy expenditure. If the diary shows that they are eating a lot of high-fat foods such as doughnuts, french fries, and chocolate, the necessary adjustments can be made in eating habits. If their diaries indicate that they tend to nibble while watching television, they can either change their environment (i.e., make food less accessible and find something else to do while watching TV) or change their leisure habits to reduce the amount of time spent watching television. Finally, diaries may show that they're far too inactive to achieve their weight-control goals. For example, if they sit at a desk all day and then spend evenings on the couch, they'll never be able to lose the desired pounds of fat weight and keep them off.

DEVELOPING A PLAN AND PUTTING IT INTO ACTION

If an individual's goal is to take off and keep off unwanted fat weight, they should eat sensibly and exercise regularly. Knowing what constitutes a sensible diet and a sound exercise program is critical to achieving optimal results.

- *Eat sensibly.* A sound diet for weight reduction will be relatively low in calories and still provide all the nutrients essential for normal body function. It will contain foods that appeal to individual taste and can be easily incorporated into an individual's lifestyle. According to the American Dietetic Association, a diet should never fall below a level of approximately 10 to 12 Calories (kcal) per lb of body weight. A sensible diet must foster new, healthier eating habits (e.g., limiting fat consumption, avoiding fried foods, reducing salt intake) that can be maintained over the long haul.

One of the first steps in deciding what to eat is to determine how much food (the number of calories) should be consumed to cause fat loss. The simplest way to calculate daily caloric-intake needs is to multiply an individual's present body weight (in lbs) by 15 Calories (12 Calories to meet the minimum basal needs, plus 3 Calories to account for the energy needed to support a physically active lifestyle). For example, a 150-lb individual needs 2,250 Calories daily to sustain current body weight. The next step is to reduce the daily maintenance total by 250 Calories – the amount necessary to achieve a 1-lb weight loss per week when it's combined with an exercise program that burns an additional 250 Calories a day (fielding a net negative caloric balance of 500 Calories daily). Because 1 lb of body fat has 3,500 Calories, the individual will lose 1 lb a week (7 x 500 = 3,500) – a moderate rate of loss that is more likely to be sustained than a "quick-fix" approach.

Accordingly, if a person maintains a caloric intake of 2,000 Calories daily, he or she will lose 1 lb each week. Although decreasing caloric intake by only 250 Calories (the equivalent of eliminating one slice of pizza from a person's diet daily) may not seem like much, research suggests that more drastic reductions may have negative, long-term consequences. For example, if caloric intake is reduced too dramatically, there would not be sufficient energy to support an active lifestyle, and the chances of sticking to a stringent eating regimen are very low. Over time, extremely large cuts in caloric intake may cause the body to metabolize muscle tissue instead of fat. As a guideline, the American Dietetic Association recommends that daily caloric intake should never fall below 1,000 to 1,200 Calories for normal, healthy adults.

Once it has been established how much individuals should eat to achieve weight-control goals, the next step is to identify what to eat. The ideal "weight-control" diet should be high in complex carbohydrates and low in fat. The following are some helpful, practical steps individuals can take to positively restructure their eating habits:

◊ Limit servings to 1 portion. Have all meals served on a plate in the kitchen, not family-style at the table. After taking 1 portion, wrap up and store leftovers immediately to discourage nibbling. Serve meals on small plates so it doesn't look as if food is being restricted.

◊ Eat slowly. Take small bites, chew food longer, and put down utensils between bites. It takes at least 20 minutes for the satiety center in the brain to trigger a feeling of fullness. By that time, most people have finished the first helping and are beginning seconds.

◊ Forget about being a committed member of the "clean-plate club" – stop eating when full. Try to focus only on eating during a meal. Break any habits that may encourage overeating (e.g., eating while reading or watching television).

◊ <u>Keep high-fat foods out of the house</u>. If other people insist on having high-fat items, at least try to keep them out of sight to reduce temptation. Likewise, don't keep dishes of candy, nuts, or other treats in convenient, easy-to-reach places.

One final factor relating to sensible eating involves frequency of meals. How often individuals eat can impact whether they compromise their commitment to eating sensibly. By eating frequently and, thereby, maintaining stable blood-sugar levels, the onset of hunger pangs that often drive even the most well-intentioned individual to snack or binge can be prevented (or at least minimized). Research suggests that if individuals want to maintain balanced levels of blood sugar, they should eat at least 3 regular meals or 5 to 6 mini-meals daily. Skipping meals or eating almost all daily calories in a single meal can hinder or minimize reductions in body fat.

• *Exercise regularly.* Eating sensibly is only one primary component of a sound weight-control program. For successful, lifelong weight control, sensible eating and regular exercise go hand-in-hand. For most persons, the optimal approach to weight loss combines mild caloric restriction (energy intake of not lower than 1,200 kcal/day), a negative caloric balance (not to exceed 500 to 1,000 kcal/day), and an exercise program that promotes a daily caloric expenditure of more than 300 kcal (Table 21-1). Multiple short bouts of exercise have been shown to be as effective, or more effective, than longer continuous sessions in promoting reductions in body weight and fat stores, if the total caloric expenditure is comparable.

In addition, strength-training exercise can either help to maintain or build muscle tissue or, at a minimum, counter the tendency for a severely calorie-restricted diet to cause a significant loss of muscle. A minimum of 1 set involving the major muscle groups should be performed at least 2 times per week. Such regimens should include 8 to 10 different exercises at a load that permits 8 to 12 repetitions per set for healthy, sedentary adults or 10 to 15 repetitions per set for persons older than 50 years of age. Also, exercise can improve physical appearance, even if a significant amount of weight is not lost. Because muscle is more dense than fat, individuals can look more fit and trim without changing total-body weight.

While a personally enjoyable physical activity will help to promote some degree of weight loss, an exercise program that combines aerobic conditioning, increased physical activity in daily living, and strength training represents the best approach for using exercise to control body composition. The goal should be a gradual weight loss of not more than 2 lbs per week without metabolic derangements such as ketosis.

Table 21-1. Exercise Recommendations for Overweight and Obese Adults*	
Frequency	Initially, at least 3 days/week; preferably on alternating days to allow muscle recuperation/recovery Progress to 5 days/week, or daily
Duration	40 to 60 minutes/session (or 2 sessions/day of 20 to 30 minutes)
Intensity	40/50% to 70% $\dot{V}O_{2max}$ or HRR[†], or perceived exertion (0 to 11 scale) of 2 (weak) to 4 (moderate). Initially, emphasize increasing duration rather than intensity with the goal of optimizing caloric expenditure.
Energy Expenditure	≥300 Calories/day
Type	Large muscle groups, rhythmic-type contractions; aerobic in nature (walking is highly recommended) Use low-impact modes of activity Increase physical activity in daily living Minimize highly competitive sports; emphasize enjoyable activities Resistance training may serve as a valuable adjunct to aerobic exercise

† HRR = Heart rate reserve calculated as: (maximal heart rate – resting heart rate) x 40% to 70%, plus resting heart rate.

* Adapted from American College of Sports Medicine. *ACSM's Guidelines for Exercise Testing and Prescription*, 6th ed. Philadelphia, PA: Lippincott Williams & Wilkins, 2000.

FRAUDULENT GADGETS/CLAIMS

THE MYTH OF SPOT REDUCTION

In the U.S., where the health and aesthetic disadvantages of excess adiposity are well-recognized, "spot reducing" has become a multimillion-dollar industry, with deceptive advertisements promising that people can "take inches off the waist, thighs, or buttocks – without vigorous exercise or dieting, and in just minutes a day." The concept is based on the notion that it is possible to "burn off" fat from a particular part of the body by selectively exercising that area (Figure 21-2). However, numerous studies have now refuted this claim.

EFFORTLESS EXERCISE

Several years ago, investigators examined the validity of the weight-reducing claims made for the mechanical vibrating machines commonly found in health clubs and spas (Figure 21-3). The researchers theorized that if fat is oxidized, total-body oxygen consumption should be increased. And, if it is "massaged away," there should be some trace of it in the blood. The results of one study showed that blood fats remained essentially unchanged, whereas the average caloric cost of the 15-minute exercise session, including the recovery period, was

Figure 21-2. Electrically powered ring roller exercise device purportedly provides simultaneous "massage reduction" to the hip, leg, stomach, and back. A variety of effortless exercise devices have been touted as "easy ways" to improve the figure and reduce selected areas.

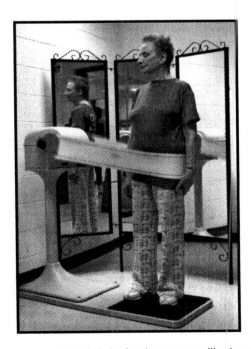

Figure 21-3. A woman leans back against a vibrator belt, hoping the massage will reduce the hips and buttocks.

only 11.4 Calories more than an equivalent period of seated rest (approximately 1/23 of an ounce of fat). The investigators concluded, "The vibrator is not to be taken seriously as a device to assist in fat reduction or shifting of fat deposits within the body."

WEIGHT-REDUCING CLOTHING

Special weight-reducing exercise garments, including heated belts and rubberized suits, are semipermeable or impermeable to moisture, and are associated with increased sweating and evaporative heat loss. Typically, these garments promote excessive dehydration by heat, localized pressure, or tissue compression. Although circumference measures and body weight may be temporarily reduced (until rehydration occurs), these losses are unrelated to actual or lasting reductions in body weight and fat stores.

ELECTRICAL MUSCLE STIMULATORS

Promoters of some electrical muscle stimulators (EMS) suggest that their modified devices can actually replace vigorous exercise. For example, advertisements claim that "microelectroimpulses" provide the same figure-toning effects as "3,000 sit-ups without moving an inch" or "10 miles of jogging while lying flat on your back." Like many fraudulent units, EMS devices have a legitimate legacy, as they are often used by physical therapists in the treatment of chronic diseases and related medical conditions. Nevertheless, the Food and Drug Administration considers muscle stimulators that are promoted or used for "body shaping and contouring" to be misbranded and fraudulent. In addition to the deceptive claims, EMS devices can be hazardous if misused. Potential complications include burns and electric shocks; moreover, the latter may have catastrophic consequences if strong current passes through the heart, brain, or spinal column.

FAT BLOCKERS/HERBAL SUPPLEMENTS

Recently, "fat blockers" have been promoted to allow individuals to eat their favorite foods and still lose weight. Presumably, the varied ingredients, including zinc, St.-John's-wort, synephrine, chromium, and a compound called chitosan, will absorb most of the fat in the diet, and facilitate its excretion. Without exception, research studies have failed to confirm the effectiveness of these products which could have serious adverse side effects. For example, ingredients like synephrine could be harmful to persons with heart disease, diabetes, or hypertension.

A variety of "all-natural" herbal supplements have also been touted as effective in enhancing weight loss. One of the primary ingredients, mahuang, contains ephedra (ephedrine), which is a potent stimulant that can influence the nervous and cardiovascular systems and can cause a marked increase in heart rate and blood pressure. Although anecdotal reports suggest these may, in some persons, promote modest weight loss, a number of deaths and serious adverse reactions, such as chest pain, seizures, and heart attack, have been reported with these products.

LOW-CARBOHYDRATE DIETS

Sugar Busters!, The Zone, Dr. Atkins' New Diet Revolution, Protein Power, and The Carbohydrate Addict's Diet are some of the latest fad diets that have become popular – and controversial. The basic claim of these diets is that carbohydrates make you fat and that insulin causes obesity. These diets focus on blood-sugar levels, and blame carbohydrates for causing a sudden rise in blood-sugar levels. As blood-sugar levels rise, insulin is released, and sends sugar to the brain and to the muscles to be burned for energy, while the excess gets stored as fat. The theory is that if you eat more protein and fat and limit your intake of carbohydrate, the rapid rise in blood sugar is avoided and less sugar will be stored for fat. These diets also claim that by eating a high-fat/high-protein diet, the body will metabolize fat instead of carbohydrates for energy. However, there is no scientific evidence to back up the authors' claims. The rapid weight loss that people may experience while on these diets is primarily from water and protein losses, not fat.

Low calorie diets that limit carbohydrate intake can have serious nutrition and health consequences. They eliminate many food groups that provide essential nutrients, energy, and fiber to the diet (e.g., breads, grains, cereals, fruits, and vegetables). They also do not teach or promote good nutritional habits. The dieter learns very little regarding wise food choices or about making lifestyle changes that will help to maintain weight loss. In addition, these diets can cause dehydration that persists until the diet is over. Finally, low-calorie diets provide limited carbohydrates for glycogen replacement. As a result, the dieter quickly becomes glycogen depleted, making exercising difficult, especially when combined with dehydration. These factors help set any exercising dieter up for ultimate failure.

A CASE STUDY

Ms. I.M. Overwaite, a 40-year-old secretary, is 5 feet 3 inches and weighs 140 pounds. She has 30 percent body fat and lives a sedentary lifestyle, although she is a member of a local health/fitness club. Her diet log shows that she usually either skips breakfast or has a doughnut and coffee with cream. She drinks coffee all morning to keep her going. Lunch and dinner are often high-fat selections from fast-food restaurants. Her assessed need for daily caloric intake is about 2,100 Calories (140 times 15 Calories).

- Overwaite wants to reduce her body weight by 25 lbs to reach a weight of 115 lbs. However, a body weight of 125 lbs happens to be the lowest weight that she has been able to achieve and maintain (as an adult) for a period of 6 months or more.
- Overwaite reduces her intake by 250 Calories for a daily total of 1,850. She starts eating a breakfast of water or juice, a bagel, fruit, and/or cereal, and limits herself to 2 cups of coffee each morning. To avoid going to fast-food restaurants, Overwaite brings her lunch to work and carries lean-meat sandwiches on whole grain bread, fruit, soups, pretzels, salads and water, iced tea, or juice. For dinner, she tries to prepare meals each weekend to freeze for weeknights. This way, Overwaite can quickly warm pasta, chicken breasts, or fish. To stay away from the vending machine, she stashes snacks at her desk, including dry cereal, fruit, cut-up vegetables, and graham crackers. At home, she now has skim milk, fat-free salad dressings, low-fat cheeses, and reduced-fat crackers. Occasionally, she will satisfy her sweet tooth with frozen yogurt.
- Overwaite begins a daily exercise program at her health/fitness club. Three days a week, she exercises on either a stair-climbing machine or an elliptical-striding machine for 20 minutes, followed by a 5-minute workout on an upper-body machine.

Two days a week, she works out on a recumbent cycle and completes a 5-machine strength circuit (chest press, lat row, leg press, shoulder press, lat pulldown) for 30 minutes combined. In addition, she has purposefully increased her physical activity during her daily routine (e.g., eliminating multiple home extension phones, using the stairs at work, parking farther away from the store when shopping, and gardening 2 evenings a week).

• Ten weeks into her program, Overwaite has lost 15 lbs, and her current body weight is 125 lbs. She feels energized, looks better, and is motivated to maintain her new, healthy eating and exercise habits.

A WINNING GAME PLAN

The most appropriate approach for achieving permanent weight loss is a sensible diet combined with a program of sound exercise that includes planned aerobic conditioning, increased lifestyle physical activity, and strength training. While such a weight-control "game plan" may not produce as rapid a weight loss as the more popularly promoted, very low-calorie diets, it will provide individuals with a medically sound and effective strategy for "winning the losing game." Almost without exception, very low-calorie diets, largely as a result of their detrimental effects on resting metabolic rate, set individuals up for weight regain and failure. A sensible diet-exercise approach to weight reduction tends to produce a rate of weight loss of about 1 to 2 pounds per week (the rate recommended by most experts). Although it might take longer for some of your clients to reach their desired weight-control goals, any weight lost in this manner tends to be truly lost, not momentarily misplaced.

Recommended Reading

American College of Sports Medicine. *ACSM's Exercise Management for Persons with Chronic Diseases and Disabilities*. Champaign, IL: Human Kinetics Publishers, Inc., 1997.

American College of Sports Medicine. *ACSM's Resource Manual for Guidelines for Exercise Testing and Prescription*, 4th ed. Philadelphia, PA: Lippincott Williams & Wilkins, 2001.

American College of Sports Medicine. Position Statement on Proper and Improper Weight Loss Programs. *Medicine & Science in Sports & Exercise* 15(1):9, 1983.

American Council on Exercise. *Clinical Exercise Specialist Manual: ACE's Source for Training Special Populations*. San Diego, CA: American Council on Exercise, 1999.

Anderson, R, Brownell, KD, Haskell, WL. *The Health & Fitness Club Leader's Guide*. Dallas, TX: American Health Publishing Co., 1992.

Bryant, CX, Peterson, JA. Weight loss: Unfolding the truth. *Fitness Management* 10(6):42-44, 1994.

Clark, N. *Nancy Clark's Sports Nutrition Guidebook*, 2nd ed. Champaign, IL: Human Kinetics Publishers, Inc., 1997.

Franklin, BA. Losing weight without vigorous exercise or dieting: Unfounded gadgets, gimmicks, and fraudulent claims. *Journal of the Hong Kong College of Cardiology* 9(Suppl.):71-77, 2001.

Franklin, BA. The downside of our technological revolution? An obesity-conducive environment. *American Journal of Cardiology* 87:1093-1095, 2001.

Hill, JO, Melanson, EL. Overview of the determinants of overweight and obesity: Current evidence and research issues. *Medicine & Science in Sports & Exercise* 31(11 Suppl.):S515-S521, 1999.

Manore, MM. Running on empty: Health consequences of chronic dieting in active women. *ACSM's Health & Fitness Journal* 2(2):24-31, 1998.

Manore, MM, Thompson, JL. *Sport Nutrition for Health and Performance*. Champaign, IL: Human Kinetics Publishers, Inc., 2000.

McInnis, KJ. Exercise for obese clients: Benefits, limitations, guidelines. *ACSM's Health & Fitness Journal* 4(1):25-31, 2000.

Nieman, DC. *The Exercise-Health Connection*. Champaign, IL: Human Kinetics Publishers, Inc., 1998.

Nieman, DC. *Fitness and Sports Medicine: An Introduction*, 3rd ed. Palo Alto, CA: Bull Publishing Company, 1995.

Parr, RB. Weight loss: What works and what doesn't. *ACSM's Health & Fitness Journal* 2(2):12-17, 1998.

Peterson, JA, Bryant, CX (eds). *The StairMaster Fitness Handbook*, 2nd ed. Champaign, IL: Sagamore Publishing Company, Inc., 1995.

Porcari, JP. Fat-burning exercise: Fit or farce. *Fitness Management* 10(8):40-41, 1994.

Ross, R, Freeman, JA, Janssen, I. Exercise alone is an effective strategy for reducing obesity and related comorbidities. *ACSM's Exercise and Sport Sciences Reviews* 28(4):165-170, 2000.

CHAPTER 22

EXERCISE AND AGING

*T*he ranks of the elderly are rapidly increasing. There are currently almost 35 million Americans over the age of 65 (nearly 13 percent of the population or approximately one in every eight Americans). According to one estimate, there are more people in the world over the age of 65 today, than the total of all those who previously lived to this age! Moreover, in the United States, the over-85 age group is the fastest growing segment of the population.

According to experts in the field of gerontology, the primary issue among older adults is that of the quality of life. It has been estimated by the National Center for Health Statistics that a significant portion of an individual's "golden years" is spent dealing with a variety of health problems, chronic diseases, and ailments. Inescapably, human beings experience a decline in the function of most physiologic systems of the body as they age. These normal, yet irreversible, physiological changes that occur over an individual's lifetime are collectively referred to as the aging process.

EFFECTS OF TIME

The cardiovascular system undergoes changes as a person ages. These changes, coupled with alterations occurring in both the pulmonary and muscular systems, are responsible for a steady decline in maximal oxygen uptake ($\dot{V}O_{2max}$) as a person ages (Figure 22-1). Some of the more prominent alterations that occur include:

- A decrease in the sympathetic nerve activity to the heart that results in a lower attainable maximal heart rate and a reduced strength of heart contraction.
- A decrease in the elasticity of the major blood vessels that results in elevated blood pressure (at rest and during activity).
- An increase in the stiffness of cardiac muscle leads to a reduction in the pumping efficiency of the heart.

Aging also causes major changes in the pulmonary system. A decline in the structural integrity of the alveoli (the functional unit of the lungs) reduces the surface area for gas exchange and thereby limits the diffusion capacity for oxygen to the blood. The elasticity of lung tissue and the strength of respiratory muscles decrease and rib cage stiffness increases with aging. The combined effect is an increase in the energy cost of breathing.

The musculoskeletal system undergoes numerous changes as individuals age. A progressive, steady decline in muscle mass and strength (especially of the lower extremities)

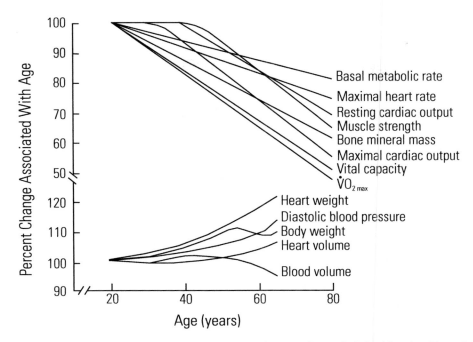

Figure 22-1. Aging is accompanied by a decrease in cardiorespiratory and musculoskeletal function. Many of these changes also occur during the transition from a trained to an untrained state. (Modified from Nieman, DC. *Fitness and Sports Medicine: An Introduction,* 3rd ed. Palo Alto, CA: Bull Publishing Company, 1995.)

occurs with age, leading to deficiencies in gait and balance, loss of functional mobility, increased risk of falling, and, ultimately, a loss of independence. Muscle mitochondrial and enzymatic changes, which reduce the ability of the muscles to extract oxygen from the blood, occur as a result of aging. Aging is also associated with a decrease in bone mineral content, which occurs in both sexes and increases the risk for osteoporosis and bone fractures. With age, increased stiffness of connective tissue results in a loss of joint flexibility and mobility.

These are a brief overview of a few of the various physiological changes that occur with aging. While most bodily systems experience an age-related decline in function, there is some good news. A significant portion (some estimates have been as high as 50 percent) of this physiological decline can be attributed to disuse atrophy resulting from physical inactivity. In the words of Hippocrates, the father of medicine, "All parts of the body which have function, if used in moderation and exercised in labors in which each is accustomed, become thereby healthy, well-developed, and age more slowly; but, if unused and left idle, they become liable to disease, defective in growth, and age quickly."

EFFECTS OF EXERCISE

A critical question concerning the aging process is: Can regular exercise slow down the biological changes that occur over the course of an individual's lifetime? The answer appears to be a resounding "yes," although the extent to which exercising on a regular basis can affect the response of certain bodily systems to aging is generally unknown. Interestingly, many of the changes that are associated with aging are similar to those that occur during

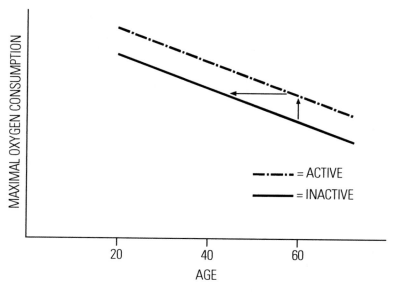

Figure 22-2. Influence of endurance exercise training on an inactive 60-year-old. The typical increase in maximal oxygen consumption (~20%) transforms the individual's aerobic fitness to what it was at the age of 40, corresponding to a 20-year functional rejuvenation.

prolonged bed rest and weightlessness. Among the more common changes are a decline in cardiovascular and pulmonary function, a reduction in muscle size and strength, an increase in body fat, and a decrease in bone mass. At the least, a physically active lifestyle can positively affect these age-related declines that, in large part, may be attributed to the fact that most people become less active as they age.

CARDIORESPIRATORY ADAPTATIONS

Numerous research studies have shown that elderly individuals who exercise can achieve an impressive cardiorespiratory training effect. For example, even though $\dot{V}O_{2max}$ declines in everyone as we get older, physically active individuals are able to slow their average rate of decline in $\dot{V}O_{2max}$ by up to 50 percent. This means that an active 60-year-old person can be as aerobically fit as a 40-year-old sedentary person (Figure 22-2). In addition, older individuals who remain physically active do not experience the typical rise in blood pressure that occurs with aging.

MUSCULOSKELETAL ADAPTATIONS

Several recent studies have shown that strength training can forestall the rate of deterioration of the musculoskeletal system in older persons. In these studies, individuals who engaged in a resistance-training program maintained their strength. In fact, strength levels actually increased dramatically. In comparison, inactive individuals typically show a 20 percent loss in strength by age 65. Participants in the resistance-training groups in these studies also demonstrated an increase in muscle mass. Finally, proper strength training has been shown to maintain or increase joint flexibility, because it involves exercising through a full range of motion.

Body Composition Adaptations

Exercise can reduce the accumulation of body fat that accompanies aging and can slow, if not reverse, the concomitant loss of fat-free mass. Older people can maintain the level of body fat they had in their youth if they remain consistently physically active and adhere to an appropriate diet throughout their lives. Thus, strength training can attenuate the loss of lean muscle mass that often accompanies aging.

Lifestyle Changes

Exercising on a regular basis can have a positive effect on the overall quality of life in older adults in many ways, including:

- Regular exercise can provide older individuals with the functional capacity necessary to perform common activities of daily living such as shopping, ambulation, self-care, and cooking meals.
- Physical activity can help an older person adapt to the changing social roles that sometimes accompany advancing age. For example, an activity program may replace work in the life of the individual.
- Social interaction can be promoted through exercise programs. Physical activity can help in adjusting to a traumatic event (e.g., retirement, the death of a loved one) by providing an avenue for social interaction and combating feelings of depression.
- Regular exercise can assist individuals in adjusting to retirement. For example, it can be a relatively inexpensive activity for those on a reduced income. In addition, maintaining physical fitness enables older persons to remain independent, thereby incurring fewer of the costs for assistance that arise if they need home management and personal care.
- Old age frequently requires the elderly to scale down their housing or move into an apartment or retirement community. Because many retirement communities do not take people who are physically dependent, individuals who maintain their physical fitness levels will have more diverse options in choosing living arrangements. In several multilevel retirement communities, for example, the average cost for assisted living (e.g., help in making the bed, meals, home finances) is estimated to be more than double the monthly average cost required to live independently.

Developing an Exercise Program

To ensure that older individuals are medically safe to exercise, they should first see a physician and undergo a physical examination and evaluation *before* a physical activity program is initiated. The extent of the evaluation depends on an individual's age, health status, and the strenuousness of the anticipated exercise regimen. Men over age 45, women over age 55, and all individuals at moderate-to-high risk (i.e., individuals with two or more coronary risk factors, one or more signs/symptoms listed in Table 22-1, or with known cardiovascular, pulmonary, or metabolic diseases) are strongly encouraged to undergo a medically supervised, graded exercise test, especially if vigorous exercise is contemplated.

Table 22-1. Major Signs or Symptoms Suggestive of Cardiovascular and Pulmonary Disease*

- Pain, discomfort (or other anginal equivalents) in the chest, neck, jaw, arms, and other areas that may be due to myocardial ischemia
- Shortness of breath at rest or with mild exertion
- Dizziness or syncope (fainting)
- Orthopnea or paroxysmal nocturnal dyspnea (difficult or labored breathing)
- Ankle edema (swelling)
- Palpitations or tachycardia (elevated heart rate)
- Intermittent, severe leg pain (claudication)
- Known heart murmur
- Unusual fatigue

These symptoms must be interpreted in the clinical context in which they appear because they are not all specific for cardiovascular, pulmonary, or metabolic diseases.

* Adapted from American College of Sports Medicine. *ACSM's Guidelines for Exercise Testing and Prescription*, 6th ed. Philadelphia, PA: Lippincott Williams & Wilkins, 2000.

The next step is to develop a comprehensive exercise program based on scientifically documented information. A safe and effective exercise prescription enables individuals to achieve as much as possible (effectiveness), as quickly as possible (efficiency), and without undue risk of injury, which is most important. If an exercise regimen is to be relatively risk-free for older individuals, it must be tailored to age, gender, and current level of fitness.

A safety-oriented exercise program also involves starting at an intensity appropriate for the individual and then progressing gradually. The temptation to do too much too soon should be avoided. Moderation is essential. A major cause of musculoskeletal injuries is overuse – placing demands on the body that it simply is not capable of handling. A sound exercise program always includes provisions for stretching the major muscles and joints before and after exercising. It also ensures that individuals get proper rest along with exercise. Rest enables individuals to recover from the demands of exercise placed on their bodies.

The final step is for individuals to listen to their bodies as they exercise. They must respond accordingly to specific warning signs or symptoms of exertional intolerance, which include chest or stomach pain or discomfort, dizziness, palpitations (e.g., high or irregular heart rates), and/or fainting spells (Table 22-2).

Warmup and cool-down activities should be an essential part of all exercise programs – particularly those involving older participants. The purpose of warmup activities is to prepare the body, especially the cardiovascular and musculoskeletal systems, for the conditioning or stimulus phase of the exercise session. The cool-down phase assures that venous return to the heart is maintained during recovery, reducing the possibility of postexercise hypotension and related complications. Light aerobic endurance activities, coupled with stretching activities, provide the fundamental basis for both the warmup and cool-down phases.

The length of the warmup and cool-down periods depends on several factors, including the type of activity, the anticipated exercise intensity, and the age and fitness of the participant.

Table 22-2. Signs and Symptoms of Exertional Intolerance

Unusual or severe fatigue
Nausea
Difficult or labored breathing (dyspnea)
Dizziness
Lightheadedness
Palpitations (heart rhythm irregularities)
Excessive tachycardia or bradycardia (fast or slow heart rates)
Fainting (syncope)
Tightness or pain in the chest
Unsteadiness
Severe pallor
Mental confusion
Intermittent, severe leg pain (claudication)
Loss of muscle control
Persistent joint or muscle pain

In general, the warmup and cool-down phases, at a minimum, should last approximately 5 to 10 minutes each. If the individual has less time than usual for working out, it is recommended that the time allotted for the aerobic phase of the workout be reduced, while retaining sufficient time for the warmup and cool-down phases.

AEROBIC CONDITIONING

Based on the existing scientific evidence relevant to prescribing exercise for healthy adults and the need for such guidelines, the American College of Sports Medicine (ACSM) developed a recent position paper (1998) on exercise prescription that included the following recommendations regarding the quantity and quality of exercise for developing and maintaining cardiorespiratory fitness and desirable body composition in a healthy adult:

1. *Frequency of training:* 3 to 5 days per week.
2. *Intensity:* 40% to 85% of maximal oxygen uptake ($\dot{V}O_{2max}$), or maximum heart rate reserve, or 55% to 90% of maximal heart rate. It should also be noted that exercise of a relatively low-to-moderate intensity may provide important health benefits and may result in increased fitness in some individuals (i.e., clients who were previously sedentary and unfit).
3. *Duration of training:* 20 to 60 minutes of continuous or intermittent aerobic-activity (a minimum of 10-minute) bouts accumulated throughout the day. The actual time spent in exercise generally depends on the relative intensity of the activity. For example, activities involving a lower intensity should be conducted over a longer period of time. The emphasis should be placed on the total amount of work performed, which can be estimated by the caloric expenditure associated with the activity.
4. *Mode of activity:* An appropriate modality for developing cardiorespiratory fitness

is any activity that uses the large muscle groups, can be maintained continuously, and is rhythmic and aerobic in nature (e.g., running, jogging, walking, stair stepping, aquatics, elliptical cross-training, bicycling, rowing, cross-country skiing, and various endurance game activities). At the beginning of an exercise program, low-impact activities such as walking, cycling, and stair stepping are recommended.

5. *Rate of progression:* In most instances, the ability of the body to adapt to the stresses imposed upon it (sometimes referred to as the training effect) allows individuals to gradually increase the total work done over time. In continuous exercise, increasing the work performed can be achieved by increasing either the intensity of the exercise, the duration, or both. Major conditioning effects are typically observed during the first 6 to 8 weeks of an exercise program. An individual's exercise prescription should be adjusted as these occur. The degree of adjustment depends on the individual involved, additional feedback from periodic assessments, and/or the exercise performance of the individual during the exercise sessions.

MUSCULOSKELETAL CONDITIONING

Musculoskeletal conditioning includes exercises to facilitate an adequate level of flexibility, as well as for developing an appropriate level of muscular fitness. Flexibility was previously discussed in the sections on the warmup and cool-down phases of an exercise session. Achieving and maintaining an adequate range of motion should always be an objective of a comprehensive exercise prescription, especially for older adults. Flexibility is important for several reasons, because it may reduce an individual's potential for injury and improve his or her ability to perform certain physical and sports-related tasks.

The warmup phase of the exercise session should include light activities to increase both heart rate and internal body temperature, followed by flexibility exercises that are specifically designed to stretch the musculature around the body's major skeletal joints. Attempting to stretch a cold muscle can be dangerous to the soft tissues surrounding the muscle. No matter how controlled the movement, forcing a muscle through a full, normal range of motion (and beyond) without appropriately warming it up is both unsafe and counterproductive. A general exercise prescription for achieving and maintaining flexibility should adhere to the following guidelines:

Frequency	-	daily
Intensity	-	to a position of mild discomfort
Duration	-	10 to 30 seconds for each stretch
Repetitions	-	2 to 6 for each stretch
Type	-	static, with a major emphasis on the low-back and hamstrings area because of the high prevalence of low-back pain syndrome in our society

Specific guidelines for developing muscular fitness are not as universally accepted as those for attaining flexibility. Considerable debate exists regarding the most appropriate protocol for developing muscular strength and muscular endurance (collectively referred to as muscular fitness). What is generally accepted, however, is the fact that, like any system of the body, the muscular system responds to the demands placed upon it. There is also a growing awareness that resistance training, performed at least at a moderate intensity sufficient to develop and maintain lean body tissue, should be an integral part of a comprehensive adult fitness program.

According to the ACSM, the recommended minimum amount of resistance training to achieve a training effect in older adults is 8 to 10 exercises involving the major muscle groups of the body performed at least two days per week. Each exercise should be performed in one set of 10 to 15 repetitions. Considerable evidence suggests that for resistance training to be safe, effective, and efficient, individuals should:

- Adhere to the proper techniques for performing a particular exercise.
- Exercise to the point of volitional muscular fatigue.
- Perform every exercise through a full, pain-free range of motion.
- Exercise both agonist and antagonist muscle groups.
- Perform the eccentric (lowering), as well as the concentric (raising), phases of a lift in a controlled manner.
- Include exercises for all the major muscle groups of the body, not just a few selected muscle groups.
- Work out (if possible) with a training partner who can provide feedback, support, and motivation.
- Never perform a breath-holding maneuver while strength training, because it can transiently raise blood pressure to a potentially unsafe level, cause symptoms of lightheadedness or dizziness, or both.

(*Note:* For more detailed information regarding strength training for older adults, refer to Chapter 12.)

LIVING SMART

Depending on an individual's point of reference, reflecting on the aging process may present a dismal picture. In fact, a generation ago much confusion and fatalism existed regarding aging. Old age was viewed as the time of inevitable and irreversible decline. By no means, however, is the future as bleak as it might first appear. With respect to the effects of the aging process, individuals can control their own destiny to a great extent. Fortunately, much of the deterioration that was once attributed to aging is now linked to physical inactivity. According to several noted gerontologists, an essential ingredient to healthy aging is regular physical activity. Of all age groups, older individuals stand the most to gain by adopting an active lifestyle. Not only do active persons live longer, but disability is postponed and compressed into fewer years near the end of life (i.e., an improved quality of life).

Regular exercise can and does slow down many of the debilitating effects of advancing years. The master guideline with regard to exercise and aging is that it is never too late to start. It is not "you're too old to exercise," it is "you're too old not to exercise." The risk for many health problems and diseases commonly associated with aging (hypertension, depression, osteoporosis, diabetes, etc.) is decreased with regular exercise. Irrefutable evidence exists to support the fact that mixing strict adherence to sound exercise principles with a personal commitment to common sense and patience could well serve as an appropriate recipe for improving and sustaining an independent lifestyle for the elderly. In other words, "living smart" is the fundamental priority for "living well" ... at any age.

Recommended Reading

American College of Sports Medicine. Position Stand. Exercise and physical activity for older adults. *Medicine & Science in Sports & Exercise* 30:992-1008, 1998.

Bortz, WM. *We Live Too Short and Die Too Long.* New York, NY: Bantam Books, 1991.

Corbin, DE. Exercise Programming for Older Adults. In: American College of Sports Medicine, *ACSM's Resource Manual for Guidelines for Exercise Testing and Prescription*, 4th ed. Philadelphia, PA: Lippincott Williams & Wilkins, 2001.

Elia, EA. Exercise and the elderly. *Clinical Sports Medicine* 10:141-155, 1991.

Evans, W, Rosenberg, I. *Biomarkers.* New York, NY: Simon & Schuster, 1991.

Franklin, BA. The fountain of youth in physical fitness. *ACSM's Health & Fitness Journal* 1(2):32, 1997.

Green, JS, Crouse, SF. The effects of endurance training on functional capacity in the elderly: A meta-analysis. *Medicine & Science in Sports & Exercise* 27:920-926, 1995.

Kavanagh, T, Shephard, RJ. Can regular sports participation slow the aging process? Data on masters athletes. *The Physician and Sportsmedicine* 18(6):94-104, 1990.

Nieman, DC. *Fitness and Sports Medicine: An Introduction*, 3rd ed. Palo Alto, CA: Bull Publishing Company, 1995.

Pollock, ML, Carroll, JF, Graves, JE, et al. Injuries and adherence to walk/jog and resistance training programs in the elderly. *Medicine & Science in Sports & Exercise* 23:1194-1200, 1991.

Pollock, ML, Gaesser, GA, Butcher, JD, et al. The recommended quantity and quality of exercise for developing and maintaining cardiorespiratory and muscular fitness, and flexibility in healthy adults. *Medicine & Science in Sports & Exercise* 30:975-991, 1998.

Pollock, ML, Mengelkoch, LJ, Graves, JE, et al. Twenty-year follow-up of aerobic power and body composition of older track athletes. *Journal of Applied Physiology* 82:1508-1516, 1997.

Rogers, MA, Evans, WJ. Changes in skeletal muscle with aging: Effects of exercise training. In: Holloszy, J (ed). *Exercise and Sport Sciences Reviews.* Baltimore, MD: Williams & Wilkins, 1993.

Taunton, JE, Martin, AD, Rhodes, EC, et al. Exercise for the older woman: Choosing the right prescription. *British Journal of Sports Medicine* 31:5-10, 1997.

Vita, AJ, Terry, RB, Hubert, HB, Fries, JF. Aging, health risks, and cumulative disability. *New England Journal of Medicine* 338(15):1035-1041, 1998.

CHAPTER 23

● ●

EXERCISE ADHERENCE

*I*t's well-documented that exercise has a positive effect on the quality of life. Stress reduction, disease prevention or management, and looking and feeling better are a few of the benefits of regular exercise. However, before an exercise program can have a measurable impact on a person's life, it must meet at least two criteria. First, it must place an appropriate demand on the various physiological systems of the body (cardiovascular, muscular, and metabolic) so that favorable adaptation and improvement can occur. Second, an exercise regimen must be designed to maximize an individual's willingness to stick with the program.

Of the two criteria, placing a demand on the body is fairly straightforward, whereas creating a commitment to exercise is substantially more difficult. Developing an appropriate exercise prescription involves following established quantitative guidelines (e.g., workout "X" number of days per week, for "Y" number of minutes per session, at "Z" level of intensity). But, organizing an exercise program that enhances long-term adherence is another matter. Research shows that dropout rates among those who voluntarily enter exercise programs are highest during the first 90 days, reaching nearly 50 percent within one year (Figure 23-1). Exercise is

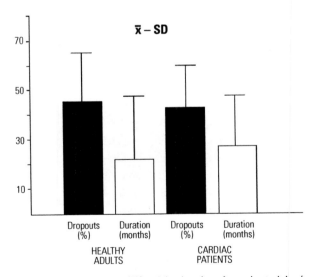

Figure 23-1. Relationship between the dropout rate (%) and the duration of exercise training (months) in healthy adults (7 studies) and patients with coronary artery disease (14 studies) with a total of 3887 cardiac patients. Values are expressed as the mean ± standard deviation (x ± SD). The vertical axis represents the dropout rate (%) as well as the average duration (months). (Reprinted with permission from American College of Sports Medicine. *ACSM's Guidelines for Exercise Testing and Prescription*, 6th ed. Philadelphia, PA: Lippincott Williams & Wilkins, 2000.)

not unlike other health-related behaviors (e.g., smoking cessation, weight loss, and dietary modification) in that approximately half the individuals who initiate a change of behavior will continue, regardless of the type of exercise program or their initial health status.

The importance of exercise adherence to achieving the many physiological and psychosocial benefits of physical activity seems obvious. One of the key precepts for developing an optimal level of fitness is that participants must engage in exercise on a regular basis. Once individuals stop exercising regularly, their fitness gains diminish and health benefits decline. Eventually, a person's level of fitness will return to what it was before he/she started the personal conditioning program.

Two key questions arise with regard to sticking with an exercise regimen: Why do people drop out of exercise programs, and what can be done to increase an individual's exercise adherence? Unfortunately, the answers are not clear-cut. Just as people join an exercise program for varying reasons, they also drop out for different reasons. A factor that affects one individual may not be as important to another. A list of factors that may negatively impact exercise adherence is presented in Table 23-1.

According to many experts, four of the most critical factors regarding exercise adherence are: (1) injuries, (2) time, (3) boredom, and (4) results. Not surprisingly, individuals won't stick with exercise programs in which they get hurt. The old adage, "no pain, no gain," makes no sense to most people. Individuals prefer to engage in exercise regimens that are time-efficient, which will allow them to continue to enjoy valued hobbies and other interests. Fortunately, individuals can experience the innumerable benefits of exercise without enduring marathon workouts.

Common sense dictates that people prefer to participate in exercise programs that are enjoyable. Boredom can have a devastating impact on an exercise commitment. At the

Table 23-1. Factors That May Negatively Affect Exercise Adherence

Personal Factors	Program Factors	Other Factors
Smoker	Inconvenient time/location	Lack of support from
Inactive leisure time	Excessive cost	significant other
Inactive occupation	High-intensity exercise	Inclement weather
Blue collar worker	Lack of exercise variety	Excessive job travel
Type A personality	(e.g., running only)	Injury
Increased physical strength	Exercises alone	Medical problems
Extroverted	Lack of positive feedback or	Job change/move
Introverted	reinforcement	Transportation
Poor credit rating	Inflexible exercise goals	difficulties
Overweight and/or overfat	Low enjoyability ratings	
Poor self-image	Poor exercise leadership	
Depression		
Hypochondria		
Anxiety		

least, the activity should allow an exerciser to disassociate from the negative aspects of the exercise experience (fatigue, muscle soreness) and to refocus on more positive factors. For example, the high-tech features on many contemporary exercise machines are designed not only to provide physiological and performance feedback, but also to engage the exerciser in a diversion from the physical effort required for the exercise.

Achieving meaningful results is perhaps the most important adherence factor for many individuals. Individuals typically participate in exercise programs to achieve specific goals (e.g., weight loss, stress reduction, improved strength, etc.). Obviously, they're more likely to continue expending the time and energy involved if their efforts produce desired and meaningful results.

STRATEGIES FOR INCREASING EXERCISE ADHERENCE

The fundamental basis of any exercise program that aims to increase retention is that the program must meet the unique needs of each participant. A number of possible steps that may lead to enhanced participant interest, enthusiasm, and, ultimately, long-term adherence include:

- *Recruit physician support of the health and fitness program.* Perhaps the single most important factor determining participation in exercise is a strong recommendation from a primary care physician. Basic physician counseling is highly effective in motivating individuals to make other significant lifestyle changes (e.g., smoking cessation).
- *Provide exercise facilities and locker rooms that are appropriately maintained.* The cleanliness of the equipment and facilities is critical to most participants. Fortunately, achieving this is easily within reach of most health/fitness facilities. For example, bright lights, light-colored walls, and bright carpets all suggest a clean environment. In addition, a facility should have a satisfactory ventilation system and appropriate control over temperature and humidity. Regular maintenance and calibration of all exercise equipment should be a standard practice.
- *Clarify individual needs to establish the motive to exercise.* An initial semi-structured interview will allow you to determine exactly what a client hopes to gain from an exercise program. During the interview, you should clarify the individual's needs and expectations, and establish a personalized schedule to monitor progress and reassess goals.
- *Emphasize short-term goals.* Goal setting should be viewed much like climbing a ladder, with an emphasis placed on reasonable distances between rungs. Individuals should be oriented toward short-term objectives that are specific, clearly defined, and realistically attainable. The key is to keep clients focused on short-term and intermediate goals, rather than the final objective.
- *Minimize injury/complications with a mild-to-moderate exercise prescription.* If personal trainers increase the activity dosage for novice exercisers too abruptly, they will often become discouraged with physical conditioning regimens due to either muscular soreness or orthopedic injury. Using an exercise prescription form (Figure 23-2) is an ideal way to ensure that your recommendations are understood

---

Name of MD _____

Name _____ Age _____ Starting Date _____

Clinical Status*:
Normal   Arrhythmia   Angina   CABG   CAD   HTN   MI   PTCA   VR

Note: This prescription is valid only if you remain on the same medications (type and dose), and you are in the same clinical status as on the day your exercise test was conducted.

Contraindications: Angina at rest, fever, illness
Temperature and weather extremes (below 30°F or more than 80°F with high humidity)

Activities to Avoid: Sudden strenuous lifting or carrying
Exertion that leads to holding your breath

Exercise Type: Aerobic types of exercise that are continuous, dynamic, and repetitive in nature

Frequency: Times/day_____ Days/week_____

Duration: Total duration of exercise session _____ min

To be divided as follows:

Warmup (light flexibility/stretching routine): _____ min

Aerobic training activity: _____ to _____ min

Cool-down (slow walking and stretching): _____ min

Intensity:

Target heart rate _____ to _____ beats/min

_____ to _____ beats/10 sec

Perceived exertion should not exceed "strong/heavy"

Reevaluation

Your next graded exercise test is due:_____
Call our office to schedule an appointment. Phone:_____

Exercise Physiologist:_____

---

* Clinical Status abbreviations: CABG = coronary artery bypass graft; CAD = coronary artery disease; HTN = hypertension; MI = myocardial infarction (i.e., heart attack); PTCA = percutaneous transluminal coronary angioplasty; VR = valve replacement.

Figure 23-2. Exercise prescription form for healthy adults or cardiac patients.

and followed. Excessive intensity (>90% $\dot{V}O_{2max}$), frequency (>5 days/week), or duration (>45 minutes/session) of training offer the participant little additional gain in aerobic capacity ($\dot{V}O_{2max}$), yet the incidence of orthopedic injury increases substantially. A recommended prescription for individuals who are just beginning an exercise program is to "accumulate" 30 or more minutes of exercise every

Exercise Warnings

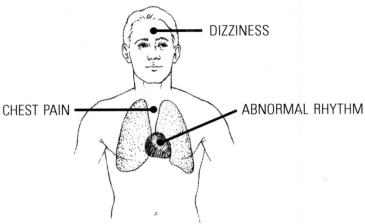

Figure 23-3. Abnormal signs and symptoms suggesting exercise intolerance.

other day, at a rating of perceived exertion (0 to 11) of 1 to 5 ("very weak" to "strong/heavy"). Research has shown similar training effects in subjects who completed three 10-minute bouts of moderate-intensity exercise per day versus those who performed a single "continuous" exercise bout of 30 minutes. In addition, warming up before exercising, wearing proper walking or running shoes while working out, and training on appropriate terrain (avoiding hard and uneven surfaces) should help minimize dropout rates due to injury. Finally, clients should be counseled to discontinue exercising and seek medical advice if they experience warning signs or symptoms of exertional intolerance, including abnormal heart rhythms (palpitations), chest pain or pressure, or dizziness (Figure 23-3).

- *Encourage group participation.* Group commitments tend to be stronger than those made individually. Often, the encouragement of a group can provide an individual with the incentive to continue exercising during periods of decreasing interest. Diminished levels of long-term adherence have been reported in programs where an individual exercises alone, as compared with those that incorporate group dynamics. Most people (approximately 90%) prefer group as opposed to individual exercise. Social reinforcement through camaraderie and companionship are potent motivators.

- *Emphasize fun and variety in the exercise program.* The type of exercise program has also been shown to influence long-term exercise adherence. For example, regimented calisthenics often become monotonous and boring, leading to poor exercise adherence. Another example of the negative effect a monotonous exercise routine can have on adherence involves individuals who purchase stationary exercise cycles for home use. Despite an initial enthusiasm for working out, many of these individuals quickly become exercise dropouts. Exercise conditioning regimens that offer the greatest variety and enjoyment are usually those that are most successful.

- *Employ periodic fitness testing to assess the client's response to the training program.* Favorable physiologic adaptations to regular endurance exercise include a decreased heart rate, blood pressure, and perceived exertion during submaximal exercise; increased physical work capacity and $\dot{V}O_{2max}$; reduced body weight and fat stores; and an improved serum lipid/lipoprotein profile. Such changes are powerful motivators that can produce renewed enthusiasm and dedication. Fortunately, each variable can readily be assessed with the proper testing equipment.

- *Include family members, significant others, and/or friends.* The attitude and support of those with whom an individual interacts most frequently helps determine whether that person will adhere to an exercise program. A client's significant other, as well as family and friends, can play an important role in this regard. The importance of this influence became evident in 1 study that showed the husband's adherence to the exercise program was directly related to the wife's attitude toward the program. Of those men whose spouses had a positive attitude toward the exercise program, 80% demonstrated good-to-excellent adherence, while only 20% exhibited fair-to-poor adherence (Figure 23-4). In contrast, when the spouse was neutral or negative, 40% showed good-to-excellent adherence and 60% demonstrated fair-to-poor adherence. These findings suggest that program counseling and educational gatherings, which include both participants and their significant others, help reduce misunderstandings and create positive attitudes that support exercise adherence.

- *Use progress charts to record exercise achievements.* The importance of immediate, positive feedback to reinforce desirable health-related behaviors is well-documented. A progress chart that allows participants to record daily and cumulative exercise achievements (e.g., mileage) can facilitate this objective. One example is the computerized progress report system used by the Cooper Institute for Aerobics Research in Dallas, Texas, which provides exercisers with an updated record of the number of "aerobic points" they have earned, miles they have run, and related training accomplishments. A practical alternative, however, is a progress chart that allows participants to record daily workout mileage. If the chart is strategically placed near the running track or a locker room, it can become a matter of pride to motivate individuals to increase their exercise totals.

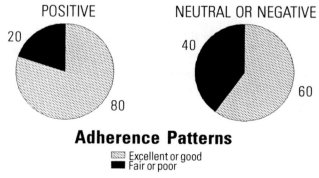

Figure 23-4. Relationship of wives' attitudes to husbands' adherence to an exercise-training program. Adapted from Heinzelman, F, Bagley, RW. Response to physical activity programs and their effects on health behavior. *Public Health Report* 85:905-911, 1970. (Reprinted with permission from American College of Sports Medicine. *ACSM's Guidelines for Exercise Testing and Prescription*, 6th ed. Philadelphia, PA: Lippincott Williams & Wilkins, 2000.)

- *Complement the standard exercise program format with recreational activities.* The standard warmup, endurance, and cool-down sequence employed in most adult fitness programs offers little in terms of fun or variety. This format can be enhanced by adding recreational activities to the collective exercise "experience." Whenever feasible, exercise leaders should consider modifying the recreational activity to minimize skill and competition and maximize participant success. For example, altering conventional volleyball rules to allow 1 bounce of the ball per side can facilitate longer rallies and provide additional fun, while minimizing the skill level required to enjoy the game. Many team games and individual sports can be adapted in a similar fashion. Through such modifications, the exercise leader will be better able to emphasize the primary goal of the activity – enjoyment of the game.
- *Play music during exercise sessions.* Appropriate background music may mask general fatigue and stimulate participants to exercise more energetically. Many individuals feel that stimulating music enhances their workouts, while reducing their perceived level of exertion at any given intensity of exercise. The proliferation of headset use appears to further substantiate the efficacy of using music as a motivator during exercise workouts.
- *Establish regularity of workouts.* If individuals start their workouts at the same time each day, they will be more likely to make exercise a habit. The availability of morning, evening, and weekend sessions should serve to further increase the compatibility of an exercise commitment with the varied schedules of participants.
- *Recognize client accomplishments through a system of rewards.* Peer recognition is another powerful motivator. Recognition of lifestyle, health, or exercise achievements can be made in the form of inexpensive trophies, plaques, ribbons, or certificates. An annual awards ceremony or banquet can also positively affect exercise adherence.
- *Provide qualified, enthusiastic exercise leaders.* Although numerous factors affect exercise adherence, arguably the single most important variable is the personal trainer or exercise professional. Health and fitness staff members should be well-trained, compassionate, sensitive, empathetic, tactful, innovative, and enthusiastic. Table 23-2 lists several behavioral strategies of the effective exercise professional. Workshop and certification offerings by professional associations (e.g., the American College of Sports Medicine [ACSM] and the American Council on Exercise [ACE]) can promote quality control, knowledge, and proficiency standards for program personnel.

ENCOURAGE LIFESTYLE PHYSICAL ACTIVITY

Despite nearly three decades of the so-called "exercise revolution," structured exercise programs have been only marginally effective in getting people to be more physically active. Why? Perhaps it's because planned exercise may extend the day or compete with other valued interests and responsibilities of daily life. Indeed, recent studies have shown that new members of fitness clubs typically use these facilities less than twice a month. According to the U.S. Surgeon General, more than 60 percent of American adults are not regularly physically active, and 25 percent of men and women report no leisure-time physical activity.

Table 23-2. Behavioral Strategies of an Effective Exercise Professional

1. Show sincere interest. Learn why clients have gotten involved in the program, and what they hope to achieve.
2. Remove as many barriers to program entrance and participation as possible. If cost, distance, childcare, or other factors make it difficult for clients to attend, help find ways to deal with them.
3. Be optimistic and enthusiastic in your instruction and guidance, and project a positive, caring attitude.
4. Develop a personal association with each client.
5. Learn clients' names and greet them with a handshake.
6. Consider the reasons why adults exercise (e.g., health, rehabilitation, recreation, weight loss, social, personal appearance, etc.) and allow for individual differences by providing clients with choices.
7. Don't overlook the importance of meaningful follow-up. Call or send a note if someone fails to show up for an appointment, or if someone has successive, unexplained absences. A phone call after your initial meeting may help sway a potential client who has not yet committed to joining your program.
8. Practice what you preach. Participate in the exercise sessions yourself.
9. Honor special days (e.g., birthdays) or exercise accomplishments with T-shirts, ribbons, or certificates.
10. Attend to all orthopedic and musculoskeletal problems immediately.
11. Counsel participants on proper foot apparel and exercise clothing.
12. Introduce first-time exercisers to the veterans on the gymnasium floor.
13. Reinforce and provide frequent feedback on appearance and lifestyle alterations. Personal feedback that helps track progress toward personal goals is particularly appropriate. Any interaction with a client is also a useful time to assess potential relapse and to intervene accordingly.
14. Use goal setting as a motivational tool. Build on areas of client-perceived interest (e.g., how would he/she like to be "better" or "improved").
15. Show your optimism, which can help create a positive self-fulfilling prophecy where clients succeed largely because of their belief that they can.
16. Give clear and concise information. Listen, summarize, and clarify to make sure that your recommendations have been correctly understood.

Over the last decade, researchers have reevaluated the scientific evidence linking physical inactivity with a variety of chronic diseases. These analyses suggest that the intensity or dosage of exercise needed to achieve health-related benefits is probably less than that required to improve fitness. Accordingly, frequent bouts of moderate-intensity activity (e.g., brisk walking, household chores, gardening, recreational sports) can be as effective as vigorous exercise, provided that the daily energy expenditure is comparable (Figure 23-5). In other words, the desk-bound executive who regularly jogs may not be any better off than the person who does periodic low-intensity activity throughout the day.

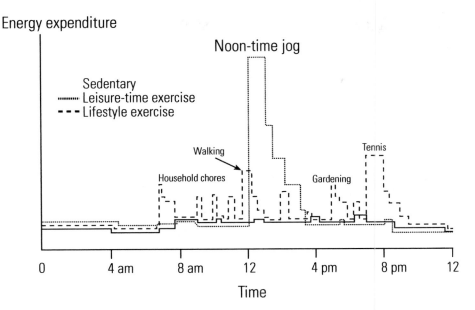

Figure 23-5. Theoretical patterns of physical activity for a sedentary person, an individual who engages in regular, leisure-time exercise (e.g., a noon jog), but is otherwise sedentary, and an individual who does less-intense, periodic activity throughout the day. Lifestyle activities may include moderate-intensity household chores, walking, gardening, and tennis. These may be as effective in promoting health benefits, provided that the total daily energy expenditure is comparable. (Adapted from Gordon, NF, et al. Life style exercise: A new strategy to promote physical activity for adults. *Journal of Cardiopulmonary Rehabilitation* 13(3):161-163, 1993.)

Recent research studies have confirmed that a lifestyle approach to physical activity can be as effective as a traditional exercise program. These findings are encouraging in that they support a wide range of choices for physical activity. Specific suggestions may include taking the stairs instead of the elevator and walking to the store instead of driving.

To assist your clients in tracking their daily activities, you might recommend that they consider buying a pedometer. These are easy to use and can be worn on the belt, at the midline of the thigh. The base models just count steps, whereas the newer electronic versions (which range from about $25 to $35) convert steps to miles and calories burned and include a built-in stopwatch. The conversion: 10,000 steps is roughly 5 miles or 500 Calories.

How much exercise is enough? Inactive people take 2,000 to 4,000 steps per day, moderately active people take 5,000 to 7,000 steps per day, and active people take at least 10,000 steps per day. And, glancing down at the pedometer and checking progress can provide the client with the motivation to go for an extra walk when they are short of their daily goal.

Although lifestyle exercise is not being suggested to replace more traditional workouts, it's a wonderful complement to any health and fitness program. Exercise professionals should consider broadening their client's recommendations from the traditional frequency, intensity, duration, and mode of training that are associated with structured exercise programs to promoting increased activity in daily living. The Activity Pyramid has been suggested as one way to facilitate this objective (Figure 23-6).

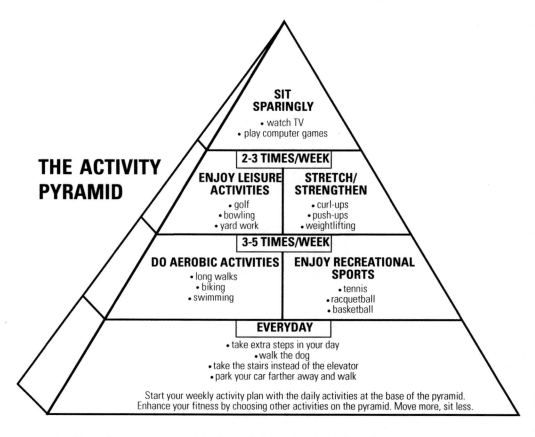

THE ACTIVITY PYRAMID

SIT SPARINGLY
- watch TV
- play computer games

2-3 TIMES/WEEK

ENJOY LEISURE ACTIVITIES
- golf
- bowling
- yard work

STRETCH/ STRENGTHEN
- curl-ups
- push-ups
- weightlifting

3-5 TIMES/WEEK

DO AEROBIC ACTIVITIES
- long walks
- biking
- swimming

ENJOY RECREATIONAL SPORTS
- tennis
- racquetball
- basketball

EVERYDAY
- take extra steps in your day
- walk the dog
- take the stairs instead of the elevator
- park your car farther away and walk

Start your weekly activity plan with the daily activities at the base of the pyramid.
Enhance your fitness by choosing other activities on the pyramid. Move more, sit less.

Figure 23-6. The Activity Pyramid. Copyright © 1999 Park Nicollet *Health Source®* Park Nicollet Institute. Reprinted bypermission.

WORKING TOGETHER

From a physical and mental health standpoint, an active lifestyle can easily be distinguished from a sedentary one. To help your clients receive the numerous benefits of exercise, however, you *must* get them to exercise on a regular basis. Sticking with a structured exercise program is one of the most beneficial and important things that individuals can do. By the same token, you should endeavor to do whatever you can to enhance the lifestyle exercise of your clients.

Recommended Reading

American College of Sports Medicine. *ACSM's Resource Manual for Guidelines for Exercise Testing and Prescription*, 4th ed. Philadelphia, PA: Lippincott Williams & Wilkins, 2001.
DeBusk, RF, Stenestrand, U, Sheehan, M, et al. Training effects of long versus short bouts of exercise in healthy subjects. *American Journal of Cardiology* 65:1010-1013, 1990.
Dishman, RK (ed). *Advances in Exercise Adherence*. Champaign, IL: Human Kinetics Publishers, Inc., 1994.

Franklin, BA. Program factors that influence exercise adherence: Practical adherence skills for the clinical staff. In: Dishman, RK (ed), *Exercise Adherence*. Champaign, IL: Human Kinetics Publishers, Inc., 1988.

Gordon, NF, Kohl, HW, Blair, SN. Life style exercise: A new strategy to promote physical activity for adults. *Journal of Cardiopulmonary Rehabilitation* 13(3):161-163, 1993.

Heinzelman, F, Bagley, RW. Response to physical activity programs and their effects on health behavior. *Public Health Report* 85:905-911, 1970.

Pollock, ML, Gettman, L, Milesis, C, et al. Effects of frequency and duration of training on attrition and incidence of injury. *Medicine & Science in Sports & Exercise* 9:31-36, 1977.

Rejewski, WJ, Kenney, EA. *Fitness Motivation: Preventing Participant Dropout.* Champaign, IL: Life Enhancement Publications, 1988.

APPENDIX

APPENDIX A

●●●●●●●●●●●●●●●●●●●●●●●●●●●●●

GLOSSARY OF TERMS

Note: This glossary includes an overview of common terms pertaining to exercise, health, medicine, nutrition, physiology, etc.

Acclimation

A program undertaken to induce acclimatization to new environmental conditions, such as increases in temperature or altitude.

Acclimatization

The body's gradual adaptation to a changed environment, such as higher temperatures or lower barometric pressures (at high altitude).

Acute

Sudden, short-term, sharp, or severe.

Adaptation

The adjustment of the body (or mind) to achieve a greater degree of fitness (i.e., training effect) to its environment. An adaptation is more persistent than an immediate response to the new stimuli of the environment.

Adherence

Maintaining a lifestyle change. Used to describe a person's continuation in an exercise program.

Adipose tissue

Fat tissue.

Aerobic

Using oxygen.

Aerobic activities

Activities using large muscle groups at moderate-to-vigorous intensities that permit the body to use oxygen to supply energy and to maintain a steady state for more than a few minutes.

Aerobic endurance

The ability to continue aerobic activity over a period of time.

Aerobic power

See maximal oxygen uptake.

Agonist

A muscle that directly engages in an action around a joint which has another muscle that can provide an opposing action (antagonist).

Amenorrhea

The absence of menstruation; prevalence is approximately 10 to 20 percent among athletic women, particularly runners, and roughly 5 percent in the general population.

Amino acids

The building blocks of protein. Twenty different amino acids are required by the body.

Anabolic

Pertaining to the putting together of complex substances from simpler ones, especially to the building of body proteins from amino acids.

Anabolic steroids

A group of synthetic, testosterone-like hormones that promote anabolism (tissue building), including muscle hypertrophy. Medical uses include promotion of tissue repair in severely debilitated older or elderly patients, but their use in athletics is considered unethical and carries numerous serious health risks (e.g., liver damage, decreased HDL-cholesterol).

Anabolism

The process performed by the cells of combining simple substances to build living matter. For example, combining amino acids into proteins to build muscle cells.

Anaerobic

Not using oxygen.

Anaerobic activities

Activities using muscle groups at high intensities that exceed the body's capacity to use oxygen to supply energy and that create an oxygen debt by using energy produced without oxygen.

Anaerobic endurance

The ability to continue activity over a period of time (much shorter time than with aerobic activity).

Anaerobic threshold

The point where increasing energy demands of exercise cannot be met by the use of oxygen, and blood lactate begins to increase disproportionately. This is paralleled by abrupt increases in two ventilatory variables, CO_2 production and minute ventilation.

Anatomy

The science of the structure of the human body.

Anemia

A subnormal number of red blood cells or low hemoglobin content. Symptoms may include fatigue, pale complexion, lightheadedness, palpitations, and loss of appetite.

Angina

A gripping, vice-like, or suffocating pain or pressure in the chest (angina pectoris), caused most often by insufficient flow of oxygen to the heart muscle during exercise or stress. Exercise should be stopped, and medical attention should be sought to clarify the reason for the symptoms.

Anorexia

Lack of appetite. Anorexia nervosa is a psychological and physiological condition characterized by inability or refusal to eat, leading to severe weight loss, malnutrition, hormone imbalances, and other potentially life-threatening biological consequences.

Antagonist

A muscle that can provide an opposing action to the action of another muscle (the agonist) around a joint.

Anthropometry

The science dealing with the measurement (size, weight, proportions) of the human body.

Aquatics

Exercise or sports activities in or on the water.

Arrhythmia

Any abnormal rhythm of the heart beat. Because some causes of arrhythmia may have threatening health consequences, exercisers experiencing irregular heart beats should be referred for medical evaluation.

Arteriosclerosis

Thickening and hardening of the artery walls by one of several diseases.

Artery

Vessel which carries oxygenated blood away from the heart to the tissues of the body.

Arthritis

Inflammation of the joints which causes pain, stiffness, and limitation of motion. May be symptomatic of a systemic disease, such as rheumatoid arthritis which can affect all age groups.

Asthma

A pulmonary condition caused by constriction of the bronchial tubes from allergies, physical activity, or other irritants; characterized by wheezing, coughing, and labored breathing (dyspnea).

Atherosclerosis

A common form of arteriosclerosis, in which the arteries are narrowed by deposits of cholesterol and other fibrous material in the inner walls of the artery.

Atrophy

Reduction in size or degeneration of a body part, organ, tissue or cell.

Ballistic movement

An exercise movement in which part of the body is "thrown" against the resistance of antagonist muscles or against the limits of a joint. The latter, especially, is considered dangerous to the integrity of ligaments and tendons.

Basal metabolic rate

The minimum energy required to maintain the body's life function at rest. Usually expressed in kilocalories per hour per square meter of body surface.

Biofeedback

A process that permits a person to see or hear indicators of physiological variables, such as blood pressure, skin temperature, or heart rate, which may allow the person to exert some control over those variables. Often used to teach relaxation techniques.

Blood pressure

The pressure exerted by the blood on the wall of the arteries. Maximum and minimum measures are used: Systolic pressure reaches a maximum just before the end of the pumping phase of the heart; diastolic pressure (minimum) occurs late in the refilling phase of the heart. Measures are in millimeters of mercury (as 120/80 mm Hg).

Body composition

The proportions of fat, muscle, and bone making up the body. Usually expressed as percent of body fat and percent of lean body mass.

Body density

The specific gravity of the body, which can be tested by underwater weighing. Compares the weight of the body to the weight of the same volume of water. Result can be used to estimate the percentage of body fat.

Body mass index (BMI)

This variable is used to assess weight relative to height. Body mass index is calculated by dividing body weight in kilograms by height in meters squared (kg/m^2). A BMI of 25.0 to 29.9 kg/m^2 is considered overweight, and a BMI equal to or greater than 30.0 kg/m^2 is classified as obese.

Bradycardia

Slow heart beat. A well-conditioned heart will often deliver a pulse rate of less than 60 beats per minute at rest, which would be considered bradycardic by standard definitions.

Bulimia

A clinical eating disorder characterized by repeated episodes of binge eating, often followed by purging which may include self-induced vomiting and the use of laxatives and diuretics.

Bursa

A cushioning sac filled with a lubricating fluid that alleviates friction where there is movement between muscles, between tendon and bone, or between bone and skin.

Bursitis

The inflammation of a bursa, sometimes with calcification in underlying tendons.

Calisthenics

A system of exercise movements, without equipment, for the building of strength, flexibility, and physical grace. The Greeks formed the word from "kalos" (beautiful) and "sthenos" (strength).

Calorie

The calorie used as a unit of metabolism (as in diet and energy expenditure) equals 1,000 small calories, and is often spelled with a capital C to make that distinction. It is the energy required to raise the temperature of one kilogram of water one degree Celsius. Also called a kilocalorie (kcal).

Calorie cost

The number of calories burned to produce the energy for a given task. Usually measured in calories (kcal) per minute.

Capillary

The tiny blood vessels (about the diameter of one red blood cell) that receive blood flow from the arteries, interchange gasses and nutrients between the blood and the tissues, and return the blood to the veins.

Carbohydrate

Chemical compound of carbon, oxygen, and hydrogen, usually with the hydrogen and oxygen in the right proportions to form water. Common forms are starches, sugars, cellulose, and gums. Carbohydrates are more readily used for energy production than are fats and proteins.

Carbon dioxide

A colorless, odorless gas that is formed in the tissues by the oxidation of carbon, and is eliminated by the lungs. Its presence in the bloodstream stimulates breathing.

Cardiac

Pertaining to the heart.

Cardiac output ($\dot{Q}$)

The volume of blood pumped out by the heart per minute. It equals the stroke volume times the heart rate.

Cardiac rehabilitation

A multidisciplinary program of exercise, risk factor reduction, education, and counseling that is designed to prepare cardiac patients to return to productive lives with a reduced risk of recurrent cardiac events.

Cardiopulmonary resuscitation (CPR)

A first-aid method to restore breathing and heart action through mouth-to-mouth breathing and rhythmic chest compressions. CPR instruction is offered by local Heart Association and Red Cross units, and is a minimum requirement for most fitness-instruction certifications.

Cardiorespiratory endurance

See aerobic endurance.

Cardiovascular

Pertaining to the heart and blood vessels.

Carotid artery

The principal artery in both sides of the neck. A convenient place to detect a pulse.

Catabolism

The process performed by the cells of breaking down complex substances into simpler parts. For example, breaking down carbohydrates or fats for use in energy expenditure.

Cellulite

A commercially created name for lumpy or dimpled fat deposits. Actually this fat behaves no differently than other types of body fat; it is just aligned against irregular bands of connective tissue.

Cholesterol

A steroid alcohol found in animal fats. This pearly, fatlike substance is implicated in the narrowing of the arteries in atherosclerosis. Plasma levels of cholesterol are considered normal below 200 milligrams per 100 milliliters of blood. Higher levels are thought to pose risks to the arteries.

Chronic

Continuing over time.

Circuit training

A series of exercises, performed one after the other, with little rest between. Resistance training in this manner increases strength while potentially providing some modest contribution to cardiovascular endurance as well.

Collateral circulation

Blood circulation through small side branches that can supplement (or substitute for) the main vessel's delivery of blood to certain tissues (e.g., the heart).

Compliance

Maintaining a prescribed exercise program. (Often used in a medical setting.)

Concentric action

Muscle action in which the muscle is shortening under its own power. This action is commonly called "positive" work or, redundantly, "concentric contraction."

Concussion

An injury from a severe blow or jar. A brain concussion may result in temporary loss of consciousness and memory loss. Severe concussion causes prolonged loss of consciousness and may impair breathing, dilate the pupils and disrupt other regulatory functions of the brain.

Conditioning

Long-term physical training.

Connective tissue
A fibrous tissue that binds together and supports the structures of the body.

Contraindication
Any condition which indicates that a particular course of action (or exercise) would be inadvisable.

Cool-down
A gradual reduction of the intensity of exercise to allow physiological processes to return to normal. Helps avoid blood pooling in the legs and may reduce muscular soreness.

Coronary arteries
The small arteries, circling the heart like a crown, that supply blood to the heart muscle. These are about the size of cooked spaghetti.

Coronary heart disease (CHD)
Atherosclerosis of the coronary arteries.

Cross-sectional study
A study made at one point in time.

Defibrillator
A device used to reverse weak, uncoordinated beating (fibrillation) of the heart and facilitate restoration of a normal heart beat. Part of the "crash cart" at cardiac rehabilitation program sites.

Dehydration
The condition resulting from the excessive loss of body water.

Detraining
The process of losing the benefits of training by returning to a sedentary lifestyle.

Diabetes mellitus
A metabolic disorder characterized by high blood-sugar levels (hyperglycemia). The disease develops when there is insufficient production of insulin by the pancreas (Type I) or inadequate utilization of insulin by the cells (Type II).

Diastole
Relaxation phase of the heart.

Diastolic blood pressure
The minimum blood pressure that occurs during the refilling of the heart.

Diet
The food one eats. May include a selection of foods to help accomplish a particular health or fitness objective.

Disordered eating
Abnormal eating behavior that ranges from severe restriction of food intake to clinical disorders such as bulimia and anorexia.

Diuretic

Any agent that increases the flow of urine. Sometimes used inadvisedly for quick weight loss, diuretics can cause dehydration.

Dry-bulb thermometer

An ordinary instrument for indicating temperature. Does not take into account humidity and other factors that combine to determine the heat stress experienced by the body.

Duration

The time spent in a single exercise session. Duration, along with frequency and intensity, is a factor influencing the effectiveness of exercise.

Dyspnea

Difficult or labored breathing.

Eccentric action

Muscle action in which the muscle resists while it is forced to lengthen. This action is commonly called "negative" work or "eccentric contraction"; but, because the muscle is lengthening, the word "contraction" is misapplied.

Efficiency

The ratio of energy used to the work accomplished. Exercisers utilizing the same amounts of oxygen may differ in their speed or amount of weight moved in a given time because of differing efficiencies.

Electrocardiogram (EKG, ECG)

A graph of the electrical activity caused by the stimulation of the heart muscle. The millivolts of electricity are detected by electrodes on the body surface and are recorded by an electrocardiograph.

Electrolyte

A substance which, in solution, is capable of conducting electricity. Certain electrolytes are essential to the electrochemical functioning of the body.

Endurance

The capacity to continue a physical performance over a period of time.

Energy

The capacity to produce work.

Epidemiological studies

Statistical study of the relationships between various factors that determine the frequency and distribution of disease. For example, such studies have linked regular exercise to reduced cardiovascular and all-cause mortality.

Epiphyseal plates

The sites of new bone growth, separated from the main bone by cartilage during the growth period. This is a potential injury site to be avoided in prescribing exercise to prepubescent individuals.

Epiphyses

The ends of long bones, usually wider than the shaft of the bone.

Ergometer

A device that can measure work consistently and reliably. Stationary exercise cycles were the first widely available devices equipped with ergometers, but a wide variety of endurance-training machines now have ergometric capacity.

Essential amino acids

Those amino acids that the body cannot make on its own. They are: isoleucine, leucine, lysine, methionine, phenylalanine, tryptophan, and valine.

Essential hypertension

Hypertension without an identifiable cause. Also called primary hypertension.

Estrogen

The sex hormone that predominates in the female, but also has functions in the male. It is responsible for the development of female secondary sex characteristics, which have an effect on female responses to exercise.

Exercise

Physical exertion of sufficient intensity, duration, and frequency to achieve or maintain fitness, or other health or athletic objectives.

Exercise prescription

A recommendation for a course of exercise to meet desirable individual objectives for fitness. Includes activity types, duration, intensity, and frequency of exercise.

Exercise program director

Certification as exercise program director by the American College of Sports Medicine indicates the competency to design, implement, and administer preventive and rehabilitative exercise programs, to educate staff in conducting tests and leading physical activity, and to educate the community about such programs. Must have all the competencies of the certified health/fitness instructor, exercise leader, and exercise specialist. Current cardiopulmonary resuscitation (CPR) certification is also a requirement.

Exercise specialist

A person certified by the American College of Sports Medicine as having the competency and skill to supervise preventive and rehabilitative exercise programs and prescribe activities for patients. Must also have the ACSM competencies for health/fitness instructor and exercise leader. CPR certification is also a requirement.

Expiration

Breathing air out of the lungs.

Extension

A movement that moves the two ends of a jointed body part away from each other, as in straightening the arm.

Extensor

A muscle that extends a jointed body part. For example, when the triceps muscle contracts, it extends the lower arm.

Faint

See syncope.

Fascia

Connective tissue which surrounds muscles and various organs of the body.

Fast-twitch fibers

Muscle fiber type that contracts quickly and is used mostly in intensive, short-duration exercises, such as weightlifting or sprints.

Fat

1. A white or yellowish tissue that stores reserve energy, provides padding for organs, and smooths body contours. 2. A compound of glycerol and various fatty acids. Dietary fat is not as readily converted to energy as are carbohydrates.

Fat-free weight

Lean body mass.

Fatigue

A loss of power to continue a given level of physical performance.

Female triad

Refers to the interrelatedness of three medical disorders: disordered eating, amenorrhea, and osteoporosis. These medical disorders most often occur in young women who are driven to excel in their chosen sports and pressured to fit a lean body image to obtain their performance goals.

Fibromyalgia

Widespread pain in the muscles and surrounding connective tissues, usually accompanied by fatigue and malaise.

Fitness

The state of well-being consisting of optimum levels of strength, flexibility, weight control, cardiovascular capacity, and positive physical and mental health behaviors that prepare a person to participate fully in life, to be cognizant of controllable health risk factors, and to achieve physical objectives consistent with his/her potential.

Fitness center

A place furnished with space and equipment, where professional leadership and supervision are offered to further the fitness objectives of participants.

Fitness instructor

Technically called a health/fitness instructor. A person who directs classes or individuals in the performance of exercise. Certification by the American College of Sports Medicine (ACSM) indicates the competency to identify risk factors, conduct submaximal exercise tests, recommend exercise programs, lead classes, and counsel exercisers. Accordingly, the ACSM health/fitness instructor is also responsible for the knowledge, skills, and abilities of the ACSM-certified exercise leader. Works with persons without known disease. CPR certification is required.

Fitness testing
Measuring the indicators of the various aspects of fitness.

Flexibility
The range of motion around a joint.

Flexion
A movement that moves the two ends of a jointed body part closer to each other, as in bending the arm.

Foot-pound
The amount of work required to lift 1 pound 1 foot.

Frequency
How often a person repeats a complete exercise session (e.g., three times per week). Frequency, along with duration and intensity, affects the effectiveness of exercise.

Functional capacity
See maximal oxygen uptake.

Glucose
Blood sugar. The transportable form of carbohydrate, which reaches the cells.

Glycogen
The storage form of carbohydrate. Glycogen is used in the muscles for the production of energy.

Golgi tendon organ (GTO)
Organs at the junction of muscle and tendon that send inhibitory impulses to the muscle when the muscle's contraction reaches certain levels. The purpose may be to protect against separating the tendon from bone when a contraction is excessive.

Graded exercise test (GXT)
A treadmill or cycle-ergometer test that monitors heart rate, blood pressure, ECG, and other data. Work load is gradually increased until an increase in workload is not followed by an increase in oxygen consumption; this identifies the individual's maximal oxygen uptake. Allows the prescribing of exercise to the individual's actual, rather than estimated, heart rate or aerobic capacity. Requires medical supervision.

Growth hormone
Human growth hormone (HGH), somatotropin, is produced by the pituitary to promote growth in body cells. To treat children with growth disorders, it has been obtained from primate sources or may be artificially synthesized. There are reports of abuse by athletes, although there is no clear benefit in taking HGH and there are potential serious side effects, such as acromegaly, from dosages only slightly larger than those given to children.

Hamstrings
The group of muscles at the back of the thigh, and their tendons.

Health history
See medical history.

Health-risk appraisal
A procedure that gathers information about a person's behaviors, family history, and other characteristics known to be associated with the incidence of serious disease, and uses that information to compare the individual's present risks with the lower risks that could be achieved by changing certain behaviors.

Heart attack
An acute manifestation of heart disease, associated with permanent tissue damage or necrosis.

Heart rate
Number of heart beats per minute.

Heart rate reserve
The difference between the resting heart rate and the maximal heart rate.

Heat cramps
Muscle twitching or painful cramping, usually following heavy exercise with profuse sweating. The legs, arms, and abdominal muscles are most often affected.

Heat exhaustion
Caused by dehydration (and sometimes salt loss). Symptoms include dry mouth, excessive thirst, loss of coordination, dizziness, headache, paleness, shaking, and cool and clammy skin.

Heat stroke
A life-threatening illness where the body's temperature-regulating mechanisms fail. Body temperature may rise to over 104°F; the skin appears red, dry, and warm to the touch. The victim has chills, sometimes nausea and dizziness, and may be confused or irrational. Seizures and coma may follow unless temperature is brought down to 102 degrees or lower within an hour.

Heat syncope
Fainting from the heat. When excess blood is shunted to the skin for cooling and the person becomes inactive enough to allow blood to pool in the legs, the heart may not receive enough blood to supply the brain. Once the person is in a horizontal position, consciousness is regained quickly.

High blood pressure
See hypertension.

High-density lipoprotein (HDL)
A type of lipoprotein that seems to provide protection against the buildup of atherosclerotic fat deposits in the arteries. Exercise seems to increase the HDL fraction of total cholesterol. HDL contains high levels of protein and low levels of triglycerides and cholesterol. An HDL above 60 mg/dL is considered a "negative" risk factor.

Homeostasis

The tendency of the body to maintain its internal systems in balance. Example: A buildup of carbon dioxide increases the respiration rate to eliminate it and draw in more oxygen.

Hormone

A chemical, secreted into the blood stream, that specifically regulates the function of a certain organ of the body. Usually, but not always, secreted by an endocrine gland.

Horsepower (HP)

A work rate measure equal to 746 watts or about 550 foot-pounds per second.

Hyperglycemia

Abnormally high level of glucose in the blood (high blood sugar). The clinical hallmark of diabetes mellitus. Usually defined as a blood-sugar value exceeding 110 mg/dL.

Hypertension

Persistent high blood pressure. Readings of 140/90 millimeters of mercury are considered a threshold for high blood pressure by some authorities.

Hyperthermia

Body temperatures exceeding normal. See heat cramps, heat exhaustion, heat stroke, heat syncope.

Hypertonic

Describes a solution concentrated enough to draw water out of body cells.

Hypertrophy

Enlargement of a body part or organ by an increase in the size of the cells that comprise it.

Hypervitaminosis

Undesirable symptoms caused by an excess consumption of certain vitamins.

Hypoglycemia

Abnormally low level of glucose in the blood (low blood sugar). May lead to shaking, cold sweats, goose bumps, hypothermia, hallucinations, strange behavior, and, in extreme cases, convulsions and coma.

Hypothermia

Body temperature below normal. Usually due to prolonged exposure to cold temperatures.

Hypotonic

Describes a solution dilute enough to allow its water to be absorbed by body cells.

Hypoxia

Insufficient oxygen delivery to the tissues, even though blood flow may be adequate.

Iliac crest

The upper, wide portion of the hip bone.

Infarction

Death of a section of tissue from the total obstruction of blood flow (ischemia) to the area.

Inflammation

Body's local response to injury. Acute inflammation is characterized by pain, with heat, redness, swelling, and loss of function. Uncontrolled swelling may cause further damage to tissues at the injury site.

Informed consent

A procedure for obtaining a client's signed consent to a research project or a fitness center's prescription. Includes a description of the objectives and procedures, with associated benefits and risks, stated in plain language, with a consent statement and signature line in a single document.

Inspiration

Breathing air into the lungs.

Intensity

The rate of performing work; power. A function of energy output per unit of time. Examples: Aerobic exercise may be measured in oxygen consumed, METs, or heart rate; short-duration anaerobic exercise may be measured in foot-pounds per minute or other units of work measurement. Intensity, along with duration and frequency, determines the effectiveness of exercise.

Interval training

An exercise session in which the intensity and duration of exercise are consciously alternated between vigorous and moderate work. Often used to improve aerobic capacity and/or anaerobic endurance in exercisers who already have a base of endurance training.

Ischemia

Inadequate oxygen delivery to a body part, generally caused by constriction or obstruction of a blood vessel.

Isokinetic contraction

A muscle contraction against a resistance that moves at a constant velocity, so that the maximum force of which the muscle is capable throughout the range of motion may be applied.

Isometric action

Muscle action in which the muscle attempts to contract against a fixed limit. This is sometimes called "isometric contraction," although there is not appreciable shortening of the muscle.

Isotonic contraction

A muscle contraction against a constant resistance, as in lifting a weight.

Joint capsules

A saclike enclosure around a joint that holds synovial fluid to lubricate the joint.

Ketosis

An elevated level of ketone bodies in the tissues. This condition may occur during periods of starvation or in persons with diabetes, and is a common symptom among dieters on very low carbohydrate diets.

Kilocalorie (kcal)
> A measure of the heat required to raise the temperature of 1 kilogram of water 1°C. A large calorie (kcal), used in diet and metabolism measures, that equals 1,000 small calories.

Kilogram (kg)
> A unit of weight equal to 2.204623 pounds; 1,000 grams (g).

Kilogram-meter (kgm)
> The amount of work required to lift 1 kilogram 1 meter.

Kilopond-meter (kpm)
> Equivalent to a kilogram-meter, in normal gravity.

Lactate
> Lactic acid.

Lactic acid
> The end product of the metabolism of glucose for the anaerobic production of energy.

Lean body mass
> Lean body weight.

Lean body weight
> The weight of the body, less the weight of its fat.

Ligament
> The fibrous, connective tissue that connects bone to bone, or bone to cartilage, to hold together and support joints.

Lipid
> A number of body substances that are fat or fatlike.

Lipoprotein
> Combination of a lipid and protein. Cholesterol is transported in the blood plasma by lipoproteins.

Longitudinal study
> A study which observes the same subjects over a period of time.

Lordosis
> The forward curving of the spine at the neck (cervical spine) and lower back (lumbar spine). Often used to refer to an abnormally increased curvature of the lumbar spine.

Low blood sugar
> See hypoglycemia.

Low-density lipoprotein (LDL)
> A lipoprotein carrying a high level of cholesterol, moderate levels of protein, and low levels of triglycerides. Associated with the buildup of atherosclerotic deposits in the arteries.

Lumbar

Pertaining to the lower back, defined by the five lumbar vertebrae, just above the sacrum.

Maintenance load

The intensity, duration, and frequency of exercise required to maintain an individual's present level of fitness.

Max V̇O₂

See maximal oxygen uptake.

Maximal heart rate

The highest heart rate that an individual can attain. A general rule of thumb for estimating maximal heart rate is 220 (beats per minute) minus the person's age (in years).

Maximal oxygen uptake

The highest rate of oxygen consumption of which a person is capable. Usually expressed in milliliters of oxygen per kilogram of body weight per minute. Also called maximal aerobic power, maximal oxygen consumption, aerobic capacity, and maximal oxygen intake. The abbreviation for maximal oxygen uptake is $\dot{V}O_{2max}$.

Maximal tests

An exercise test to exhaustion or to levels of oxygen uptake or heart rate that cannot increase further with additional work loads.

Medical history

A list of a person's previous illnesses, present conditions, symptoms, medications, and health risk factors. Used to prescribe appropriate exercise programs. Persons whose responses indicate they may be in a moderate-to-high risk category should be referred for medical evaluation before beginning a vigorous exercise program.

Medical referral

Recommending that a person see a qualified medical professional to review his or her health status to determine whether medical evaluation and treatment are needed or whether a particular course of exercise and/or diet change is safe.

Menopause

The point in time that the cessation of menstrual function occurs. Women typically stop menstruating between the ages of 45 and 55.

MET

Stands for metabolic equivalent. A measure of energy output equal to the metabolic rate of a resting subject. Approximates an oxygen uptake of 3.5 milliliters per kilogram of body weight per minute, or a caloric expenditure of ~50 kilocalories per square meter of body surface per hour. Hard exercise, for example, requires up to 8 METs of energy expenditure, which equals 8 times the resting energy requirement.

Metabolism

The total of all the chemical and physical processes by which the body builds and maintains itself (anabolism) and by which it breaks down its substances for the production of energy (catabolism).

Minimum daily requirement (MDR)
> The minimum amounts of protein, vitamins, and minerals considered necessary to maintain health.

Monounsaturated fat
> Dietary fat of which the molecules have one double bond open to receive more hydrogen. Found in many nuts, olive oil, and avocados.

Motor neuron
> A nerve cell that conducts impulses from the central nervous system to a group of muscle fibers to produce movement.

Motor unit
> A motor neuron and the muscle fibers activated by it.

Muscle group
> Specific muscles that act together at the same joint to produce a movement.

Muscle spindle
> Organ in a muscle that senses changes in muscle length, especially stretches. Rapid stretching of the muscle results in messages being sent to the nervous system to contract the muscle, thereby limiting the stretch.

Musculoskeletal
> Referring to the muscles, bones, joints, and related structures (e.g., tendons, ligaments, etc.) that function in the movements of the human body.

Musculotendinous
> Pertaining to or composed of muscle and tendon.

Myocardial infarction
> A common form of heart attack, in which the complete blockage of a coronary artery causes the death or necrosis of a part of the heart muscle.

Myositis
> Inflammation of a skeletal muscle.

Myositis ossificans
> The deposit of bony materials in the muscle. Bruises from contact sports may result in this condition. Severe bruises should be iced and evaluated by a physician.

Nutrients
> Food and its specific elements and compounds that can be used by the body to build and maintain itself and to produce energy.

Nutrition
> The processes involved in consuming and using food substances.

Obesity
> Excessive accumulation of body fat.

One repetition maximum (1 RM)
> The maximum resistance at which a person can execute one repetition of an exercise movement.

Osmolarity

The concentration of a solution participating in osmosis. For example, a sugar-water solution of high osmolarity is concentrated enough to draw water through the membranes of the digestive tract to dilute the sugar.

Osmosis

The movement of fluid through a membrane, tending to equalize the concentrations of the solutions on both sides.

Ossification

The formation of bone. The turning of cartilage into bone (as in the joints).

Osteoarthritis

A noninflammatory joint disease of older persons. The cartilage in the joint wears down, and there is bone growth at the edges of the joints. Results in pain and stiffness, especially after prolonged exercise.

Osteoporosis

Decreased bone mineral content causing reduced bone density that results in an increased risk of fracture due to skeletal fragility and compromised bone microarchitecture.

Overload

Subjecting a part of the body to efforts greater than it is accustomed to, in order to elicit a training response. Increases may be in intensity or duration.

Overuse

Excessive repeated exertion or shock that results in injuries, such as stress fractures of bones or inflammation of muscles and tendons.

Oxygen (O_2)

The essential element in the respiration process to sustain life. The colorless, odorless gas makes up about 21 percent of the air, by weight at sea level.

Oxygen consumption

See oxygen uptake.

Oxygen debt

The oxygen required to restore the capacity for anaerobic work after an effort has used those reserves. Measured by the extra oxygen that is consumed during the recovery from the work.

Oxygen deficit

The energy supplied anaerobically while oxygen uptake has not yet reached the steady state which matches energy output. Becomes oxygen debt at end of exercise.

Oxygen uptake

The amount of oxygen used up at the cellular level during exercise. Can be measured by determining the volume of air moved and amount of oxygen exhaled as compared with the amount inhaled, or estimated by indirect means.

Peak heart rate

The highest heart rate reached during an exercise or physical activity session.

Perceived exertion

See rating of perceived exertion.

pH

A measure of acidity, relating to the hydrogen ion (H^+) concentration. A pH of 7.0 is neutral; acidity increases with lower numbers, and alkalinity increases with higher numbers. Body fluids have a pH of about 7.3.

Physical conditioning

A program of regular, sustained exercise to increase or maintain levels of strength, flexibility, aerobic capacity, and body composition consistent with health, fitness, or athletic objectives.

Physical fitness

The physiological contribution to wellness through exercise and nutrition behaviors that maintain high aerobic capacity, optimal body composition, and adequate strength and flexibility to minimize risk of chronic health problems and to enhance the quality of life.

Physical work capacity (PWC)

An exercise test that measures the amount of work done at a given, submaximal heart rate. The work is measured in oxygen uptake, kilopond meters per minute, or other units. It can be used to estimate maximal heart rate and oxygen uptake. Less accurate, but safer and less expensive than the graded exercise test.

Plyometric

A type of exercise that suddenly preloads and forces the stretching of a muscle an instant prior to its concentric action. An example is jumping down from a bench and immediately springing back up.

PNF stretch

See proprioceptive neuromuscular facilitation stretch.

Polyunsaturated fat

Dietary fat whose molecules have more than one double bond open to receive more hydrogen. Found in safflower oil, corn oil, soybeans, sesame seeds, sunflower seeds.

Power

Work performed per unit of time. Measured by the formula: work equals force multiplied by distance divided by time. A combination of strength and speed.

Primary risk factor

A risk factor that is strong enough to operate independently, without the presence of other risk factors (refer to risk factor and secondary risk factor). For heart disease, there are five primary risk factors: elevated blood cholesterol, high blood pressure (hypertension), cigarette smoking, obesity, and physical inactivity (sedentary lifestyle).

Prime mover

The muscle or muscle group that is causing the movement around a joint.

Progressive resistance exercise

Exercise in which the amount of resistance is increased to further stress the muscle after it has become accustomed to handling a lesser resistance.

Pronation

Assuming a facedown position. Of the hand, turning the palm backward or downward. Of the foot, lowering the inner (medial) side of the foot so as to flatten the arch. The opposite of supination.

Proprioceptive neuromuscular facilitation (PNF) stretch

Muscle stretches that use the proprioceptors (muscle spindles) to send inhibiting (relaxing) messages to the muscle that is to be stretched. Example: The contraction of an agonist muscle sends inhibiting signals that relax the antagonist muscle so that it is easier to stretch. (Term was once applied to a very specific therapeutic technique, but now is being widely applied to stretch techniques such as slow-reversal-hold, contract-relax, and hold-relax.)

Proprioceptor

Self-sensors (nerve terminals) that give messages to the nervous system about movements and position of the body. Proprioceptors include muscle spindles and Golgi tendon organs.

Protein

Compounds of amino acids that make up most of the body's cells and perform other physiological functions.

Pulmonary

Pertaining to the lungs.

Quadriceps

A muscle group at the front of the thigh connected to a common tendon that surrounds the knee cap and attaches to the tibia (lower leg bone). The individual muscles are the rectus femoris, vastus intermedius, vastus lateralis, and vastus medialis. Acts to extend the lower leg.

Radial pulse

The pulse at the wrist.

Rating of perceived exertion

A means to quantify the subjective feeling of the intensity of an exercise. Borg category (6 to 20) or category-ratio (0 to 11) scales, charts which describe a range of intensity from resting to maximal energy outputs, are used as a visual aid for exercisers in adjusting their efforts in the effective training zone.

Recommended dietary allowance (RDA)

The protein, vitamin, and mineral amounts considered adequate to meet the nutrition needs of 95 percent of the healthy population. Established by the National Research Council of the National Academy of Sciences. The RDA is calculated to exceed the needs of most people.

Rectus femoris

The long, straight muscle in the front of the thigh that attaches to the knee cap. Part of the quadriceps muscle group.

Rehabilitation

A program to restore physical and psychological well-being to persons disabled by illness or injury.

Renal

Pertaining to the kidney.

Repetition

A single completed exercise movement. Repetitions are usually done in multiples.

Residual volume

The volume of air remaining in the lungs after a maximum expiration. Must be calculated in the formula for determining body composition through underwater weighing.

Resistance

The force which a muscle is required to work against.

Respiration

Exchange of oxygen and carbon dioxide between the atmosphere and the cells of the body. Includes ventilation (breathing), exchange of gasses to and from the blood in the lungs, transportation of the gasses in the blood, the taking in and utilizing of oxygen, and the elimination of waste products by the cells.

Response

An immediate, short-term change in physiological functions (such as heart rate or respiration) brought on by exercise.

Retest

A repetition of a given test after the passage of time, usually to assess the progress made in an exercise program.

Risk factor

A behavior, characteristic, symptom, or sign that is associated with an increased risk of developing a health problem. Example: Smoking is a risk factor for lung cancer and coronary heart disease.

Sarcopenia

The loss of skeletal muscle mass that generally accompanies aging.

Saturated fat

Dietary fats of which the molecules are saturated with hydrogen. They are usually hard at room temperature and are readily converted into cholesterol in the body. Sources include animal products as well as hydrogenated vegetable oils.

Screening

Comparing individuals to set criteria for inclusion in a fitness program or for referral to a medical professional.

Secondary risk factor

A risk factor that acts when certain other risk factors are present.

Sedentary

Sitting a lot; inactive or unfit; not involved in any regular physical activity that might produce significant fitness benefits.

Set

A group of repetitions of an exercise movement done consecutively, without rest, until a given number, or volitional fatigue, is reached.

Shin splints

Pain in the front of the lower leg from inflammation of muscle and tendon tissue caused by overuse.

Sign

An indicator of disease found during a physician's examination or tests; an objective indicator of disease.

Slow-twitch fibers

Muscle fiber type that contracts slowly and is used mostly in moderate-intensity, endurance exercises, such as distance running.

Somatotropin

See growth hormone.

Spasm

The involuntary contraction of a muscle or muscle group in a sudden, violent manner.

Specificity

The principle that the body adapts very specifically to the training stimuli it is challenged with. The body will perform best at the specific speed, type of contraction, muscle-group usage, and energy-source usage it has become accustomed to in training.

Spot reducing

An effort to reduce fat at one location on the body by concentrating exercise, manipulation, wraps, etc. on that location. Research indicates that any fat loss is generalized over the body, however.

Sprain

A stretching or tearing of ligaments. Severity ratings of sprains are: first-degree, partial tearing; third-degree, complete tears.

Static contraction

See isometric action.

Steady state

The physiological state, during submaximal exercise, where oxygen uptake and heart rate level off, energy demands and energy production are balanced, and the body can maintain the level of exertion for an extended period of time.

Strain

A stretching or tearing of a musculotendinous unit. Degrees of severity include: first-degree, stretching of the unit; second-degree, partial tearing of the unit; third-degree, complete disruption of the unit.

Strength

The amount of muscular force that can be exerted. (Speed and distance are not factors of strength.)

Stress

The general physical and psychological response of an individual to any real or perceived adverse stimulus, internal or external, that tends to disturb the individual's homeostasis. Stress that is excessive or reacted to inappropriately may cause disorders.

Stress fracture

A partial or complete fracture of a bone because of the inability of the remodeling process to keep up with the effects of continual, rhythmic, nonviolent stresses on the bone.

Stress management

A group of skills for dealing with the stresses imposed on an individual to help him or her avoid suffering psychological distress and/or physical disorders.

Stress test

See graded exercise test.

Stress urinary incontinence

The involuntary passage of urine during physical exertion or activities such as laughing, coughing, or sneezing.

Stretching

Lengthening a muscle to its maximum extension; moving a joint to the limits of its extension.

Stroke volume

The volume of blood pumped out of the heart by the ventricles in one contraction.

Submaximal

Less than maximum. Submaximal exercise requires less than one's maximum oxygen uptake, heart rate, or minute ventilation (i.e., the amount of oxygen that passes in and out of the respiratory system per minute). Usually refers to intensity of the exercise, but may be used to refer to duration.

Supination

Assuming a horizontal position facing upward. In the case of the hand, it also means turning the palm to face forward. The opposite of pronation.

Symptom

Any evidence by which a person perceives that he/she may not be well; subjective evidence of illness.

Syncope

Fainting. A temporary loss of consciousness from insufficient blood flow to the brain.

Syndrome

A group of related symptoms or signs of disease.

Systole

The contraction, or time of contraction, of the heart.

Systolic blood pressure

Blood pressure during the contraction of the heart muscle.

Tachycardia

Excessively rapid heart rate. Usually describes a pulse of more than 100 beats per minute at rest.

Taper down

See cool-down.

Target heart rate (THR)

The heart rate at which one aims to exercise to improve cardiorespiratory fitness. According to the ACSM, this should approximate 40% to 85% of the maximum heart rate reserve.

Tendon

The fibrous connective tissue that connects muscle to bone.

Tendonitis

Inflammation of a tendon.

Testing protocol

A specific plan for conducting an exercise stress test; usually following an accepted standard.

Testosterone

The sex hormone that predominates in the male, is responsible for the development of male secondary sex characteristics and is involved in stimulating the hypertrophy of muscle.

Training

Subjecting the body to repeated stresses with interspersed recovery periods to elicit gradual physiologic adaptation (e.g., improved oxidative enzymes) in its capacity to handle such stresses.

Training zone

See target heart rate.

Twitch

A brief muscle contraction caused by a single volley of motor neuron impulses.

Unsaturated fat

Dietary fat of which the molecules have one or more double bonds to receive more hydrogen atoms. Replacing saturated fats with unsaturated fats in the diet can help reduce cholesterol levels.

Valsalva maneuver

A strong exhaling effort against a closed glottis, which builds pressure in the chest cavity that interferes with the return of the blood to the heart. May deprive the brain of blood and cause fainting.

Vasoconstriction

The transient narrowing of a blood vessel, causing a decrease in blood flow to a body part.

Vasodilation

The transient enlarging of a blood vessel, causing an increase in blood flow to a body part.

Vein

A vessel that returns deoxygenated blood from the various parts of the body back to the heart.

Ventilation

Breathing.

Vertigo

Sensation that the surroundings are spinning or that the individual is revolving; a particular kind of dizziness.

Vital capacity

Maximal breathing capacity; the amount of air that can be expired after a maximum inspiration; the maximum total volume of the lungs, less the residual volume.

Vital signs

The measurable signs of essential bodily functions, such as respiration rate, heart rate, temperature, blood pressure, etc.

Vitamins

A number of unrelated organic substances that are required in trace amounts for the metabolic processes of the body and that occur in small amounts in many foods.

$\dot{V}O_{2max}$

Maximum volume of oxygen consumed per unit of time. In scientific notation, a dot appears over the V to indicate "per unit of time."

Warmup

A gradual increase in the intensity of exercise to allow physiological processes to prepare for greater energy outputs. Changes include a rise in body temperature, cardiovascular- and respiratory-system changes, an increase in muscle elasticity and contractility, etc.

Watt

A measure of power equal to 6.12 kilogram-meters per minute.

Wellness

A state of health more positive than the mere absence of disease. Wellness programs emphasize self-responsibility for a lifestyle that facilitates the individual's optimal physical, mental, and spiritual well-being.

Wet-bulb thermometer

A thermometer with a bulb that is enclosed in a wet wick, so that evaporation from the wick will lower the temperature reading more in dry air than in humid air. The comparison of wet- and dry-bulb readings can be used to calculate relative humidity.

Wet-globe temperature

A temperature reading that approximates the heat stress that the environment will impose on the human body. Takes into account not only temperature and humidity, but radiant heat from the sun and cooling breezes that would speed evaporation and convection of heat away from the body. Reading is provided by an instrument that encloses a thermometer in a wet, black copper sphere.

Work

Force multiplied by distance. Measured in foot-pounds and similar units. Example: Both lifting a 200-pound barbell 8 feet and lifting a 400-pound barbell 4 feet, each require 1,600 foot-pounds of work.

Work measures

See foot-pound, kilogram-meter.

Workout

A complete exercise session, ideally consisting of warmup, moderate-to-vigorous aerobic and/or strength exercises, and cool-down.

Work rate

Power. The amount of work done per unit of time. Can be measured in foot-pounds per second, watts, horsepower, etc.

APPENDIX B

• •

NUTRITIONAL SUPPLEMENTS: FACT VS. FICTION

*L*ike Ponce de Leon who searched for the "fountain of youth," millions of fitness enthusiasts and athletes are searching for the enhancers – the "magic lift." Aggressive and ethically questionable marketing has promoted the use of nutritional supplements for enhancing physical appearance and/or improving performance capabilities. Marketing and sales of nutritional supplements has become a lucrative business in the United States. Statistics show that the sale of ergogenic supplements yields nearly $4 billion in revenue annually. Robust sales occur even though the advertised ergogenic benefits are often based on little or no scientific evidence and despite the fact that these "performance-enhancing pills, powders, and potions" may have harmful side effects.

Among the more popular, magic-lift supplements being promoted are androstenedione, chromium, creatine, and dehydroepiandrosterone (DHEA). In Appendix B, we will review each of these "hot" supplements and address the following questions:

- What is it and how is it used?
- How is it supposed to work?
- Does it work?
- Are there potential health risks associated with its use?
- Does sufficient evidence exist to recommend its use?

ANDROSTENEDIONE

Androstenedione is a male sex hormone produced naturally by the body, which can be converted to testosterone. It is also marketed and sold as a natural supplement under various trade names (all of which have some form of the word "andro" in their names). Androstenedione is believed to have first been used by East German sports scientists to enhance the performance capabilities of their Olympic athletes. The popularity of androstenedione skyrocketed in 1998 after it was revealed that record-setting, baseball slugger Mark McGuire used the supplement.

The marketers and manufacturers of "andro" (as it is popularly called) claim that a 100-mg dose of andro can increase plasma concentrations of testosterone by a factor of four within 90 minutes. Additional claims include increases in muscle size, strength, energy, immune function, libido (sex drive), and general well-being. It has been suggested that, as with other steroids, andro improves the body's ability to rapidly recover from strenuous physical activity, allowing users to train more frequently and at higher intensities. Presumably, the result of such training would be a substantial increase in muscle size and strength.

Dr. Charles Yesalis, a leading expert on the topic of anabolic steroids, contends that andro should be placed on the list of substances covered by the Anabolic Steroid Control Act of 1990, and its use should be controlled until the long-term health effects are determined. Given its close link to testosterone, it seems logical that androstenedione has the potential to bring about the same harmful side effects associated with anabolic steroid use. Potential users should recognize that even though andro is sold legally over the counter, it has been banned by the National Collegiate Athletic Association, the International Olympic Committee, and the National Football League.

CHROMIUM

Chromium, an essential trace mineral, aids insulin in the transfer of glucose, amino acids, and fat from the bloodstream into the cells. Chromium can be found in many unrefined foods such as whole grain breads and cereals, nuts, prunes, and mushrooms. The estimated, safe range of chromium intake for adults is 50 to 200 micrograms per day. With a typical American diet, two-thirds of the recommended daily allowance (RDA) of chromium is consumed.

Chromium supplementation became popular after it was found that exercise increases chromium loss, raising the concern that chromium deficiency may be common among physically active individuals. Despite little evidence existing to suggest that chromium deficiency is a widespread problem, chromium picolinate (a supplemental form of chromium) has gained popularity recently as a potent stimulus for simultaneous muscular development and fat loss. The few research studies conducted on chromium supplementation have not found it to either increase lean muscle mass or decrease relative body fatness.

In 1996, the Federal Trade Commission (FTC) forced three of the leading marketers of chromium picolinate to stop making undocumented claims, including that the pills promote weight loss, burn fat, build muscle, lower cholesterol, regulate blood sugars, and treat or prevent diabetes. The FTC concluded that these health claims had not been substantiated by scientific studies, and that no reliable evidence existed that most Americans do not consume enough chromium. In a recent position paper, the American College of Sports Medicine (ACSM) concluded that "based on available evidence, chromium supplementation is not necessary." ACSM recommends that individuals consume a diet high in unrefined foods and include a wide variety of foods to obtain adequate amounts of chromium.

CREATINE

Creatine is one of the "hottest" supplements among fitness enthusiasts. Part of the reason for its popularity is the growing evidence which suggests that taking creatine supplements may improve the ability to perform short-term, vigorous exercise.

The effect of creatine on short-term, high-intensity exercise is hardly surprising, given the relationship between creatine and skeletal muscle. All skeletal muscle tissue contains creatine, and dietary creatine is found in both meat and fish. In its phosphorylated form, creatine plays a key role in the formation of adenosine triphosphate (ATP), the body's energy source. During exercise, a portion of the muscle's creatine is depleted. Without sufficient amounts of creatine, which is manufactured in the liver and kidneys and stored in the skeletal muscles, the cycle that creates this energy is unable to produce enough ATP to meet the demand for short bursts of high-intensity exercise. Creatine supplements have been shown to increase the total creatine content (creatine and creatine phosphate) of muscle by an average of 20 to 30 percent.

Several studies suggest that ingestion of 20 to 25 grams of creatine monohydrate per day for five to six days improves muscular performance during activities that require short periods of high-intensity power and strength (e.g., weightlifting, sprinting). Sufficient evidence suggests that, under certain conditions, creatine supplementation can enhance performance in these activities. If individuals can train at higher intensity levels, they may be able to add strength and power at accelerated rates over time. Creatine can also lead to weight gain, but the mechanism responsible for the added weight has not been adequately investigated. Before individuals start buying and taking creatine supplements, however, they should consider the following:

- For a 175-lb individual, approximately 20 grams per day (4 doses of 5 grams each consumed over the course of the day) should increase muscle creatine levels within 5 to 7 days.
- To encourage the storage of creatine in the muscles, 90 grams of carbohydrates should be consumed with each 5-gram dose.
- A more gradual technique would be to consume 3 grams of creatine a day for approximately 1 month.
- Once these levels are achieved, 2 grams of creatine supplementation per day will maintain muscle creatine levels.
- The long-term effects of taking creatine have not been established. Most studies have examined the short-term (30 days or less) effects.
- All of the studies conducted have involved adults only. Creatine's effects on children are unknown.
- Concerns exist about possible liver and kidney damage if large quantities (>40 grams per day) of creatine are consumed.
- Stomach cramping and diarrhea have been reported as adverse side effects of creatine supplementation.
- Creatine supplementation is not recommended for individuals involved in aerobic endurance activities, since accompanying increases in body mass could impair performance.
- Creatine supplementation alone, in the absence of physical training, has been shown to be ineffective.

The U.S. Food and Drug Administration (FDA) issued the following statement regarding creatine use: "Much remains unknown about whether creatine is absolutely safe for long-term use at levels currently being recommended. Both current and potential users should consult their physicians to identify any potential health problems."

Dehydroepiandrosterone

Dehydroepiandrosterone (DHEA) is a substance secreted by the adrenal glands that is ultimately converted to testosterone and estrogen. As with many hormones, decreasing amounts of DHEA are produced as the body ages. DHEA production typically peaks around age 30 and steadily declines thereafter. By age 60, DHEA production is reduced to approximately 10 percent of what it was at age 30. Proponents of DHEA claim that it offers the following beneficial effects:

- Stops or slows the aging process.
- Stops or slows the development of Alzheimer's disease.
- Builds muscle.
- Helps individuals lose body weight and fat.
- Improves sex drive.
- May help treat cancer and AIDS.

Unfortunately, all of these claims have one thing in common: None of them have been scientifically substantiated by well-designed studies. While a relatively large body of research on DHEA has been conducted using animals, these studies have limited value and cannot necessarily be extrapolated to human DHEA life-cycle patterns. Animals have negligible levels of endogenous DHEA. In 1996, the FDA banned the sale and distribution of DHEA for therapeutic uses until its safety and effectiveness could be reviewed. To circumvent the ban, manufacturers began marketing and selling DHEA as a nutritional supplement rather than a therapeutic drug.

The most sensible approach to take with a poorly studied supplement such as DHEA is to be extremely cautious. Because DHEA is a natural substance, the FDA has no regulatory power to control its distribution. Manufacturers are allowed to say (or not say) virtually anything they wish concerning their product. The decision to take DHEA should be based on a risk/benefit analysis. At present, few data are available to support the positive claims associated with DHEA use. While DHEA users have reported few adverse side effects, one side effect is irreversible masculinization in women (hair loss, excessive facial hair growth, and deepening of the voice). In addition, male users of DHEA have reported irreversible gynecomastia (development of breasts in men), which may be the result of elevated estrogen levels. The long-term effects of DHEA use remain unclear. Because of its tendency to cause elevations of serum estrogen and testosterone levels, DHEA may significantly increase the risk of uterine and prostate cancer.

The potential risks associated with DHEA use appear to substantially outweigh any possible benefits. Given the lack of scientific evidence to support performance-enhancing abilities and potentially severe side effects, DHEA supplementation is not recommended. The National Institute on Aging (NIA) has launched an educational campaign to urge consumers to approach "anti-aging" hormone supplements with caution. Consumers can contact the NIA at 1-800-222-2225 or www.nih.gov\nia to order a free fact sheet on hormone supplements.

Truth in Advertising?

Many nutritional supplements are marketed using deceptive, misleading, or fraudulent advertising. Although many claims are unsubstantiated, such substances can be marketed without the FDA review of safety and effectiveness. Another problem with these "magic pills, powders, and potions" is that the concentration of active ingredients can greatly differ from product to product due to the lack of regulatory control. Although some supplements may confer beneficial effects, most are associated with varied adverse side effects. When a supplement label refers to "research" that has proven a supplement's powers, it may actually be referring to animal studies, not research on humans.

As a fitness professional, it is beyond your scope of practice to recommend nutritional supplement use to your clients — from both a professional and legal liability standpoint.

Recommended Reading

Armsey Jr, TD. Nutrition supplements: Science vs. hype. *The Physician and Sportsmedicine* 25(6):77-92, 1997.

Clarkson, PM. Nutritional supplements for weight gain. *Sports Science Exchange 68* by Gatorade Sports Science Institute 11(1), 1998.

Clarkson, PM. The skinny on weight loss supplements & drugs: Winning the war against fat. *ACSM's Health & Fitness Journal* 2(4):18-26, 1998.

Dehydroepiandrosterone (DHEA). *Medical Letter Drug Therapy* 38(985):91-92, 1996.

Eichner, ER. Ergogenic aids: What athletes are using and why. *The Physician and Sportsmedicine* 25(4):70-83, 1997.

Lukaski, HC, Bolonchuk, WW, Siders, WA, Milne, DB. Chromium supplementation and resistance training: Effect of body composition, strength, and trace element status of men. *American Journal of Clinical Nutrition* 63:954-965, 1996.

National Institute on Aging. *Pills, Patches, and Shots: Can Hormones Prevent Aging?* Bethesda, MD, 1997.

Volek, JS. Creatine supplementation and its possible role in improving physical performance. *ACSM's Health & Fitness Journal* 1(4):23-29, 1997.

Williams, M. The gospel truth about dietary supplements. *ACSM's Health & Fitness Journal* 1(1):24-29, 1997.

Williams, MH. *The Ergogenics Edge: Pushing the Limits of Sports Performance.* Champaign, IL: Human Kinetics Publishers, Inc., 1998.

APPENDIX C

PROFESSIONAL FITNESS CERTIFICATION PROGRAMS

*I*t is well-documented that exercise can have a positive impact on the physical and mental health of participants. Numerous studies have confirmed the critical role that regular physical activity plays in preventing (and oftentimes treating) many common medical conditions (e.g., hypertension, diabetes, coronary heart disease, and some forms of cancer). Not surprisingly, as the positive effects of regular exercise have become more publicized, the need for qualified fitness professionals to help ensure that individuals safely and effectively achieve the desired benefits from their exercise efforts has skyrocketed.

The demand for knowledgeable exercise professionals has come from two primary sources: managers of health/fitness facilities and their members. Obviously, most managers are aware that the key to any successful organization is its people. Managers strive to employ staff members who demonstrate the knowledge, skills, and abilities necessary to carry out their job responsibilities in a highly professional manner. They are also aware that members expect to receive attention and instruction from individual staff members whose qualifications and professional competencies are beyond reproach. With the growing awareness of the health and fitness benefits of appropriately prescribed exercise, users of health/fitness facilities feel that they deserve such assistance and that it should be an integral part of their club experience.

Accordingly, one of the key issues for both fitness facility managers and consumers is how to determine if an individual is qualified to assist people on basic health, wellness, and exercise-related issues. This level of expertise can be viewed as the combined by-product of formal academic preparation, professional experience, and a legally defensible certification.

Unfortunately, a precise formula or guideline does not exist regarding how much of each attribute a person should possess to be considered a "qualified" professional. Under most circumstances, having formal academic preparation requires that an individual earn an educational degree in exercise science or a related field from an accredited institution. Achieving professional experience, on the other hand, is an ongoing process that involves various forms of on-the-job training. In many situations, individuals are required to have completed the first link in the chain of professional competence (formal academic preparation) before they are given the opportunity to pursue the second (professional experience).

Professional certification, the third major attribute necessary to be considered "professionally qualified," is perhaps the most confounding of the three factors. Professional certification is an increasingly common mode of verifying that an individual possesses specific competencies or qualifications. In this arena, a number of organizations purporting to represent a diverse array of interests and qualifications bestow "formal certification" on individuals who have met certain knowledge-based standards that have been independently established by each organization. A list of the prominent certifying organizations is presented in Table C-1. *

The practice of certifying professionals is a formidable and ever-expanding task. A sizable number of professional organizations offer primary and secondary certifications in areas of study related to exercise science. In fact, more than 60 different organizations currently offer some form of certification for health/fitness professionals. Despite the proliferation of certification opportunities, however, several major issues relating to certification have arisen, including who should pursue professional certification and how health/fitness facilities can make certification work for them.

GAINING A COMPETITIVE EDGE

Addressing the issue of whether health/fitness professionals should expend the energy and resources to be certified is relatively easy. In a word, "yes." Certification offers several potential benefits to exercise professionals, including higher salaries and an enhanced level of respect from their peers and clients. In addition, certified professionals also appear to have a competitive advantage in the hiring process. Finally, and perhaps most importantly, the process of certification protects the public by identifying professionals who demonstrate competence in providing safe and effective exercise programs.

Table C-1. Prominent Certifying Organizations in the Health/Fitness Industry

- *American Council on Exercise (ACE).* Offers 4 types of certification: group fitness instructor, personal trainer, lifestyle and weight management consultant, and clinical exercise specialist. Contact: (800) 825-3636 / www.acefitness.org.
- *American College of Sports Medicine (ACSM).* Offers 2 and 3 levels of certification within 2 specific tracks: clinical track and health and fitness track, respectively. Contact: (317) 637-9200 / www.acsm.org.
- *National Strength Conditioning Association (NSCA).* Offers certification for 2 groups: strength and conditioning professionals and personal trainers. Contact: (800) 815-6826 / www.nsca-lift.org.
- *International Weightlifting Association (IWA).* Offers certification in strength training. Contact: (800) 934-4487 / www.iwacourses.com.
- *National Academy of Sports Medicine (NASM).* Offers a professional certification course for personal fitness trainers. Contact: (800) 656-2739 / www.nasm.org.

---

* Authors' note: Although professional certification for health/fitness professionals is currently voluntary in the United States, several renowned industry leaders predict that, in the not-too-distant future, health/fitness professionals may be required to be licensed and/or registered.

IDENTIFYING THE BEST MATCH

The most logical way to evaluate certifying agencies is to develop a list of significant factors to consider when assessing a specific certification alternative. Once the information has been gathered, a basis for identifying meaningful differences can be established. At least eight factors should be used to analyze the certification process options, including (1) the type of certifying organization, (2) the services offered by a particular agency, (3) the requirements an organization imposes for certification, (4) the rigors of a specific certification process, (5) the relevancy of a particular type of certification, (6) the focal point of the certification, (7) the quality of the methods used to test the competencies of the individual, and (8) the fundamental basis for the certification.

- *Type of certifying organization.* The key issues that should be addressed include the kind of certifying agency (e.g., an association of professionals with a common interest, a training organization, an educational institution, a commercial enterprise or an individual entrepreneur) and the financial motives of the certifying agency (e.g., for-profit vs. not-for-profit).
- *Services offered by a certifying agency.* What features does the certifying agency offer (e.g., certification, training, continuing education, renewable certifications)? If training is offered, how qualified is the agency's instructional staff? Does a conflict of interest exist if the agency offers both training and certification?
- *Requirements for certification.* What prerequisites have been established for being accepted into the certification process (e.g., educational degrees, professional experience)? Does the certification procedure include a written exam, a practical exam, or a combination of both? In the latter case, what is the relative importance of each type of exam? Does the certification process require internship experience? If so, what does the internship entail?
- *Rigors of the certification process.* How much time does the certification process require? What does the process cost?
- *Relevancy of the certification process.* Is the process relevant to your job responsibilities (e.g., a personal trainer, a supervisor of trainers, or a facility manager? Does the process deal with issues relevant to the clientele you plan to serve after being certified (e.g., healthy exercisers versus individuals with specific medical conditions)?
- *Focal point of the certification process.* Does the process focus on job-related knowledge and skill components (e.g., aerobic fitness, muscular fitness, flexibility, body composition, weight control, stress management, enhanced sports performance, leading an exercise class, and/or serving as a personal trainer)?
- *Quality of certification testing methods.* Are the testing methods used to certify individuals both valid and reliable? Are the certifying exams (written and/or practical) administered in an appropriate manner (i.e., secure, trustworthy, professional, ethical)?
- *Fundamental basis for certification.* What credentials, competencies, and skills should an individual possess to be certified? Does the certification award include an ethics code that, if violated, can result in the revocation of the certification?

MAKING THE PROPER CHOICE

Fitness professionals who want to inspire confidence in the clients they serve and who plan to stay on top of the ever-expanding body of knowledge in their field should strongly consider applying for certification from a nationally recognized organization. Choosing the right certification process should be the result of an informed and thoughtful procedure. In the end, it will pay substantial dividends in both profitability and client satisfaction.

Recommended Reading

American College of Sports Medicine. *ACSM's Guidelines for Exercise Testing and Prescription*, 6th ed. Philadelphia, PA: Lippincott Williams & Wilkins, 2000.

American College of Sports Medicine. *ACSM's Health/Fitness Facility Standards and Guidelines*, 2nd ed. Champaign, IL: Human Kinetics Publishers, Inc., 1997.

National Organization for Competency Assurance. *Certification: A NOCA Handbook*. Washington, DC, 1996.

Patton, RW, Grantham, WF, Gerson, RF, Gettman, LR. *Developing and Managing Health/Fitness Facilities*. Champaign, IL: Human Kinetics Books, 1989.

APPENDIX D

INFORMED CONSENT

*I*nformed consent is the voluntary written acknowledgment on the part of your client of the purposes, procedures, and specific risks associated with an activity in which he or she intends to participate.

As a fitness professional, you are required not only to know about fitness evaluation and exercise prescription, you also need to understand the legal environment in which you operate when performing fitness tests and to be competent to make exercise recommendations to your clients based upon the results of the tests. You probably are very comfortable with the fitness instruction and evaluation of personal training, however, you need to be just as comfortable – and skilled – with the legal aspects.

WHAT IS THE PURPOSE OF THE INFORMED CONSENT?

When your client reads and signs an informed consent form, they are acknowledging that they have been informed about all the risks of the activities associated with the fitness testing or prescription of exercise. The informed consent form does not guarantee the client that nothing will go wrong. In fact, it provides the client with a preview of what could go wrong and the risk of injury associated with the activity, allowing the client to make an "INFORMED CONSENT" to participate. The risk of participation for most clients will be so small that the benefits outweigh the risks. An informed consent form is for YOUR LEGAL PROTECTION!

WHAT COMPONENTS ARE NEEDED FOR AN INFORMED CONSENT FORM?

The informed consent form should include an explanation of the tests being performed, the risks and possible discomforts involved, the benefits a client may expect and any alternatives that may be advantageous for him or her to consider. A section of the form should be allocated for recording all questions asked by the client and the answers given to the client. All informed consent forms must be signed by the client and witnessed by an independent third party.

WHO CAN SIGN AN INFORMED CONSENT FORM?

The courts only recognize an adult's signature on an informed consent form. Anyone under the age of 18 should have a parent or legal guardian sign for them or cosign the informed consent. Not only should the client be of lawful age, they may not be mentally incapacitated, and must know and fully understand the importance of the risks associated (no matter how remote the possibility) with participation in the exercise and fitness training program, and must be able to provide the consent voluntarily, without duress. Be aware that in some states, even with a parent's signature cosigning the informed consent, a minor can file a suit after they become an adult.

WHAT DO YOU DO IF YOUR CLIENT DOES NOT WISH TO SIGN AN INFORMED CONSENT FORM?

The client has no obligation to sign an informed consent form. However, you should feel no obligation to continue with an assessment or prescription of an exercise program should an individual refuse to sign. While a client may give their consent verbally (even if witnessed by an independent third party), verbal consent is not recognized in all legal jurisdictions and is not recommended.

WILL AN INFORMED CONSENT FORM KEEP YOU FROM BEING SUED?

No! There is a major difference between being named in a lawsuit and being found liable for actions taken or omitted. While you can be sued, the issue in law is whether you conducted yourself in a negligent manner or if you conducted tests or provided information that was outside the scope of the informed consent. What an informed consent does is establish that the client has been given an explanation of what can happen and that he or she has the option of not continuing. This is not a perfect legal security blanket, but it has been shown to be very useful when forced into a legal situation.

WHAT PERIOD OF TIME DOES THE INFORMED CONSENT COVER?

Generally, the informed consent form only covers the evaluation and advice that is provided at the time of the assessment or meeting. Should an individual return for a second evaluation or new exercise prescription, it is generally recommended that the client sign a new informed consent form, even if it is a duplicate of the original.

The following samples of informed consent forms are intended to be examples of the layout and type of information required in an informed consent form. There is no intent to offer legal advice or recommend these forms for your use. We recommend you consult your business attorney for legal advice and to review all the forms you will be using while operating your personal training business.

FORM 1

INFORMED CONSENT FOR PARTICIPATION IN AN EXERCISE PROGRAM
FOR APPARENTLY HEALTHY ADULTS
(WITHOUT KNOWN OR SUSPECTED HEART DISEASE)

Name: _____

1. PURPOSE AND EXPLANATION OF PROCEDURE

I hereby consent to voluntarily engage in an acceptable plan of exercise conditioning. I also give consent to be placed in program activities that are recommended to me for improvement of my general health and well-being. These may include dietary counseling, stress reduction, and health education activities. The levels of exercise I will perform will be based upon my cardiorespiratory (heart and lungs) fitness as determined through my recent graded exercise evaluation. I will be given exact instructions regarding the amount and kind of exercise I should do. I agree to participate 3 times per week in the formal program sessions. Professionally trained personnel will provide leadership to direct my activities, monitor my performance, and otherwise evaluate my effort. Depending upon my health status, I may or may not be required to have my blood pressure and heart rate evaluated during these sessions to regulate my exercise within desired limits. I understand that I am expected to attend every session and to follow staff instructions with regard to exercise, diet, stress management, and smoking cessation. If I am taking prescribed medications, I have already so informed the program staff and further agree to so inform them promptly of any changes my doctor or I make with regard to use of these. I will be given the opportunity for periodic assessment with laboratory evaluations at 6 months after the start of my program. Should I remain in the program thereafter, additional evaluations will generally be given at 12-month intervals. The program may change the foregoing schedule of evaluations, if this is considered desirable for health reasons.

I have been informed that during my participation in exercise, I will be asked to complete the physical activities unless symptoms such as fatigue, shortness of breath, chest discomfort, or similar occurrences appear. At that point, I have been advised it is my complete right to decrease or stop exercise and that it is my obligation to inform the program personnel of my symptoms. I hereby state that I have been so advised and agree to inform the program personnel of my symptoms, should any develop.

I understand that while I exercise, a trained observer will periodically monitor my performance and perhaps measure my pulse and blood pressure or assess my feelings of effort for the purposes of monitoring my progress. I also understand that the observer may reduce or stop my exercise program when any of these findings so indicate that this should be done for my safety and benefit.

2. RISKS

I understand and have been informed that there exists the remote possibility during exercise of adverse changes, including abnormal blood pressure, fainting, disorders of heart rhythm, and very rare instances of heart attack or even death. I have been told that every effort will be made to minimize these occurrences by proper staff assessment of my condition before each exercise session, by staff supervision during exercise, and by my own careful control of exercise efforts. I have also been informed that emergency equipment and personnel are readily available to deal with unusual situations should these occur. I understand that there is a risk of injury, heart attack, or even death as a result of my exercise, but knowing those risks, I desire to participate as herein indicated.

3.   BENEFITS TO BE EXPECTED AND ALTERNATIVES AVAILABLE TO EXERCISE

I understand that this program may or may not benefit my physical fitness or general health. I recognize that involvement in the exercise sessions will allow me to learn proper ways to perform conditioning exercises, use fitness equipment, and regulate physical effort. These experiences should benefit me by indicating how my physical limitations may affect my ability to perform various physical activities. I further understand that if I closely follow the program instructions, I will likely improve my exercise capacity after a period of 3 to 6 months.

4.   CONFIDENTIALITY AND USE OF INFORMATION

I have been informed that the information obtained in this exercise program will be treated as privileged and confidential and will, consequently, not be released or revealed to any person without my express written consent. I do, however, agree to the use of any information that is not personally identifiable with me for research and statistical purposes, so long as same does not identify me or provide facts that could lead to my identification. Any other information obtained, however, will be used only by the program staff in the course of prescribing exercise for me and evaluating my progress in the program.

5.   INQUIRIES AND FREEDOM OF CONSENT

I have been given an opportunity to ask certain questions as to the procedures of this program. Generally, these requests have been noted by the interviewing staff member, and his/her responses are as follows:

_____

_____

I further understand that there are also other remote risks that may be associated with this program. Despite the fact that a complete accounting of all those remote risks has not been provided to me, I still desire to participate.

I acknowledge that I have read this document in its entirety or that it has been read to me if I have been unable to read same.

I consent to the rendition of all services and procedures as explained herein by all program personnel.

Participant's signature _____ Date _____

Witness's signature _____

Test supervisor's signature _____

Note: The law varies from state to state. No form should be adopted or used by any program without individualized legal advice. Reprinted by permission from Herbert, 1990.

FORM 2

INFORMED CONSENT FOR EXERCISE TESTING OF APPARENTLY HEALTHY ADULTS
(WITHOUT KNOWN HEART DISEASE)

Name: _____

1.   PURPOSE AND EXPLANATION OF TEST

I hereby consent to voluntarily engage in an exercise test to determine my circulatory and respiratory fitness. I also consent to the taking of samples of my exhaled air during exercise to properly measure my oxygen consumption. I also consent, if necessary, to have a small blood sample drawn by needle from my arm for blood chemistry analysis and for the performance of lung function tests, and I consent to have body fat (skinfold pinch) tests. It is my understanding that the information obtained will help me evaluate future physical activities and sports activities in which I may engage.

Before I undergo the test, I certify to the program that I am in good health and have had a physical examination conducted by a licensed medical physician within the last _____ months. Further, I hereby represent and inform the program that I have completed the pretest history interview presented to me by the program staff and have provided correct responses to the questions as indicated on the history form or as supplied to the interviewer. It is my understanding that I will be interviewed by a physician or other person, prior to my undergoing the test, who will in the course of interviewing me determine if there are any reasons which would make it undesirable or unsafe for me to take the test. Consequently, I understand that it is important that I provide complete and accurate responses to the interviewer and recognize that my failure to do so could lead to possible unnecessary injury to myself during the test.

The test I will undergo will be performed on a motor-driven treadmill or bicycle ergometer, with the amount of effort gradually increasing. As I understand it, this increase in effort will continue until I feel and verbally report to the operator any symptoms such as fatigue, shortness of breath, or chest discomfort which may appear. It is my understanding and I have been clearly advised that it is my right to request that a test be stopped at any point if I feel unusual discomfort or fatigue. I have been advised that I should immediately upon experiencing any such symptoms, or if I so choose, inform the operator that I wish to stop the test at that or any other point. My wishes in this regard shall be absolutely carried out.

It is further my understanding that prior to beginning the test, I will be connected by electrodes and cables to an electrocardiographic recorder, which will enable the program personnel to monitor my cardiac (heart) activity. It is my understanding that during the test itself, a trained observer will monitor my responses continuously and take frequent readings of blood pressure, the electrocardiogram, and my expressed feelings of effort. I realize that a true determination of my exercise capacity depends on progressing the test to the point of my fatigue.

Once the test has been completed, but before I am released from the test area, I will be given special instructions about showering and recognition of certain symptoms that may appear within the first 24 hours after the test. I agree to follow these instructions and promptly contact the program personnel or medical providers if such symptoms develop.

2. RISKS

I understand and have been informed that there exists the remote possibility of adverse changes during the actual test. I have been informed that these changes could include abnormal blood pressure, fainting, disorders of heart rhythm, stroke, and very rare instances of heart attack or even death. I have been told that every effort will be made to minimize these occurrences by preliminary examination and by precautions and observations taken during the test. I have also been informed that emergency equipment and personnel are readily available to deal with these unusual situations should they occur. I understand that there is a risk of injury, heart attack, or even death as a result of my performance of this test, but knowing those risks, it is my desire to proceed to take the test as herein indicated.

3. BENEFITS TO BE EXPECTED AND AVAILABLE ALTERNATIVES TO THE EXERCISE TESTING PROCEDURE

The results of this test may or may not benefit me. Potential benefits relate mainly to my personal motives for taking the test, that is, knowing my exercise capacity in relation to the general population, understanding my fitness for certain sports and recreational activities, planning my physical conditioning program, or evaluating the effects of my recent physical activity habits. Although my fitness might also be evaluated by alternative means, for example, a bench step test or an outdoor running test, such tests do not provide as accurate a fitness assessment as the treadmill or bike test, nor do those options allow equally effective monitoring of my responses.

4. CONFIDENTIALITY AND USE OF INFORMATION

I have been informed that the information obtained in this exercise test will be treated as privileged and confidential and will, consequently, not be released or revealed to any person without my express written consent. I do, however, agree to the use of any information for research and statistical purposes, so long as same does not provide facts that could lead to my identification. Any other information obtained, however, will be used only by the program staff to evaluate my exercise status or needs.

5. INQUIRIES AND FREEDOM OF CONSENT

I have been given an opportunity to ask certain questions as to the procedure. Generally, these requests have been noted by the testing staff, and their responses are as follows:

_____

_____

_____

_____

_____

_____

I further understand that there are also other remote risks that may be associated with this procedure. Despite the fact that a complete accounting of all those remote risks has not been provided to me, I still desire to proceed with the test.

I acknowledge that I have read this document in its entirety or that it has been read to me if I have been unable to read same.

I consent to the rendition of all services and procedures as explained herein by all program personnel.

Date _____

Participant's signature _____

Witness's signature _____

Test supervisor's signature _____

Note: The law varies from state to state. No form should be adopted or used by any program without individualized legal advice. Reprinted by permission from Herbert, 1990.

FORM 3

ALTERNATIVE FORM FOR INFORMED CONSENT
FOR EXERCISE TESTING PROCEDURES
OF APPARENTLY HEALTHY ADULTS

Name: _____

1.   PURPOSE AND EXPLANATION OF TEST

It is my understanding that I will undergo a test to be performed on a motor-driven treadmill or bicycle ergometer, with the amount of effort gradually increasing. As I understand it, this increase in effort will continue until I feel and verbally report to the operator any symptoms such as fatigue, shortness of breath, or chest discomfort that may appear or until the test is completed or otherwise terminated. I understand and have been clearly advised that it is my right to request that a test be stopped at any point if I feel unusual discomfort or fatigue. I have been advised that I should immediately upon experiencing any such symptoms, or if I so choose, inform the operator that I wish to stop the test at that or any other point. My stated wishes in this regard shall be carried out. **IF CORRECT, AND YOU AGREE AND UNDERSTAND, INITIAL HERE. _____**

It is further my understanding that prior to beginning the test, I will be connected by electrodes and cables to an electrocardiographic recorder, which will enable the program personnel to monitor my cardiac (heart) activity. It is my understanding that during the test itself, a trained observer will monitor my responses continuously and take frequent readings of blood pressure, the electrocardiogram, and my expressed feelings of effort. I realize that a true determination of my exercise capacity depends on progressing the test to the point of my fatigue.

Once the test has been completed, but before I am released from the test area, I will be given special instructions about showering and recognition of certain symptoms that may appear within the first 24 hours after the test. I agree to follow these instructions and promptly contact the program personnel or medical providers if such symptoms develop. **IF CORRECT, AND YOU AGREE AND UNDERSTAND, INITIAL HERE. _____**

Before I undergo the test, I certify to the program that I am in good health and have had a physical examination conducted by a licensed medical physician within the last _____ months. Further, I hereby represent and inform the program that I have accurately completed the pretest history interview presented to me by the program staff and have provided correct responses to the questions as indicated on the history form or as supplied to the interviewer. It is my understanding that I will be interviewed by a physician or other person, prior to my undergoing the test, who will in the course of interviewing me determine if there are any reasons that would make it undesirable or unsafe for me to take the test. Consequently, I understand that it is important that I provide complete and accurate responses to the interviewer and recognize that my failure to do so could lead to possible unnecessary injury to myself during the test. **IF CORRECT, AND YOU AGREE AND UNDERSTAND, INITIAL HERE.**

_____

2.   RISKS

I understand and have been informed that there exists the possibility of adverse changes during the actual test. I have been informed that these changes could include abnormal blood pressure, fainting, disorders of heart rhythm, stroke, and very rare instances of heart attack or even death. I have also been informed that aside from the foregoing other risks exist. These risks include, but are not necessarily limited to, the possibility of stroke or other cerebrovascular incident or occurrence, mental, physiological, motor, visual, or hearing injuries; deficiencies, difficulties, or disturbances; partial or total paralysis; slips, falls, or other unintended loss of balance or bodily movement related to the exercise treadmill (or bicycle ergometer) that may cause muscular, neurological, orthopedic, or other bodily injury; as well as a variety of other possible occurrences, any one of which could conceivably, however remotely, cause bodily injury, impairment, disability, or death. Any procedure such as this one carries with it some risk, however unlikely or remote. THERE ARE ALSO OTHER RISKS OF INJURY, IMPAIRMENT, DISABILITY, DISFIGUREMENT, AND EVEN DEATH. **I ACKNOWLEDGE AND AGREE TO ASSUME ALL RISKS. IF YOU AGREE AND UNDERSTAND, INITIAL HERE.** _____

I have been told that every effort will be made to minimize these occurrences by preliminary examination and by precautions and observations taken during the test. I have also been informed that emergency equipment and personnel are readily available to deal with these unusual situations should they occur.

Knowing and understanding all risks, it is my desire to proceed to take the test as herein described. **IF CORRECT, AND YOU AGREE AND UNDERSTAND, INITIAL HERE.**
_____

3.   BENEFITS TO BE EXPECTED AND AVAILABLE ALTERNATIVES TO THE EXERCISE TESTING PROCEDURE

I understand and have been told that the results of this test may or may not benefit me. Potential benefits relate mainly to my personal motives for taking the test, that is, knowing my exercise capacity in relation to the general population, understanding my fitness for certain sports and recreational activities, planning my physical conditioning program, or evaluating the effects of my recent physical activity habits. Although my fitness might also be evaluated by alternative means, for example, a bench step test or an outdoor running test, such tests do not provide as accurate a fitness assessment as the treadmill or bike test, nor do those options allow equally effective monitoring of my responses. **IF CORRECT, AND YOU AGREE AND UNDERSTAND, INITIAL HERE.** _____

4.   CONSENT

I hereby consent to voluntarily engage in an exercise test to determine my circulatory and respiratory fitness. I also consent to the taking of samples of my exhaled air during exercise to properly measure my oxygen consumption. I also consent, if necessary, to have a small blood sample drawn by needle from my arm for blood chemistry analysis and for the performance of lung function tests, and I consent to have body fat (skinfold pinch) tests. It is my understanding that the information obtained will help me evaluate future physical fitness and sports activities in which I may engage. **IF CORRECT, AND YOU AGREE AND UNDERSTAND, INITIAL HERE. _____**

5.   CONFIDENTIALITY AND USE OF INFORMATION

I have been informed that the information obtained in this exercise test will be treated as privileged and confidential and will, consequently, not be released or revealed to any person without my express written consent, I do, however, agree to the use of any information for research or statistical purposes, so long as same does not provide facts that could lead to my identification. Any other information obtained, however, will be used only by the program staff to evaluate my exercise status or needs. **IF CORRECT, AND YOU AGREE AND UNDERSTAND, INITIAL HERE. _____**

6.   INQUIRIES AND FREEDOM OF CONSENT

I have been given an opportunity to ask questions as to the procedures. Generally, these requests have been noted by the testing staff, and their responses are as follows:

_____

_____

_____

_____

IF THIS NOTATION IS COMPLETE AND CORRECT, INITIAL HERE. _____

I acknowledge that I have read this document in its entirety or that it has been read to me if I have been unable to read same.

I consent to the rendition of all services and procedures as explained herein by all program personnel.

Participant's signature _____Date _____

Spouse's consent _____

Witness's signature _____

Witness's signature _____

Test supervisor's signature _____

Note: The law varies from state to state. No form should be adopted or used by any program without individualized legal advice. Reprinted by permission from Herbert, 1990.

FORM 4

INFORMED CONSENT FOR PARTICIPATION IN A PERSONAL FITNESS TRAINING PROGRAM FOR APPARENTLY HEALTHY ADULTS
(WITHOUT KNOWN OR SUSPECTED HEART DISEASE)

Name: _____

1.   PURPOSE AND EXPLANATION OF PROCEDURE

I hereby consent to voluntarily engage in an acceptable plan of personal fitness training. I also give consent to be placed in personal fitness training program activities that are recommended to me for improvement of my general health and well-being. These may include dietary counseling, stress management, and health/fitness education activities. The levels of exercise I perform will be based upon my cardiorespiratory (heart and lungs) and muscular fitness. I understand that I may be required to undergo a graded exercise test as well as other fitness tests prior to the start of my personal fitness training program in order to evaluate and assess my present level of fitness. I will be given exact personal instructions regarding the amount and kind of exercise I should do. I agree to participate 3 times per week in the formal program sessions. Professionally trained personal fitness trainers will provide leadership to direct my activities, monitor my performance, and otherwise evaluate my effort. Depending upon my health status, I may or may not be required to have my blood pressure and heart rate evaluated during these sessions to regulate my exercise within desired limits. I understand that I am expected to attend every session and to follow staff instructions with regard to exercise, diet, stress management, and other health/fitness-related programs. If I am taking prescribed medications, I have already so informed the program staff and further agree to so inform them promptly of any changes my doctor or I make with regard to use of these. I will be given the opportunity for periodic assessment and evaluation at regular intervals after the start of my program.

I have been informed that during my participation in this personal fitness training program, I will be asked to complete the physical activities unless symptoms such as fatigue, shortness of breath, chest discomfort, or similar occurrences appear. At that point, I have been advised that it is my complete right to decrease or stop exercise and that it is my obligation to inform the personal fitness training program personnel of my symptoms. I hereby state that I have been so advised and agree to inform the personal fitness training program personnel of my symptoms, should any develop.

I understand that while I exercise, a personal fitness trainer will periodically monitor my performance and perhaps measure my pulse and blood pressure or assess my feelings of effort for the purposes of monitoring my progress. I also understand that the personal fitness trainer may reduce or stop my exercise program when any of these findings so indicate that this should be done for my safety and benefit.

I also understand that during the performance of my personal fitness training program, physical touching and positioning of my body may be necessary to assess my muscular and bodily reactions to specific exercises, as well as ensure that I am using proper technique and body alignment. I expressly consent to the physical contact for these reasons.

2. Risks

I understand and have been informed that there exists the remote possibility of adverse changes occurring during exercise including, but not limited to, abnormal blood pressure, fainting, dizziness, disorders of heart rhythm, and very rare instances of heart attack, stroke, or even death. Further, I have been informed and I understand that there exists the risk of bodily injury, including, but not limited to, injuries to the muscles, ligaments, tendons, and joints of the body. I have been told that every effort will be made to minimize these occurrences by proper staff assessments of my condition before each exercise session, by staff supervision during exercise, and by my own careful control of exercise efforts. I fully understand the risks associated with exercise, including the risk of bodily injury, heart attack, stroke, or even death, but knowing those risks, it is my desire to participate as herein indicated.

3. Benefits to be Expected and Alternatives Available to Exercise

I understand that this program may or may not benefit my physical fitness or general health. I recognize that involvement in the exercise sessions and personal fitness training sessions will allow me to learn proper ways to perform conditioning exercises, use fitness equipment, and regulate physical effort. These experiences should benefit me by indicating how my physical limitations may affect my ability to perform various physical activities. I further understand that if I closely follow the program instructions, I will likely improve my exercise capacity and fitness level after a period of 3 to 6 months.

4. Confidentiality and Use of Information

I have been informed that the information obtained in this personal fitness training program will be treated as privileged and confidential and will, consequently, not be released or revealed to any person without my express written consent. I do, however, agree to the use of any information that is not personally identifiable with me for research and statistical purposes, so long as same does not identify me or provide facts that could lead to my identification. I also agree to the use of any information for the purpose of consultation with other health/fitness professionals, including my doctor. Any other information obtained, however, will be used only by the program staff in the course of prescribing exercise for me and evaluating my progress in the program.

5. Inquiries and Freedom of Consent

I have been given an opportunity to ask certain questions as to the procedures of this program. Generally, these requests have been noted by the interviewing staff member, and his/her responses are as follows:

_____

_____

_____

I further understand that there are also other remote risks that may be associated with this personal fitness training program. Despite the fact that a complete accounting of all those remote risks has not been provided to me, I still desire to participate.

I acknowledge that I have read this document in its entirety or that it has been read to me if I have been unable to read same.

I expressly consent to the rendition of all services and procedures as explained herein by all program personnel.

Date _____

Client's signature _____

Authorized representative _____

Note: The law varies from state to state. No form should be adopted or used by any program without individualized legal advice. Reprinted by permission from Koeberle, 1990.

INFORMED CONSENT
• • •

FORM 5

EXPRESS ASSUMPTION OF RISK FORM

I, the undersigned, hereby expressly and affirmatively state that I wish to participate in _____.
I realize that my participation in this activity involves risks of injury, including but not limited to _____ (list) _____ and even the possibility of death. I also recognize that there are many other risks of injury, including serious disabling injuries, that may arise due to my participation in this activity and that it is not possible to specifically list each and every individual injury risk. However, knowing the material risks and appreciating, knowing, and reasonably anticipating that other injuries and even death are a possibility, I hereby expressly assume all of the delineated risks of injury, all other possible risks of injury, and even risk of death, which could occur by reason of my participation.

I have had an opportunity to ask questions. Any questions I have asked have been answered to my complete satisfaction. I subjectively understand the risks of my participation in this activity, and knowing and appreciating those risks, I voluntarily choose to participate, assuming all risks of injury or even death due to my participation.

_____   _____
Witness   Participant

                                    Dated_____

Notes of Questions and Answers

_____

_____

_____

This is, as stated, a true and accurate record of what was asked and answered.

                                    _____
                                    Participant

To be checked by program staff

		Checked	Initials
I.	Risks were orally discussed.	_____	_____
II.	Questions were asked, and the participant indicated complete understanding of the risks.	_____	_____
III.	Questions were not asked, but an opportunity to ask questions was provided and the participant indicated complete understanding of the risks.	_____	_____

Staff member_____ Date _____

Note: The law varies from state to state. No form should be adopted or used by any program without individualized legal advice. Reprinted by permission from Herbert and Herbert, 1989.

FORM 6

Physical Activity Readiness
Questionnaire - PAR-Q
(revised 1994)

PAR - Q & You

(A Questionnaire for People Aged 15 to 69)

Regular physical activity is fun and healthy, and increasingly more people are starting to become more active every day. Being more active is very safe for most people. However, some people should check with their doctor before they start becoming much more physically active.

If you are planning to become much more physically active than you are now, start by answering the seven questions in the box below. If you are between the ages of 15 and 69, the PAR-Q will tell you if you should check with your doctor before you start. If you are over 69 years of age, and you are not used to being very active, check with your doctor.

Common sense is your best guide when you answer these questions. Please read the questions carefully and answer each one honestly: check YES or NO.

Yes	No		
☐	☐	1.	Has your doctor ever said that you have a heart condition and that you should only do physical activity recommended by a doctor?
☐	☐	2.	Do you feel pain in your chest when you do physical activity?
☐	☐	3.	In the past month, have you had chest pain when you were not doing physical activity?
☐	☐	4.	Do you lose your balance because of dizziness or do you ever lose consciousness?
☐	☐	5.	Do you have a bone or joint problem that could be made worse by a change in your physical activity?
☐	☐	6.	Is your doctor currently prescribing drugs (for example, water pills) for your blood pressure or heart condition?
☐	☐	7.	Do you know of any other reason why you should not do physical activity?

If you answered

YES to one or more questions

Talk with your doctor by phone or in person BEFORE you start becoming much more physically active or BEFORE you have a fitness appraisal. Tell your doctor about the PAR-Q and which questions you answered YES.

- You may be able to do any activity you want—as long as you start slowly and build up gradually. Or, you may need to restrict your activities to those which are safe for you. Talk with your doctor about the kinds of activities you wish to participate in and follow his/her advice.
- Find out which community programs are safe and helpful for you.

NO to all questions

If you answered NO honestly to all PAR-Q questions, you can be reasonably sure that you can:

- start becoming much more physically active—begin slowly and build up gradually. This is the safest and easiest way to go.
- take part in a fitness appraisal—this is an excellent way to determine your basic fitness so that you can plan the best way for you to live actively.

DELAY BECOMING MUCH MORE ACTIVE:

- if you are not feeling well because of a temporary illness such as a cold or a fever—wait until you feel better; or
- if you are or may be pregnant—talk to your doctor before you start becoming more active.

Please note: If your health changes so that you then answer YES to any of the above questions, tell your fitness or health professional. Ask whether you should change your physical activity plan.

Informed Use of the PAR-Q: The Canadian Society for Exercise Physiology, Health Canada, and their agents assume no liability for persons who undertake physical activity, and if in doubt after completing this questionnaire, consult your doctor prior to physical activity.

You are encouraged to copy the PAR-Q but only if you use the entire form.

NOTE: If the PAR-Q is being given to a person before he or she participates in a physical activity program or a fitness appraisal, this section may be used for legal or administrative purposes.

I have read, understood and completed this questionnaire. Any questions I had were answered to my full satisfaction.

NAME _____ PHONE _____

ADDRESS _____
                              STREET   STATE   ZIP

SIGNATURE _____ DATE _____

SIGNATURE OF PARENT_____ WITNESS_____
or GUARDIAN (for participants under the age of majority)

Supported by: Health Canada   Santé Canada

Reprinted with permission from the 1994 revised version of the Physical Activity Readiness Questionnaire (PAR-Q and YOU). The PAR-Q and YOU is a copyrighted, pre-exercise screen owned by the Canadian Society for Exercise Physiology.

ABOUT THE AUTHORS

CEDRIC X. BRYANT, PH.D., FACSM

Dr. Bryant is the chief exercise physiologist and vice president of educational services for the American Council on Exercise. Previously, Dr. Bryant was a senior vice president for StairMaster Health & Fitness Products, Inc. and served on the exercise science faculties of the United States Military Academy at West Point, Penn State University, and Arizona State University. He lectures nationally and internationally on many topics related to exercise, fitness, and health. Dr. Bryant is an accomplished writer, having authored 14 books and over 180 articles in a variety of sports medicine and fitness journals, including *ACE Certified News, Fitness Management, IDEA Personal Trainer,* the *Journal of Cardiopulmonary Rehabilitation, Medicine & Science in Sports & Exercise,* and *Shape.* An active member and fellow of the American College of Sports Medicine, Dr. Bryant currently serves as an associate editor for *ACSM's Health & Fitness Journal,* has served on ACSM's Certification Committee, was an associate editor of *ACSM's Guidelines for Exercise Testing and Prescription,* 5th edition, and is an ACSM certified exercise specialist. He is also the chairman of the scientific advisory board for the American Council on Exercise and serves on the editorial board for *ACE's Fitness Matters.*

BARRY A. FRANKLIN, PH.D., FACSM

Dr. Franklin has been the director of the Cardiac Rehabilitation Program and Exercise Laboratories at William Beaumont Hospital in Royal Oak, Michigan since 1985. He holds adjunct faculty appointments as clinical professor of exercise science at Oakland University, Rochester, Michigan; professor of physiology at the Wayne State University School of Medicine, Detroit; and professor of family medicine at the University of Michigan, Ann Arbor, Michigan. He is a past president of the Board of Trustees of the American Heart Association, Michigan Affiliate, and has been a member of the board

since 1989. He served as President of the American Association of Cardiovascular and Pulmonary Rehabilitation in 1988 and President of the American College of Sports Medicine in 1999-2000. Currently, he serves as editor-in-chief of *The American Journal of Medicine & Sports,* a journal geared to primary care physicians. He is a past editor-in-chief of the *Journal of Cardiopulmonary Rehabilitation* and serves as a member of the *American Journal of Cardiology's* editorial board. He holds editorial positions with several other scientific journals, including the *American Journal of Health Promotion, Sports Medicine,* the *Physician and Sportsmedicine,* the *Journal of Cardiovascular Nursing,* the *Exercise Standards and Malpractice Reporter,* and *Medicine & Science in Sports & Exercise.* Dr. Franklin has authored or coauthored over 300 scholastic papers, abstracts, chapters, and books, and has presented his research studies at national and international scientific meetings.

JASON M. CONVISER, PH.D., FACSM

Dr. Conviser is vice president of clinical services for Bally Total Fitness, which is the largest health club corporation in North America with over 290 fitness centers, 4 million members, and annually services 125 million member visits. Dr. Conviser is one of the nation's experts in articulating the business opportunity for the fitness industry when the traditional health care continuum is expanded to include health clubs. He specializes in developing medical/health club relationships, as well as programs to attract the deconditioned population into existing health clubs. In the last five years, he has been responsible for establishing over 100 health care and hospital/health club relationships. Dr. Conviser has written and published over 30 articles in both peer review and consumer publications. He is a frequently requested speaker at national fitness industry conventions. Dr. Conviser holds an MBA from the Kellogg Graduate School of Management at Northwestern University, with an emphasis in marketing. His Ph.D. is from the University of Wisconsin, with an emphasis in exercise physiology.